CHEESE

CHEESE

selecting, tasting, and serving
the world's finest

LAUREL
GLEN

San Diego, California

contents

introduction

Strong, subtle, fruity, dry, creamy, slightly tangy, and highly fragrant: cheese comes in an endless range of flavors.

This delicious and highly varied invention, however, was born of a very simple necessity: preserving milk. That's why mankind dreamed up cheese—in the beginning, it was no more than curdled milk with an appealing taste. Later the Romans enjoyed it uncooked with herbs and spices, or cooked with olive oil and white wine. In the Middle Ages, Benedictine monks, established on the plains at the heart of large agricultural estates, invented stronger-tasting cheeses such as Muenster or Maroilles. In the same era, Alpine farmers set up the first cheesemaking cooperatives, pooling the dairy resources of entire villages in order to manufacture enormous "millstones," or wheels, of Comté, Emmental (Swiss), or Gruyère. Production multiplied and diversified. The success of these highly innovative dairy products spread rapidly, especially among those in high places, who featured these heavenly cheeses at their dinner tables.

Kings and princes were crazy about them, as reported in several surviving anecdotes about Saint-Marcellin and Brie de Meaux. Today this gift of Nature is a splendid ambassador of the regions that produce it. Fruit of the patience, creativity, and know-how of mankind, cheese draws from cow's, ewe's, or goat's milk an infinity of flavors that tell a story—a gentian meadow, a thyme scrub, a field of apple trees, a rocky hollow, cut hay, and fresh straw.

Savored in abundance, cheese is a rustic but delicate food that, along with its accompaniments, should be chosen with care on the basis of the season and the occasion.

the cheesemaking process: perfect matches and seasons

The cows graze on the mountain pastures, as seen here in Haute-Savoie, and produce milk, the raw material from which cheese is made.

Once collected, the milk may be skimmed, a process in which part of its fat content is removed.

During coagulation, the rennet causes the milk to form clumps.

The consistency then changes to a sort of thicker paste.

The Camembert de Normandie, bearing the A.O.C. label, is hand-ladled into molds according to tradition.

The molds may have different shapes. Pont-l'Évêque, for example, is made in a square mold.

The mysterious ripening stage then begins, which gives each individual variety its particular flavor.

The Camembert de Normandie A.O.C. is placed on the ripening shelves. The rind is gradually covered with its characteristic "bloom."

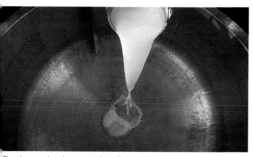

The cheesemaker then pours the milk into large copper vats.

He adds rennet to the milk so that it curdles more quickly.

When the operation is finished, we are left with the curds from which the cheese is made.

The mixture obtained is then pressed in a cloth bag in order to extract the whey from the curds.

After draining, certain cheeses are unmolded and salted by hand, such as the Bleu d'Auvergne shown here.

At the end of the manufacturing process, the cheeses are left to dry.

During the ripening process, the large wheels (*meules*, "millstones") of Emmental or Comté are regularly turned, washed, and brushed.

The *hâloir*, a cellar whose temperature and humidity remain constant, is the ideal place to ripen the cheeses to perfection.

Cheese: Time and Know-How

I N THE BEGINNING, THE MILK FROM COWS, GOATS, OR SHEEP WAS SIMPLY COOLED ON THE FARM IMMEDIATELY AFTER MILKING. NOWADAYS, AFTER THE MILK CHURNS ARE COLLECTED, THE MILK UNDERGOES NUMEROUS CHECKS TO GUARANTEE ITS QUALITY. IT IS THEN SUBJECTED TO SEVERAL TRANSFORMATIONS BEFORE IT TURNS INTO CHEESE. THESE DIFFERENT STAGES INVOLVE TIME, KNOW-HOW, AND SPECIFIC TOOLS, SOME OF WHICH HAVE HARDLY CHANGED SINCE THE DAWN OF TIME.

Coagulation

Milk naturally contains lactic ferments. When these ferments acidify, the milk may spontaneously pass from the liquid to the solid state. In order to make cheese, therefore, this natural reaction is used and even encouraged, i.e., by adding other ferments to the milk. After checking the acidity of the milk and measuring how much must be added—therein lies the art of the cheesemaker— lactic ferments or rennet are then added to the milk.

Rennet is an enzyme that causes milk to coagulate. According to the type of cheese one wishes to make, coagulation will either be "lactic," as with fresh cheeses, or predominantly "rennet," as for pressed, cooked cheeses. For soft or blue-veined cheeses such as Camembert, Brie, or blue cheeses, coagulation is "mixed," i.e., it uses both lactic ferments and rennet.

During coagulation, the milk turns either into clumps, in the case of lactic curds, or into a sort of paste, as when coagulation has been sped up by the addition of rennet. Curds formed from lactic fermentation drain by themselves, while curds formed by adding rennet, which yields a sort of elastic, compact, gelatinous mass, must be cut through and broken up.

Molding

This operation enables the future cheese to be given its definitive shape. It is performed with or without pressing. For soft cheeses, the curds are either ladled or poured from bags or skimmers into perforated molds placed on grooved tables, allowing the whey to drain off. Pressed, cooked cheeses are wrapped in a cloth and then molded into wood-bottomed shapes called *foncets* or *planchets*.

Pressing consists of hooping with wood or another material the cloth-wrapped shapes to give a final form to the cheese. Pressing causes the residual whey to drain off, so the cheese acquires an even consistency.

Draining

The curds must be separated from the whey. The quality and future keeping characteristics of the cheese will depend on this delicate operation. The draining stage is therefore a true art. When the curds are lactic in nature, as in the case of fresh cheeses, draining occurs spontaneously. Pressing can be used to expel the whey. In all cases, this operation lasts several hours.

Salting

Once the soft cheeses have finished draining, the drying stage takes place. This operation is performed in a warm, ventilated drying shed. Next, the cheese is unmolded and then salted, either by dusting it with fine salt or by dipping it in a saturated brine bath. Salt is very important because it has a triple effect—it determines the appearance and taste of the cheese, it toughens the rind and acts as a regulator by encouraging the exchange between the interior of the cheese and the ambient atmosphere, and last, its antiseptic properties protect against germs and bacteria.

Ripening

For fresh cheeses, the manufacturing process ends with draining. For all other cheeses, the mysterious ripening or finishing stage now begins. This consists of a biological maturation lasting several days to several months, depending on the cheese. This final stage in manufacturing demands razor-sharp attention, patience, and the right action at the right time on the part of the *affineur* (cheesemaker), all within the controlled atmosphere of the cellars or *hâloirs* (drying rooms). This complex operation permits the control of the development of the cheese's interior. For this, the *affineur* must check the oxygen, humidity, and temperature level of the areas specific to each cheese. The artisan turns, brushes, and sometimes washes the cheeses. Depending upon the curd type, he will use liquids such as white wine, cider, beer, brandy, or olive oil. Sometimes he will use plant products such as hay, oak-, beech-, or acacia-ash, vine shoots, and chestnut or plane-tree leaves.

LABELS—A GUARANTEE OF QUALITY

The finished cheeses must still undergo taste checks and quality controls. Scientific tests check whether they are properly made according to precise rules meeting standards of composition and hygiene. Organoleptic tests evaluate the consistency, smell, and flavor of the interior to ensure that each variety is both wholesome and tasty. In the final stage, packaging preserves the product and informs the consumer as to its name, origin, weight, fat content, etc.

In order to guarantee a quality product to the consumer, certain cheeses bear a farm label. This is a collective mark attesting to the fact that the cheese meets precise criteria. This label is synonymous with a strictly monitored level of quality. Another guarantee is the regional label common to various consumer products from certain areas, for example Emmental or Tomme de Savoie. These products must provide evidence of their origin and undergo checks throughout the entire chain, from production to distribution. Their quality is assessed by an organization independent of the profession. Farm and regional labels are guarantees of the cheeses' quality.

CHEESE BUILDS HEALTHY BONES

Even in small amounts, cheese provides energy and body-building materials. Along with milk, it is one of the best sources of calcium. Calcium content depends on the type of cheese but, according to nutritionists, there is as much calcium in 1 ounce of pressed, cooked cheese (such as Swiss) as there is in 2.8 ounces of soft cheese (such as Camembert).

That 1 ounce of cheese contains as much calcium as 35 ounces of oranges or 30 ounces of cabbage. The least-calcium-rich cheese is still ten times richer in calcium than meat, and four times richer than fish.

THE A.O.C. LABEL: SETTING A STANDARD

As with great wines, it was decided that Controlled Denomination of Origin (in French, *Appellation d'Origine Contrôlée,* or A.O.C.) labels would be awarded to great cheeses—products that were particularly representative of a region, a history, and a specific brand of know-how. Thirty-eight cheeses, remarkable both for the virtues of their region and the traditional method of their manufacture, now bear an A.O.C. label. The Institut National des Appelations d'Origine (INAO) grants approval for the awarding of the A.O.C. label, which is held by the following cheeses:

Pressed, uncooked cheeses:
Cantal, Laguiole, Morbier Fermier, Ossau-Iraty Brebis des Pyrénées, Reblochon de Savoie, Saint-Nectaire, Salers, Tomme d'Abondance.

Pressed, scalded cheeses:
Beaufort, Comté.

Goat cheeses:
Chabichou du Poitou, Chavignol or Crottin de Chavignol, Pélardon def Cévennes, Picodon de l'Ardèche or Picodon de la Drôme, Pouligny-Saint-Pierre, Rocamadour, Sainte-Maure-de-Touraine, Selles-sur-Cher, Valençay. There is also a ewe's-milk cheese, Brocciu.

Blue-veined cheeses:
Bleu d'Auvergne, Bleu de Gex or Bleu du Haut Jura or Bleu de Septmoncel, Bleu du Vercors-Sassenage, Bleu des Causses, Fourme d'Ambert or Fourme de Montbrison, Roquefort.

Soft, bloomy-rind cheeses:
Brie de Meaux, Brie de Melun, Camembert de Normandie, Chaource, Neufchâtel.

Soft, washed-rind cheeses:
L'Époisses, Langres, Livarot, Maroilles, Mont d'Or or Vacherin du Haut Doubs, Munster or Munster-Géromé, Pont-l'Évêque.

THREE KINDS OF MILK, EIGHT FAMILIES

IN FRANCE, MILK IS OBTAINED FROM COWS, GOATS, OR EWES. FROM THESE THREE KINDS OF MILK, HUNDREDS OF DIFFERENT CHEESES TAKE FORM. THEY ARE MADE ACCORDING TO EIGHT DISTINCT TECHNIQUES THAT CHARACTERIZE THE EIGHT MAJOR CHEESE FAMILIES: SOFT, BLOOMY-RIND CHEESES; SOFT, WASHED-RIND CHEESES; FRESH CHEESES; PROCESSED CHEESES; BLUE-VEINED CHEESES; GOAT CHEESES; PRESSED, SCALDED (OR COOKED) CHEESES; AND PRESSED, UNCOOKED CHEESES.

THE NAMES OF THE CHEESES DERIVE FROM THEIR PLACE OF PRODUCTION OR THE METHOD USED TO MANUFACTURE THEM. WITHIN EACH FAMILY, WE CAN APPRECIATE THE "PERSONALITIES" OF THE VARIOUS CHEESES THAT DIFFER ACCORDING TO THEIR AREA OF ORIGIN, THEIR SHAPE, THEIR RIPENING METHOD, OR THE KIND OF MILK USED IN THEIR PRODUCTION.

COW'S MILK

Abbaye de Cîteaux	PU	Chaumes	WR	Mimolette Française	
Abbaye Ste-Marie		Coeur de Thiérache	WR	or Boule de Lille	PU
du Mont-des-Cats	PU	Coeur d'Époisses	WR	Montbriac	BV
Affidélice	WR	Comté A.O.C.	PC	Morbier Fermier	PU
Aisy cendré	BR	Coulommiers Fermier	BR	Munster Fermier	
Ami du Chambertin	WR	Coulommiers Laitier	BR	A.O.C.	WR
Barousse Fermier	PU	Craquegnon Affiné à		Murol	WR
Beaufort A.O.C.	PC	la Bière La Gauloise	WR	Napoléon	PU
Bergues	WR	Crémet du Cap Blanc		Neufchâtel A.O.C.	BR
Bethmale or Oustet	PU	Nez	BR	Olivet Cendré	BR
Bleu d'Auvergne A.O.C.	BV	Croquin de la		Ossau-Iraty A.O.C.	PU
Bleu de Laqueuille	BV	Mayenne	BR	Ourliou	PU
Bleu de Sassenage		Cuyalas	PC	Pavé de Roubaix	PC
A.O.C.	BV	Dauphin Poisson	WR	Petit Sénonais	BR
Bleu de Gex A.O.C.	BV	Emmental Français	PC	Pithiviers au Foin	BR
Bleu des Causses A.O.C.	BV	Epoisses A.O.C.	WR	Plaisir au Chablis	WR
Boulette d'Avesnes	WR	Explorateur	BR	Pont-l'Évêque	
Boulette de Cambrai	FC	Feuille de Dreux or		A.O.C.	WR
Boursault	BR	Dreux à la feuille	BR	Rambol aux Noix	P
Boursin à l'Ail et aux		Feur de Bière	WR	Reblochon A.O.C.	PU
Fines Herbes	FC	Fol Épi	PC	Rigotte de Vache	BR
Brie de Meaux A.O.C.	BR	Fougeru	BR	Rouy	WR
Brie de Melun A.O.C.	BR	Fourme d'Ambert		Royal Raisin	FC
Brillat-Savarin	BR	A.O.C.	BV	Saint-Albray	PU
Brique des Pays du		Fourme de Montbrison	BV	Saint-Aubin	WR
Rhône	BR	Gaperon	PU	Saint-Félicien	BR
Camembert A.O.C.	BR	Gratte-Paille	BR	Saint-Florentin	WR
Cancoillotte	P	Laguiole A.O.C.	PU	Saint-Marcellin Blanc	BR
Cantal de Montagne		Langres A.O.C.	WR	Saint-Morgon	WR
A.O.C.	PU	Livarot A.O.C.	WR	Saint-Nectaire A.O.C.	PU
Carré d'Aurillac	BV	Maroilles or Marolles		Saint-Winoc	PU
Chaource A.O.C.	BR	A.O.C.	WR	Salers A.O.C.	PU

Saulxurois	WR
Soumaintrain	WR
Tamié de Savoie	PU
Tomette de Yenne	PU
Tomette du Pays Basque	PU
Tomme au Marc	PU
Tomme d'Abondance	
A.O.C.	PU
Tomme d'Auvergne	PU
Tomme de Pont-Astier	PU
Tomme de Savoie	
d'Alpage	PU
Tomme Fraîche de	
l'Aubrac	PU
Vache-Qui-Rit	
(Laughing Cow)	P
Vacherin du Haut	
Doubs or Mont-d'Or	
A.O.C.	WR
Vieux Pané	WR
Vieux-Gris-de-Lille	WR

EWE'S MILK

Brebiou	BR
Brin d'Amour or	
Brindamour	BR
Brocciu Corse A.O.C.	FC
Brousse	FC
Caldegousse	BR
Castagniccia	BR
Derby or Sage Derby	PU
Edam	PU
Feta	FC
Lacandou	BR

Lavort	BR
Pavin	PU
Pérail de Brebis	BR
Roquefort Fermier	
A.O.C.	BV

GOAT'S MILK

Anneau du Vic-Bilh	G
Banon à la Feuille	G
Baratte de Chèvre	G
Bonde de Gâtine	G
Bouchon de Sancerre	G
Bougon	G
Bouton de Culotte	G
Briquette de la Dombes	G
Bûche de Chèvre	G
Bûchette au Romarin	G
Cabécou de	
Rocamadour A.O.C.	G
Cabécou du Périgord	G
Cabrette du Périgord	G
Cabri Ariégeois	G
Cabri des Gors	G
Cabrioulet	G
Camisard	G
Caprinu	G
Carré de Chavignol	G
Carré du Tarn	G
Cathare	G
Chabichou du Poitou	
A.O.C.	G
Chablis Secondigny	G
Champdenier	G
Charolais	G

Chèvre au Marc	G
Chèvre du Morvan	G
Chevrion	G
Chevrotin des Aravis	G
Clacbitou du Charolais	G
Coeur d'Alvignac	G
Coeur de Chèvre	
Cendré	G
Crottin de Chavignol	
Demi-Affiné	G
Fort de la Platte	G
Groû du Bâne	G
Lingot Ardéchois	G
Lingot du Berry	G
Mâconnais	G
Pastille de Chèvre	G
Pavé des Dombes	G
Péchegros	G
Pélardon des Cévennes	G
Petit Frais de la Ferme	FC
Picodon de l'Ardèche	
A.O.C.	G
Pouligny-Saint-Pierre	
A.O.C.	G
Rocamadour A.O.C.	G
Roncier	G
Rouelle Blanche	G
Sainte-Maure de	
Touraine A.O.C.	G
Selles-sur-Cher A.O.C.	G
Taupinière	G
Truffe de Valensole	G
Valençay	G
Vieillevie	G

LEGEND

FC	Fresh cheeses		PC	Pressed, scalded cheeses
BR	Soft, bloomy-rind cheeses		BV	Blue-veined cheeses
WR	Soft, washed-rind cheeses		G	Goat cheeses
PU	Pressed, uncooked cheeses		P	Processed cheeses

BREAD AND CHEESE

WINE, CHEESE, AND BREAD FORM A MAGICAL TRIO. SINCE ALL THREE ARE PRODUCTS OF FERMENTATION, IT'S SMALL WONDER THAT THEIR FLAVORS HARMONIZE SO PERFECTLY. THE CHOICE OF BREAD DEPENDS TO A GREAT EXTENT ON THE CHARACTER OF THE CHEESE: DRY, SOFT, STRONG, SPICY . . . TO AVOID A MISMATCH, FOLLOW THIS GUIDE!

MARRIAGES OF REASON

With fermented cheeses such as Époisses or Maroilles, slightly acid wheat- or rye-based breads are just the ticket.

With a fresh goat's-milk cheese, choose a Viennese baguette cut into rounds, fine wheaten bread, unsweetened brioche, or perhaps a *fougasse* for a perfect match.

With triple-cream-type cheeses with spices or herbs, try raisin or nut bread, or even a tangy sourdough. Brie and Coulommiers appreciate the gently perfumed company of dill bread.

With Cantal, Murol, Edam, or any other pressed-curd cheese, whole-wheat bread is the perfect match. Like all veined cheeses, blue cheese loves well-toasted nut bread and raisin bread, served hot. Fresh cheeses go well with sesame or cumin bread. Also try processed cheese or a young Gouda on a dark, dense rye loaf, or plain crackers with Stilton or cheddar, two British cheeses.

THE CONSISTENCY GAME

In the pursuit of ideal matches, bread type and taste count the most. There's also the question of consistency. Thus, soft cheeses harmonize well with a soft crumb and a crunchy crust. Blue cheeses go well with a firm, slightly stale loaf. Goat and pressed-curd cheeses are excellent with tender, fresh breads. Bleu d'Auvergne is delicious with nut bread, and Langres goes well with cumin bread.

Have fun harmonizing and contrasting different types of breads and cheeses to bring out the best in both.

Using your loaf
For a marriage of flavors that's worthy of the name, bread should always be absolutely fresh, except for rye bread, which should be eaten slightly stale. The crust should be crunchy, the crumb firm and fragrant with a clean taste.

A fresh, thickly sliced country loaf is always a safe bet—it harmonizes well with all cheeses. A good, fresh baguette can also be partnered with any cheese.

WINE AND CHEESE: THE PERFECT MATCH

CONTRARY TO A MYTH THAT SEEMS TO HAVE GAINED GREAT POPULARITY, CHEESE AND WHITE WINE ARE A MARRIAGE MADE IN HEAVEN! LIVELY AND SINEWY, WHITE WINE FORMS A VOLUPTUOUS PARTNERSHIP WITH A CROTTIN DE CHAVIGNOL OR A PERFECTLY RIPE ROQUEFORT.

WHITE WEDDING

According to culinary tradition, after the fish course, served with white wine, and the meat course, accompanied by robust, sparkling reds, it's difficult to go back to a sprightly white wine, whether silky or velvety, with the cheese course. What a mistake! One need only try a Fourme d'Ambert with a glass of syrupy wine such as a Sauternes or Montlouis to be convinced. Try, too, an Époisses de Bourgogne with a fresh, sappy Pouilly Fuissé, or a Livarot with a Pinot Gris d'Alsace. Curious gastronomes and bold gourmets won't want to miss out on this surprising combination: a Gris de Lille, also known as a Puant de Lille (Lille Stinker) on account of its powerful odor, accompanied by a glass of champagne.

THE CLASSIC TACK

A safe approach is to match up wines and cheeses from the same region. You could, for example, partner a white Burgundy such as a Pouligny-Montrachet with a Langres, a Muenster with a Gewurztraminer, or a Comté with a white wine from Jura. The more adventurous won't hesitate to team a small glass of Calvados with a wedge of Pont-l'Évêque. Tomme de Savoie is only happy with its local Savoie wine. With a raw-milk Camembert, an old Calvados or a young cider are a delight. With an Ossau-Iraty, a Basque Country cheese, savor an Irouleguy wine. Serve goat cheeses with a Sauvignon. Sancerre appreciates the company of a Crottin de Chavignol. As for young Gruyère, it harmonizes perfectly with fruity Swiss white wine.

THE SHOCK OF CONTRASTS

Bear in mind this basic principle: The riper the cheese, the more biting its taste and the stronger with respect to the wine. The ideal accompaniment to a tart cheese such as Comté, Roquefort, or Bleu de Gex is a sweet wine with a high alcohol content, or even an old port or a Pineau des Charentes.

Fairly salty cheeses, such as certain Bries de Meaux, as well as soft cheeses with seasonings or herbs, like Boursin, will feel at home with a slightly acidic, fragrant wine such as a Côte-du-Rhône, or a varietal wine such as a Viognier or a chardonnay.

MATCHING TONES

With a blue-veined cheese such as a rich, strong Roquefort, try a glass of syrupy wine like Loupiac or Sauternes. A Muenster Fermier goes well with a glass of Gewurztraminer. A Maroilles at the peak of its strength will enjoy the unaccustomed but seductive company of a vintage champagne. Team a

Variety is the name of the game

Since the aroma of a cheese is sometimes quite strong, it's best to consider its texture while pondering several questions: Is the cheese's interior flowing, hard, granular, supple, moist, dry, or thick? Is it salty, subtle, floral, delicate, strong, or overwhelming in taste? Will it harmonize with a wine of complex flavors, like a Médoc, or rather with a simple, "all-in-one" wine, such as a Loire wine or a Corbières?

fruity Comté with a Château Chalon–type vin jaune, with the fine taste of fresh walnuts and tart apples—a little piece of heaven!

SIMPLICITY IS THE KEY

Cheese is an easygoing food. Don't make life difficult for yourself—sometimes it's nice simply to savor it with the last wine served. Although the absolute ideal is to serve each cheese with a different wine, this is by no means obligatory. Let's keep it simple!

VERSATILE CHEESE

CHEESE IS AN INGREDIENT IN MANY OF THE GREAT CLASSICS OF FRENCH CUISINE, SUCH AS SOUFFLÉS, GOUGÈRES (CHEESE PUFFS), AND QUICHE. WITH A BIT OF IMAGINATION, THOUGH, THE UBIQUITOUS WARM GOAT-CHEESE SALAD CAN MAKE WAY FOR PLENTY OF OTHER HIGHLY SUCCESSFUL COMBINATIONS—IT'S UP TO YOU TO DISCOVER THEM!

AN EASYGOING GUEST

Melt a thin slice of Beaufort on top of piping-hot baked potato halves. A pasta au gratin, sprinkled with a little crumbled Roquefort, emerges from the oven wafting a delicious aroma. Enrich a bacon-and-cream omelette with the flavor of Saint-Nectaire . . . The combination of cheese and main dish makes for a multitude of happy matches just begging to be discovered. Let your imagination lead you, based on each diner's taste. Accompany cheeses with crunchy nuts, a few vegetables chosen with care, or ripe, fragrant fruit for a clever but hassle-free cheeseboard!

MEAT AND CHEESE

Meat feels right at home in the company of cheese.

Try, for example, a carpaccio of raw beef sprinkled with Parmesan shavings. (Whatever you do, don't grate this cheese, or it will taste insipid.) A country ham accompanied by a fresh white cheese with chives and a few fresh figs forms a very simple meal that boasted its devotees back in ancient times. Steak au bleu (in a blue cheese, white wine, and cream sauce) is a classic with numerous fans, as is veal Orloff, in which slices of roast meat are alternated with slices of bacon and processed cheese or young Comté.

CHEESE AND FISH?

Though less expected, the partnering of cheese and fish should not be ignored. Red mullet garnished with blue-veined cheese and grilled is surprisingly flavorful. Curried sole can be accompanied by a spiced *fromage blanc* sauce. A touch of Gruyère heightens the aroma of salmon en papillote. For a more casual combination, avocado is entirely at ease in the company of shrimp and diced Brie.

Surprise your palate

Combine different tastes and contrasting textures. Team up complementary opposites such as crisp and soft, dry and slightly tangy. In this spirit, dried fruit and nuts play a starring role: blue cheeses with dates, Coulommiers with figs, Picodon with dried apricots, fresh goat cheeses with walnuts, hazelnuts, or pine nuts.

ONE CHEESE MAKES A DESSERT

Extremely simple yet full of refinement, these matches will surprise you. Thin slices of pears with the merest sprinkling of lemon juice go beautifully with a perfectly ripe Roquefort. A wedge of Morbier loves the company of dessert grapes. Quartered oranges feel at home with a just-ripe Camembert, and pink grapefruit harmonizes well with cubes of Gruyère. More surprisingly, Tomme de Savoie is perfectly partnered by slices of bananas. As for slightly dry goat cheeses, these go well with black grapes, and for a more exotic touch, fresh pineapple cubes.

THREE-WAY MARRIAGES

Rustic or sophisticated, three-way marriages with cheese are often the occasion of delicious culinary discoveries. A barely sweetened apple compote with a wedge of Camembert and a glass of cider never fails to conjure up images of Normandy. Eaten together, these three specialties from the same region complement one another perfectly. Black cherry preserves and a piece of Pyrenean sheep cheese such as Ossau-Iraty develop their flavor fully when accompanied by a glass of white Irouléguy. For a more sophisticated combination, try a mouthful of Roquefort savored with some candied fruit—angelica, pear, or melon—and a glass of fortified wine.

THE CHEESE PROFESSION

BEING A *FROMAGER* REQUIRES SPECIFIC KNOW-HOW. REMAINING SENSITIVE TO THE NEEDS OF ONE'S CHEESES, AS WELL AS ONE'S CUSTOMERS, ISN'T ALWAYS EASY.

DAY BREAKS

Rue de Sèvres: The Fromagerie Quatrehomme cheese shop raises its curtain. From the cellar to the shop, staff bustle about in preparation for the arrival of their well-informed customers, devotees of fine cheeses.

Like every other morning, each salesperson, who is responsible for her cheeses, checks her shelf for overripe Camembert, Saint-Marcellin gone bad, tired Brie, or Roquefort past its prime. Each cut portion of cheese is inspected, each cheese passing muster is wrapped in a new piece of plastic wrap in order to maintain a display guaranteeing freshness and hygiene to the consumer.

FROM THE CELLAR TO THE SHELF

Each salesperson draws up a list of cheeses to complete her shelf, which she passes on to the person responsible in the ripening cellar. In the basement of the shop, in a fine vaulted cellar with stable, controlled temperature and humidity, the fromager gathers together the requested cheeses and brings them up to the store.

Most of the time, the fromager purchases "unfinished" products that have not completely finished maturing. It's in the cellar, therefore, that this ripening process is concluded, up to the moment when the "ripe to the core" cheese is put on sale. At a good cheese seller's, you can find the most common cheeses at different stages of ripeness, more or less mature according to your taste.

SERVICE IS PARAMOUNT

"A ripe-to-the-core Camembert for this evening!"

All day long, customers file in and out of the shop and the cheese seller gives advice and answers questions.

"I'm having four friends over for dinner. What cheeses would you suggest after roast beef?"

"I'd recommend a Saint-Marcellin, which is very creamy at the moment. The Comté, which has been aged for eighteen months, has a surprising taste and fruitiness . . ."

The cheese seller has a very important advisory role as regards the choosing of particular varieties and the matching of cheeses with wine or bread, not to mention storage conditions.

"Never leave a cheese at room temperature for too long. Bring it out just one hour before it is to be eaten. Leaving it out will cause it to ripen prematurely and expose it to bacteriological risks," explains Marie Quatrehomme. A lady orders a large cheeseboard for ten people: "It's for a dinner after a show," she explains. "There must be plenty of different cheeses, since they're the centerpiece of the dinner. Can you give me unusual varieties, and include the labels?"

THE DAY ENDS

The working day draws to an end. Each family of cheeses is checked once again. The knives, spoons, and serving accessories are washed. Though the store is scrubbed from top to bottom every Monday (closing day), every evening the shelves are carefully cleaned and the daily cleaning routine is carried out. The floors are sluiced down. These precautions are essential to guarantee the cleanliness of the store. What's more, the public health inspector could arrive at any time to check that the regulations concerning the maintenance of perfect hygiene on the sales premises are being upheld.

Just what is a *fromager*?

The word *fromager* originally meant someone who produced and ripened his own cheeses. Nowadays most French retailers call themselves by this name—somewhat wrongly, since they buy their cheeses either directly from the producers or from wholesalers, at the Rungis market for example. After purchase, the "finishing" takes place—an art based on experience and know-how. The fromager must bring his products to perfect maturity and detect by sight, smell, and touch when the cheese is at its best—something only an experienced professional is capable of doing.

CHEESE AND ITS SEASONS

D URING CERTAIN TIMES OF THE YEAR, CERTAIN CHEESES ARE AT THEIR PEAK OF PERFECTION, WHILE OTHERS ARE LESS TASTY. FOR EXAMPLE, IT'S BEST TO AVOID VACHERIN IN SUMMER OR GOAT CHEESE IN WINTER. YOUR NEIGHBORHOOD SPECIALTY CHEESE RETAILER IS THE BEST PLACE TO TURN TO FOR ADVICE.

THE FINE-WEATHER SEASONS

The best seasons are indisputably spring, summer, and fall. The flavor of milk depends heavily on what the animals producing it have been eating, and thus on the quality of the grazing. The milk from a cow fed on winter hay will not have the same flavor as the milk from a cow grazing in an open field in the spring. Grazing on abundant grass with a sprinkling of gentian, violets, or buttercups, the cow will yield a much richer, more fragrant milk. Cheeses made from this milk and ripened for about four weeks will have a more pronounced and more delicious taste than winter cheeses.

There is, however, one exception to this rule: For cooked and uncooked pressed cheeses, it's not so much the season that matters, but the curd ripening time. Beaufort de Montagne and Comté made in the summer are by far the best at the end of the winter—of the following year!

IN WINTER, FROM JANUARY TO MARCH

This is the time to savor the cheeses that benefit from aging, which are now ten to eighteen months old, and the Vacherins produced after the first cold snap. You can also offer on your cheeseboard Époisses, Maroilles, Muenster, Comté, Livarot, Roquefort, Brie de Melun, Camembert, Pont-l'Évêque, and the blue varieties.

IN SPRING, FROM APRIL TO JUNE

Goats and cows begin to graze on the first grass in the pastures, so their milk is fragrant and flowery. Bries, Coulommiers, the entire goat-cheese family, and fresh cheeses are at their very best.

IN SUMMER, FROM JULY TO SEPTEMBER

The first ripened cheeses, such as soft, washed rinds and bloomy rinds, are reaching maturity. This is the season of Langres, Pont-l'Évêque, Maroilles, Camembert, Saint-Nectaire . . . And don't forget fresh cheeses, Brousses, or goat cheeses.

IN FALL, FROM OCTOBER TO DECEMBER

The regrowth of the second mowing of grass, known as the "aftermath," imparts big flavors to cheeses. The variety is tempting, since Époisses, Muenster, Cantal, Roquefort, Brie, and Camembert are perfect just now. In the heart of winter, Vacherin is at its best.

The seasons of milk?

Most cheeses are better at certain times of year. The notion of a "cheese season," however, hides a small inaccuracy. Actually, it's less the time of consumption of a cheese that counts than its time of production. For example, spring and fall milk is richer because the cows, goats, and sheep graze on grass enriched with wildflowers during these two seasons. The best cheeses, therefore, are those that are made from this milk. After that, however, it's all a question of the ripening. A cheese that needs to remain in an *hâloir* (drying room) for six months will be delicious in the middle of winter.

Don't hesitate to ask your cheese seller for advice: She alone will be able to tell you when the cheese was produced, and when it will be at its best.

In the catalog of cheeses, you'll find pictograms to help you determine the best time to enjoy each cheese.

The seasons are represented by a particular color and letters: "Sp" for Spring, "Su" for summer, "Au" for Autumn, and "Wi" for winter. Where a season is missing, it's best to avoid eating the cheese in question at that time of year.

You will also find pictograms indicating the type of milk—cow's, goat's, or ewe's—as well as suggestions on how to cut the cheese: the diagrams do not take the cheeses as a whole, but rather the piece that your cheese seller will offer you. The rule followed is simple: the rind should be divided up fairly among all the guests.

CHEESE ALL YEAR ROUND

There are enough varieties of cheese to feast on all year round. Moreover, it's said that one could sample a different French cheese every day for a year without having the same one twice. In fact, France is said to have close to 365 different varieties: Chaource, Emmental, Mimolette, Gouda, blue cheeses, all of the fresh or semiripened Tommes . . . And don't forget the factory-produced specialties and fresh cheeses!

BUYING CHEESE

Whether in a supermarket or a specialty cheese shop, cheeses must be stored in a refrigerator or display case. Check the cleanliness of the premises and the coolness of the temperature. Have a close look at the cheeses before making your final selection. Make sure that the packaging is intact, and check the sell-by date. At the specialty cheese shop, make sure that the cheeses aren't piled on top of each other, especially if they're from different families. The first wedge taken from cutting cheeses must be wrapped separately in waxed paper or in plastic wrap.

At a specialty retailer's or in a supermarket, staff must handle the cheese with care. In any case, it should be cut with care and attention.

Putting Together a Cheeseboard

For a grand dinner, prepare a ceremonial cheeseboard featuring a wide range of cheeses. Select your assortment on the basis of the interplay of the six flavors, or put a single family, carefully selected, in the limelight.

Preparing the Cheeseboard

A famous French gastronome once said that he loathed "the terrible crowding of the cheeseboard, where all the flavors merge, without managing to fraternize, in an inexpressible cacophony." Although the gastronomic ideal would be to arrange one cheese per plate—obviously impossible—the next best thing is to group the cheeses by family, a relatively easy task since in general there are no more than five or six cheeses on a cheeseboard. Balance the strengths by offering mild and strong flavors, soft and cooked-curd cheeses. Offer "ripe to the core" cheeses, based on the seasons. Avoid processed cheeses and factory-made spreading cheeses.

When you are setting up the cheeseboard, give some thought to the pleasure of the eye. Vary shapes, sizes, and colors. Orange Livarot, slices of Emmental, Brocciu au Poivre studded with peppercorns, the tall, bell-shaped Clochette, and the heart-shaped Coeur du Berry would constitute a fine group of cheeses.

Cheeseboards for a Big Night

Six main flavors govern the great family of cheeses, and should take their place on a quality cheeseboard. These are: fresh, neutral, mild, pronounced, strong, and very strong. Always arrange the cheeses in groups according to their strength. The fresh flavor refers to all fresh white cheeses with a smooth or granular texture. The neutral flavor will delight those who shy away from a pronounced taste. Factory-

The art of arranging

For ease of serving, place dry, hard cheeses that need cutting along the edge of the board. Moist, crumbly blue cheeses should preferably be placed on their own in the center, to avoid mixing different flavors. Small cheeses such as Bouton de Culotte or a goat's-milk Crottin should be placed in a corner of the board. Soft cheeses will fit in quite naturally in the remaining space. The important thing is to avoid, as much as possible, mixing everything together.

made specialties with an unassertive taste and pressed, uncooked cheeses such as Reblochon, Saint-Paulin, or fresh Tommes have a neutral taste.

The mild flavor refers to creamy cheeses such as the double or triple creams, as well as young cheeses like Saint-Nectaire, Pyrenean cow's-milk Tomme, and fairly unsalty goat or sheep cheeses. These cheeses will appeal to many owing to their mild, unaggressive character.

Those who are fond of pronounced flavors will find what they are looking for in the well-ripened soft cheeses: Chaource, Camembert, Brie, and raw-milk Coulommiers, nicely matured.

Mature Salers or semihard goat cheese has the strong flavor of cheeses ripened in a cellar over a long period. Soft, washed-rind cheeses such as Langres, Époisses, Livarot, and blue-veined cheeses will appeal to those who are fond of spicier tastes.

Arrange the very strong-tasting cheeses in a corner on their own: very ripe blues, dry goat cheeses, ones that are marinated in seasonings, Boulette d'Avesnes or Boulette de Cambrai, and Puant de Lille. All of these specialties give off a strong aroma and have a very assertive taste.

Original Cheeseboards

To defy tradition, it's fun to offer an "all goat-cheese," "all soft-cheese," or "all blue-cheese" platter. If you do this, choose your cheeses strictly at various stages of ripeness so that you will appreciate the difference. Place labels on the cheeseboard to indicate the name of each cheese.

A fine wheel of Brie, perfectly ripe, also makes an elegant platter all on its own.

You could also put together an international cheeseboard. Gorgonzola from Italy, very old Gouda from Holland, perfectly ripened English Stilton, Swiss Emmental, and Spanish Manchego could all be accompanied by bread and wine from their country of origin.

CUTTING AND TASTING CHEESE

O NCE YOU'VE BROUGHT YOUR CHEESE HOME, THERE'S THE QUESTION OF HOW TO CUT IT UP—DO YOU MAKE IT INTO CUBES, WEDGES, OR SERVE IT WITH A SPOON?

CUTTING CHEESE INTO PORTIONS

Each cheese is served "open" so that its degree of ripeness can be seen and so that guests won't feel inhibited about having to cut into it. Ideally, one should be able to taste a portion that goes from the rind to the core, according to the saying, "From the core to the rind, everyone benefits from the best!" Never scratch the rind of a cheese—its appearance testifies to its quality. Diners may remove the rind for themselves, according to their taste.

Cut into round, square, and pyramidal cheeses as if slicing a pie, starting from the center. Small goat cheeses are simply cut in two. Logs of any size are cut into rounds.

Wedge-shaped cheeses such as

Brie are cut up into equitable portions, from the point to the edge. Blue cheeses are cut fan-shaped, without cutting off their "nose."

As for Vacherin, it has its own ritual: A circular cut is made on the top in order to remove part of the rind. It is served with a spoon so that each person can dip into the creamy interior of the cheese through this opening.

THE ORDER OF TASTING

Begin the tasting with mild flavors like triple cream and Saint-Nectaire. Next, proceed to the more pronounced flavors: Saint-Marcellin, Comté de Montagne, Pélardon des Cévennes, or Chabichou. Continue with Sainte-Maure, Livarot with its strong flavors, or Muenster. Finish

The Camembert de Normandie A.O.C. is placed on the ripening shelves— its rind is gradually covered with the "bloom" to which it owes its character.

A wire (above) is used to cut goat-cheese logs. A guillotine (left) is reserved for Roquefort. A cheese grater and knives designed to shave or plane are very useful when dealing with pressed, scalded cheeses.

with Roquefort and the spicier cheeses. The cheese on your plate should be cut up into bite-size portions with a knife. It should not be spread, but simply placed, with or without its rind, on a bit of bread.

ABOUT THE RIND

Cheese lovers sometimes remove the rind so that they can devote themselves to savoring the fragrant interior, although bloomy-rind cheeses like Brie are of course eaten rind and all. In the mouth, the rind's texture contrasts with the tenderer texture of the paste and yields different flavors.

SUCCESSFUL PRESENTATION

Enhance the presentation by placing a few Virginia creeper or chestnut leaves on the cheeseboard—which can be made of cork, wood, stoneware, glass, marble, or wicker.

You'll need three to five cheeses for six to eight guests. Choose an odd number of varieties for preference—it will give your cheeseboard a more harmonious appearance. If the number of guests is

With or without butter?
A perfectly ripe, creamy cheese should be sufficient by itself. A dry, firm, slightly salty goat cheese might nevertheless benefit from a thin layer of butter on the bread. It's all a question of taste. Certain people can't do without butter. Gourmets consider it to be a heresy that renders Roquefort insipid and does nothing for Camembert.

greater, it's preferable to provide two platters, one exclusively for mild- and neutral-tasting cheeses, the other for spicier ones. Likewise, two knives on the cheeseboard will prevent the mixing of flavors. For a fresh white cheese or a Vacherin, provide a dessert spoon. A few condiments such as baby gherkins or cumin would be the ideal accompaniments for the cheeseboard. A basket of different sorts of bread—country, rye, cumin, Viennese baguette—should be placed nearby. Butter should be available in a butter dish for those who can't do without it.

The gadget below serves to cut extra-thin slices of hard cheese. It's used in particular for making *raclette*.

Traditional cheese knives used at the table (below) can be recognized by their two tines opposite the blade.

STORING CHEESE

WHETHER YOU CHOOSE YOUR CHEESE IN A SUPERMARKET OR BUY IT AT A SPECIALTY CHEESE SHOP, YOU'LL NEED TO TRANSPORT IT WITH CARE AND FOLLOW A FEW BASIC RULES WHEN STORING IT.

AT THE MARKETPLACE

In France, the sale of foods at open-air or covered markets is subject to the same hygiene regulations that govern ordinary supermarkets. This means that the goat cheeses on sale must not be subjected to temperatures over 46°F; bloomy-rind cheeses, 54°F; and ultra-fresh, i.e., fresh white cheeses and Petits-Suisses, over 43°F. It's up to you to check that the cheeses look fine.

THE JOURNEY HOME

While traveling home, you should make sure that the cheeses are not exposed to excessive heat or crushed at the bottom of your shopping basket. The ideal way to protect them is in an insulated bag kept apart from other shopping bags. Your precious cheeses can remain inside one of these bags for at least two hours.

For longer journeys, you can ask to have your cheeses vacuum-packed. This process will neutralize smells and prevent ripening for several days.

THE IDEAL CELLAR

Cheese does not fare well in a dry atmosphere, which will cause it to lose all its moisture and flavor. A good cellar with a temperature of 46°F, with just the right degree of humidity, is the perfect storage solution. Remember to turn the soft cheeses every other day. The other ones will improve gradually in the cellar.

THE REFRIGERATOR

If you don't have a cellar, then a refrigerator is the solution. Place the cheeses under cheese bells, grouped according to family. In a hermetically sealed plastic container, they tend to ferment very quickly. Store them in the lowest part of the refrigerator (the vegetable compartment).

With a temperature of 46°–50°F, this section is similar to the moist, cool atmosphere of a cellar.

IT'S A WRAP

Each cheese should be individually wrapped in its original paper. This prevents the spread of unpleasant odors, keeps the cheese from drying out, and prevents microbial contamination from raw, unwashed foods. Stored like this, the cheese will keep for about a week.

Don't forget to take the cheese out of the refrigerator and let it sit at room temperature for at least an hour before serving it.

CAUTION: LISTERIA

Listeria are bacteria present in numerous foods such as meat and other deli products. Consumed in small amounts, listeria are not toxic. Nevertheless, certain types are pathogenic and can cause a serious illness, listeriosis, in susceptible people such as pregnant women. Raw-milk products are no more easily contaminated than others. Listeria cannot withstand high temperatures, and are therefore destroyed by the pasteurization process. However, contamination may occur from brief contact with contaminated food, whether during the manufacturing process or in your refrigerator. Listeria multiply readily and survive the freezing process. To limit risks, you need to follow a few simple precautions. Wash your hands and clean utensils after contact with raw foods. Store raw foods separately from cooked foods. Protect foods by wrapping them or storing them in clean, sealed containers. Clean out your refrigerator twice a month and take the opportunity to wipe it out with a weak bleach solution.

French and European cheeses

COW'S-MILK CHEESE PRODUCTION IN FRANCE

Cows range over all the plains and valleys of the French countryside. It's hardly surprising, therefore, that cheeses made from their milk are produced more or less everywhere. With a few notable exceptions—in Brittany in particular—the west side of France is clearly less well represented.

1 Abbaye de Cîteaux

2 Abbaye Notre-Dame de Belval and Monastère de Troisvaux

3 Affidélice

4 Aisy cendré

5 Ami du Chambertin

6 Banon

7 Beaufort AOC

8 Bleu d'Auvergne AOC

9 Bleu des Causses AOC

10 Boulette d'Avesnes

11 Boulette de Cambrai

12 Brie de Meaux AOC

13 Brillat-Savarin

14 Camembert de Normandie AOC

15 Cancoillotte

16 Cantal AOC

17 Carré d'Aurillac

18 Chaource

19 Comté AOC

20 Coulommiers

21 Emmental Français

22 Époisses AOC

23 Feuille de Dreux or Dreux à la feuille

24 Fourme d'Ambert AOC

25 Gaperon

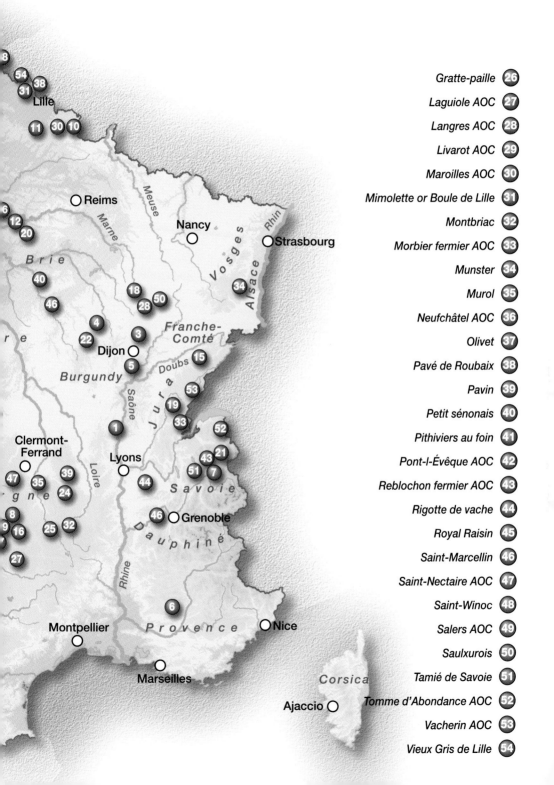

GOAT'S-MILK CHEESE PRODUCTION IN FRANCE

Goat-cheese production in France is centered in the south. Apart from a few locally produced cheeses, the most important regions are found to the south of the Loire, with a strong concentration in Poitou, Berry, Burgundy, and Mâconnais. Farther to the south, Provence, Corsica, and Pyrenees also produce several famous names.

1. Anneaux du Vic-Bihl
2. Banon
3. Baratte Chevenet
4. Baratte de Chèvre
5. Bonde de Gâtine
6. Bouchée de Chèvre
7. Bouchon de Sancerre
8. Bougon
9. Bouton de Culotte
10. Briquette de la Dombes
11. Brocciu frais AOC
12. Bûchette au Romarin
13. Cabécou de Rocamadour AOC
14. Cabrette du Périgord
15. Cabri des Gors
16. Cabrioulet
17. Caprinu
18. Carré de Chavignol
19. Carré du Tarn
20. Chabichou du Poitou AOC
21. Chabis Secondigny
22. Champdenier
23. Charolais
24. Chèvre au Marc
25. Chèvre du Morvan

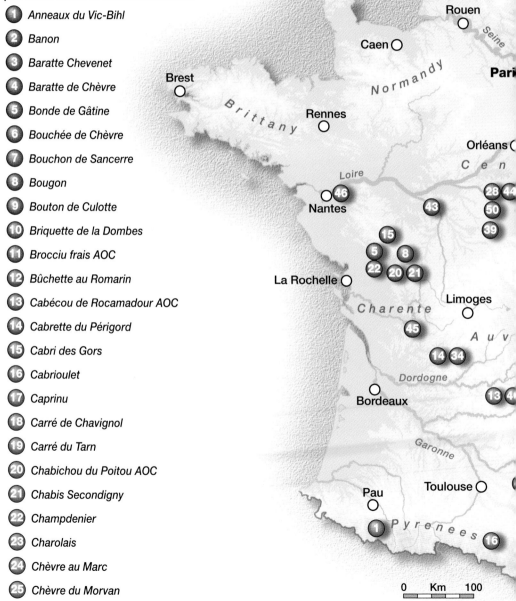

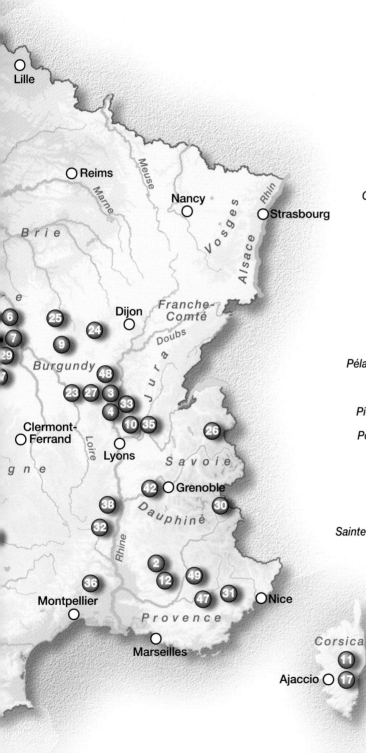

Chevrotin des Aravis ㉖

Clacbitou du Charolais ㉗

Coeur de Chèvre Cendré ㉘

Crottin de Chavignol AOC ㉙

Fort de la Platte ㉚

Groû de Bâne ㉛

Lingot Ardéchois ㉜

Mâconnais ㉝

Pastille de Chèvre ㉞

Pavé des Dombes ㉟

Pélardon des Cévennes AOC ㊱

Petit Frais de la Ferme ㊲

Picodon de l'Ardèche AOC ㊳

Pouligny-Saint-Pierre AOC ㊴

Rocamadour AOC ㊵

Rouelle Blanche ㊶

Saint-Marcellin Blanc ㊷

Sainte-Maure de Touraine AOC ㊸

Selles-Sur-Cher AOC ㊹

Taupinière ㊺

Tomme au Muscadet ㊻

Tomme de Chèvre ㊼

Tomme Sainte-Cécile ㊽

Truffe de Valensole ㊾

Valençay AOC ㊿

Vieillevie 51

SHEEP'S-MILK CHEESE PRODUCTION IN FRANCE

The sheep is a mammal well adapted to plateaus and the mid-mountains.
Sheep cheeses are therefore made in the foothills of the great massifs,
especially the sunniest ones: Causses, Alpes du Sud, Béarn,
the Basque Country, and the Corsican mountains.

1. *Banon*

2. *Brin d'Amour*

3. *Brocciu Corse AOC*

4. *Brousse Bourdin*

5. *Caldegousse*

6. *Castagniccia*

7. *Cuyalas*

8. *Lacandou*

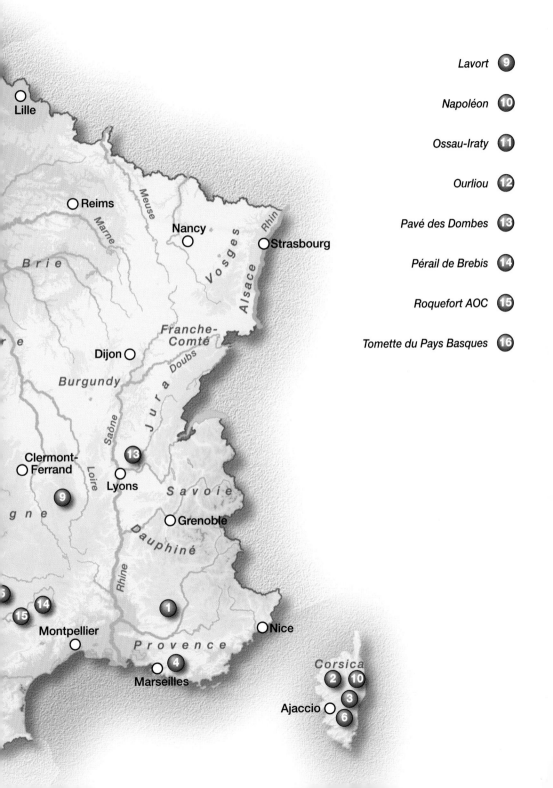

Lavort 9

Napoléon 10

Ossau-Iraty 11

Ourliou 12

Pavé des Dombes 13

Pérail de Brebis 14

Roquefort AOC 15

Tomette du Pays Basques 16

Lille

Reims

Meuse

Marne

Nancy

Rhin

Strasbourg

Vosges

Alsace

B r i e

Franche-Comté

Dijon

Doubs

Burgundy

Saône

Jura

Clermont-Ferrand

Loire

13

Lyons

S a v o i e

9

Grenoble

D a u p h i n é

Rhine

1

Montpellier

14

15

6

Nice

P r o v e n c e

Corsica

4

Marseilles

2

10

3

Ajaccio

6

CHEESE PRODUCTION IN EUROPE

*Owing to the variety of its soils, topography, and climate, and the diversity
of its animal rearing, France is the number-one producer of cheeses in Europe.
The French are also the biggest consumers of cheese (over 50 pounds per inhabitant
per year), followed by the Italians and Greeks (44 pounds).*

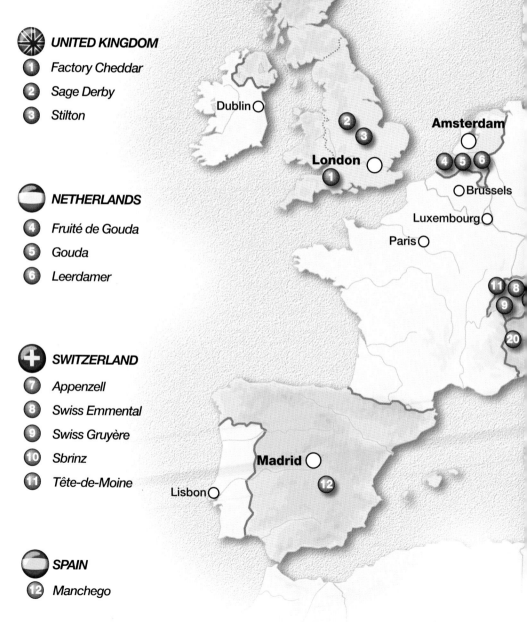

UNITED KINGDOM
1. Factory Cheddar
2. Sage Derby
3. Stilton

NETHERLANDS
4. Fruité de Gouda
5. Gouda
6. Leerdamer

SWITZERLAND
7. Appenzell
8. Swiss Emmental
9. Swiss Gruyère
10. Sbrinz
11. Tête-de-Moine

SPAIN
12. Manchego

Dublin
London
Amsterdam
Brussels
Luxembourg
Paris
Madrid
Lisbon

Copenhagen

Berlin

Warsaw

Prague

Vienna

Budapest

Zagreb

Belgrade

Bucarest

Sarajevo

Sofia

Rome

Skopje

ITALY

Gorgonzola 13
Grana Padano 14
Mascarpone 15
Mozzarella 16
Parmigiano 17
Pecorino 18
Provolone 19
Ricotta 20

GREECE

Feta 21

Athens

the eight
cheese
families

FRESH CHEESES

THE SIMPLEST AND MOST ANCIENT FORM OF CHEESEMAKING IS THE PRODUCTION OF FRESH WHITE CHEESES. EVEN OUR ANCESTORS ENJOYED THESE SMOOTH AND CREAMY PREPARATIONS BASED SIMPLY ON COAGULATED MILK, WHICH THEY EMBELLISHED WITH AROMATIC HERBS OR HONEY.

THE ORIGINAL CHEESE

All cheeses start out as fresh cheeses, more commonly termed "fresh white cheeses." At this stage, they're neither fermented nor ripened. The milk has simply been curdled by the addition of rennet. Originally, this substance was extracted from the abomasum, a small pouch in the stomach of young calves. Today a synthetic rennet is used. This fermentation causes the milk to solidify and take on a slightly acid taste. After draining this preparation, we are left with curd cheese.

FRESH AND DELICATE

This fermentation is the only step in the production of fresh white cheeses. They're called "fresh" because they're not matured in cellars like ripened cheeses. They have a high moisture content, from 60 to 85 percent. They don't keep well and must be consumed fairly quickly—their expiration date is clearly printed on the packaging. In this family, the cheeses are usually skimmed, but sometimes, cream will have been added to them. Fat content may be as high as 75 percent.

HOW SHOULD WE EAT THEM?

Fromage frais ("fresh cheese") packed in its own strainer is the best example of these fresh cheeses that have simply been drained, and of which Jonchée, Caillebotte, and Crémet are tasty regional variants. To make them smoother and creamier, they are sometimes whipped before being put into molds. Demi-Sels, Gournay, Neufchâtel Frais, and Fontainebleau are just a few of the cheeses in this category—as well as Charles Gervais's Petit Suisse, which is always a hit with French children—that never goes out of fashion.

It's by adding salt to certain of these cheeses that the range of fresh Carrés and Demi-Sels have developed. Finally, with honey, preserves, or fresh fruit, they make delicious desserts.

A QUESTION OF TERMS

The term *fromage blanc* ("white cheese") applies to two different products. It may mean a young cheese, drained and molded, which has not yet been ripened. Or it can designate a future goat cheese or a Camembert in the making. As for the term *fromage frais*, it designates a cheese that has undergone little or no ripening, and can thus refer to all types of cheeses before they are ripened. Their distinctive tastes will develop only later in the dark of the ripening cellar. The term *fromage blanc* is also used to describe a cheese that has undergone only simple lactic fermentation, such as the *fromage frais* packed in its own strainer. Slightly drained, this type of cheese is sold by weight. Eaten sweet or savory, it is prized for its slightly tart aftertaste.

A FEW HOUSEHOLD NAMES

Fontainebleau is said to have been created near the eponymous town in the Paris region. It's a handcrafted mixture of single cream and fresh white cheese, whipped by the cheesemaker. Light and delicate, this cheese is tasty with cubes of fruit. Cervelle des Canuts is a well-drained fresh white cheese to which fine chopped shallots, garlic, parsley, chervil, and chives are added. This cheese should be accompanied by toasted bread.

The verb *brousser* means "to mix or beat" in Provençal, and Brousse du Rove is a fresh white cheese whose curd is whipped hard before being drained. A century ago, it was called *fromage frais de corne* since it was served in a ram's horn (*corne*). This cheese is liquid and mild. Today it comes in plastic containers with curved rims, and should be eaten fairly soon after its production with fruit compote.

Gastamberra ("sheep's curds"), a Basque specialty, tastes like milk. Traditionally prepared at home, it comes packed in stoneware pots.

PETIT FRAIS DE LA FERME

SPANKING FRESH AND ABSOLUTELY DELICIOUS, THIS GOAT CHEESE PRODUCED IN BERRY SHOULD BE ENJOYED AS SOON AS IT COMES OUT OF THE MOLD—GOOD NEWS FOR GOURMANDS EAGER TO SAVOR ITS FRESH, AROMATIC FLAVOR.

Description
Shaped like a small cone and weighing barely 4¼ ounces, this unripened cheese is served when the curd has only just solidified—so it's marketed three or four days after its manufacture. Like a bowl of goat's milk, it gives off a lactic flavor barely tinged with a touch of acidity from the curd. Its consistency is similar to that of a fresh white cheese that has just been drained.

Serving suggestions
Gourmets particularly prize this fresh farmhouse cheese for its slight acidity and melt-in-the-mouth quality. Rindless, Petit Frais de la Ferme is eaten plain or flavored with herbs. It is also frequently served as a dessert with fruit, preserves, or runny, scented acacia honey. Children generally love it with sponge cake or ladyfingers. Serve it with a fresh, lively wine, red or white according to preference.

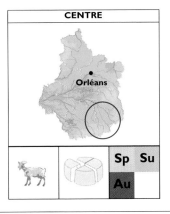

CENTRE
Orléans

		Sp	Su
		Au	

RICOTTA

THIS VERY POPULAR CHEESE ORIGINATED IN THE SOUTH OF ITALY. NOWADAYS IT IS PRODUCED HERE AND THERE IN EUROPE, AS WELL AS IN THE UNITED STATES.

Method of production
In northern Italy, in Lombardy and Piedmont, ricotta is made from cow's milk; in the south, it's made from ewe's milk, like Ricotta Romana. Ricotta is produced from November to June with the whey recovered from the manufacture of other cheeses such as provolone or Pecorino.

Serving suggestions
Fresh ricotta is slightly granular and has a strong, milky taste. It can be teamed with herbs or served as a dessert with candied fruits, or flavored with cinnamon, sugar, or cocoa. Italians eat it with salt, pepper, and a drizzle of delicately perfumed olive oil (a Tuscan variety, for example). It's also used as an ingredient in numerous recipes—ravioli, lasagna, gnocchi, and sauces, to name a few.

ITALY			
		Sp	Su
		Au	Wi

Petit Frais de la Ferme

S PANKING FRESH AND ABSOLUTELY DELICIOUS, THIS GOAT
CHEESE PRODUCED IN BERRY SHOULD BE ENJOYED AS SOON
AS IT COMES OUT OF THE MOLD—GOOD NEWS FOR
GOURMANDS EAGER TO SAVOR ITS FRESH, AROMATIC FLAVOR.

Description

Shaped like a small cone and weighing barely 4¼ ounces, this unripened
cheese is served when the curd has only just solidified—so it's marketed
three or four days after its manufacture. Like a bowl of goat's milk, it
gives off a lactic flavor barely tinged with a touch of acidity from the
curd. Its consistency is similar to that of a fresh white cheese that has just
been drained.

Serving suggestions

Gourmets particularly prize this fresh farmhouse cheese for its slight
acidity and melt-in-the-mouth quality. Rindless, Petit Frais de la Ferme
is eaten plain or flavored with herbs. It is also frequently served as a
dessert with fruit, preserves, or runny, scented acacia honey. Children
generally love it with sponge cake or ladyfingers. Serve it with a fresh,
lively wine, red or white according to preference.

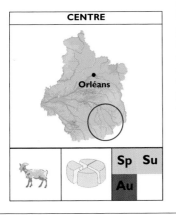

CENTRE		
Orléans		
🐐		Sp Su
		Au

Ricotta

T HIS VERY POPULAR CHEESE ORIGINATED IN THE SOUTH OF
ITALY. NOWADAYS IT IS PRODUCED HERE AND THERE IN
EUROPE, AS WELL AS IN THE UNITED STATES.

Method of production

In northern Italy, in Lombardy and Piedmont, ricotta is made from
cow's milk; in the south, it's made from ewe's milk, like Ricotta Romana.
Ricotta is produced from November to June with the whey recovered
from the manufacture of other cheeses such as provolone or Pecorino.

Serving suggestions

Fresh ricotta is slightly granular and has a strong, milky taste. It can be
teamed with herbs or served as a dessert with candied fruits, or flavored
with cinnamon, sugar, or cocoa. Italians eat it with salt, pepper, and a
drizzle of delicately perfumed olive oil (a Tuscan variety, for example).
It's also used as an ingredient in numerous recipes—ravioli, lasagna,
gnocchi, and sauces, to name a few.

ITALY		
🐄		Sp Su
		Au Wi

MASCARPONE

WITH ITS MILD FLAVOR AND SATINY TEXTURE THAT MAKE IT SUCH A PLEASURE TO EAT, THIS IS UNDOUBTEDLY ITALY'S MOST FAMOUS HIGH-FAT FRESH CHEESE. MASCARPONE, ALSO CALLED MESCHERPONE, IS MADE IN LOMBARDY FROM COW'S MILK.

Method of production

Mascarpone is made from cream with a 30 percent fat content, heated to 194°F. It is curdled with lemon juice or another acid. The coagulum is then drained and cooled. A soft cheese, mascarpone is smooth and creamy like butter, and leaves a fresh sensation in the mouth. It is sold in cardboard or plastic containers.

Serving suggestions

Quite compact in texture, this whitish or straw-yellow cheese spreads easily. Its slightly tart flavor harmonizes well with sweet foods. Mascarpone is eaten fresh, sprinkled with sugar, cinnamon, or cocoa. Some serve it with red berries or compote. Others flavor it with coffee or liqueurs such as amaretto. *Torta*, an Italian specialty, is made with alternating layers of mascarpone and gorgonzola. Mascarpone is also a key ingredient in tiramisu. Sample this cheese with a light, fruity wine.

ITALY			
🐄	🥣	**Sp**	**Su**
		Au	**Wi**

MOZZARELLA

FORMERLY MADE FROM BUFFALO'S MILK, MOZZARELLA IS NOW MADE MORE FREQUENTLY FROM COW'S MILK TO COPE WITH HEAVY DEMAND. DEPENDING ON ITS SHAPE AND THE REGION WHERE IT IS PRODUCED, THIS ITALIAN CHEESE IS CALLED BY MANY DIFFERENT NAMES: BOCCONCINI, CILIEGE, NOCIOLINI, NODINI, OR OVALINE, AMONG OTHERS.

Description

This *pasta filata* or "spun-curd" cheese has acquired quite a reputation through the years. Traditionally produced in Campania and Latium, it must contain a minimum fat content of 44 percent. At the end of the manufacturing process, the cake of curd is heated and kneaded by a transformer. Because it is sold as a fresh cheese and does not undergo any ripening, mozzarella is available in various forms. In a specialty cheese shop, it is usually stored in a light brine or is sold unbrined in a loaf shape.

Serving suggestions

Mozzarella is most often served as an appetizer in various mixed salads, or with a variety of vegetables. Baked on slices of garlic bread, it makes a typically Italian antipasto. Match it with a rosé de Provence.

ITALY			
🐃		**Sp**	**Su**
		Au	**Wi**

CRÉMET DU CAP BLANC NEZ

AMONG THE CHEESES OF NORD-PAS-DE-CALAIS, SOFT, BLOOMY-RIND CHEESES ARE NOT ALL THAT NUMEROUS. THIS ONE, ORIGINATING BY THE SEA, HAS A STRONG PERSONALITY.

Description
Dome-shaped, Crémet du Cap Blanc Nez is a double-cream cheese containing 50 to 60 precent fat. It is produced from the milk of cows that graze on salty pastures by the North Sea. The Nord-Pas-de-Calais region is home to forty or so cheese dairies, half of which are fairly small and produce local cheeses. Among the latter, Crémet owes its highly distinctive character to its maritime origins. It is ripened for ten to fifteen days, during which time its regular white-and-gold rind is formed.

Serving suggestions
Crémet's very tender texture makes it similar to other creamy cheeses such as Chaource. Unctuous without being bland, its pale yellow interior gives off a delicious grassy aroma. In top form in spring or fall, Crémet du Cap Blanc Nez is perfectly partnered with fruit. You can also sample it with a glass of fresh rosé, for example a Sancerre.

NORD-PAS-DE-CALAIS		
Lille — Cap blanc Nez		
🐄	🧀	**Sp** **Su**

FETA

WHO HAS NEVER ENJOYED THIS FAMOUS GREEK CHEESE ON A SUMMER'S EVENING, WITH A FEW BLACK OLIVES AND A MODEST WINE? FETA WAS ALREADY BEING MADE BACK IN HOMER'S TIME. TODAY, FEW DAIRY FARMERS CONTINUE TO MAKE IT IN THE TRADITIONAL MANNER. BECAUSE OF ITS INTERNATIONAL SUCCESS, THIS MODEST SHEEP'S CHEESE IS NOW FACTORY-PRODUCED ON AN EVER-INCREASING SCALE.

Description
A salty fresh white cheese, feta is smooth, white, and aromatic. Fairly firm, sometimes crumbly, it is packaged in whey or brine. Feta is traditionally produced from curdled ewe's milk. Nowadays, though, it is increasingly made from goat's or cow's milk. It contains 50 percent fat.

Serving suggestions
Choose a supple, aromatic cheese. The Greeks eat it cubed in a salad, or in a stuffing for vegetables. Tomatoes stuffed with feta are a true gourmet delight. In France, it rarely makes an appearance on the cheeseboard, but is generally used as an ingredient in cooked dishes and fresh salads. Crumbled on top of diced tomatoes and cucumbers and drizzled with olive oil, it's an essential part of a Greek salad. Serve it with a fruity red wine.

GREECE		
🐑	**Sp**	**Su**
	Au	**Wi**

Brocciu Corse A.O.C.

BROCCIU, OR BROCCIO, IS MADE IN CORSICA FROM RAW EWE'S OR GOAT'S MILK. IT'S THE ONLY A.O.C. CHEESE TO BE MADE FROM WHEY—A PART OF THE MILK THAT IS USUALLY DRAINED OFF FROM THE CURDS AND DISCARDED.

In the beginning

The Corsican word *brocciu* is related to the French *brousse*, which designates a Provençal fresh cheese, like the ewe's-milk Brousse de Brebis de Camargue. There is evidence that this product has been produced on Corsica for as long as there have been sheep on the island. Over 11½ quarts of goat's or ewe's milk are needed to obtain the whey essential for producing 2⅛ pounds of cheese. Eighty-five percent of Brocciu that is produced is eaten fresh; the rest is ripened. The cheese comes in the form of a variably-sized flattened ball, molded in a small, returnable basket. When ripened, Brocciu is covered with a fine, off-white film.

Serving suggestions

From spring to fall, choose the goat's-milk version of this fresh cheese, and in winter, the ewe's-milk variety. You should opt for a ripened Brocciu all year round. Brocciu is eaten warm or cold, accompanied by spicy wines in the forty-eight hours following its production. Salted or sweetened with honey, or sprinkled with brandy, it's a delicacy that appeals to all palates. It is also an ingredient in cakes such as *fiadone*, a Corsican cheesecake.

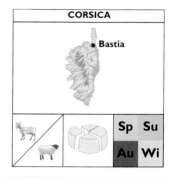

CORSICA

• Bastia

		Sp	Su
		Au	Wi

Brousse

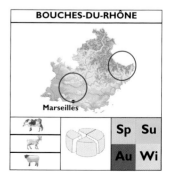

PACKED WITH ITS OWN STRAINER, BROUSSE IS A COW'S-, EWE'S-, OR GOAT'S-MILK CHEESE WITH A DISTINCTIVE MILKY, LIGHT TASTE.

In the beginning

The term *brousse* means to mix, beat, or whip. According to the traditional recipe, Brousse is whipped before being drained twice. This is done to increase the proportion of dry matter in the finished cheese. There are various names for this cheese, depending on where it is made: Brousse du Rove is produced in the Marseilles region, and Brousse de Vésubie in the Nice area. Brousse Bourdin, a factory-made variety of the traditional recipe, is produced from cow's milk.

Serving suggestions

Delicately flavored Brousse is equally good served sweetened or in savory preparations. Its packaging allows you to ripen it yourself, more or less drained, in your refrigerator. Some are fond of it with honey or preserves, while others prefer it with herbs. Accompany it with a wine from its own region, such as Coteaux d'Aix or Bandol.

BOUCHES-DU-RHÔNE

Marseilles

		Sp	Su
		Au	Wi

BOULETTE DE CAMBRAI

FRESH AND UNUSUAL, THIS RAW OR PASTEURIZED COW'S-MILK CHEESE IS A GASTRONOMIC FIND. TUROPHILES CAN ENJOY IT ALL YEAR ROUND.

Choosing wisely
Pear-shaped and hand-molded, Boulette de Cambrai is not ripened. Its rather mild taste is enlivened with spices and seasonings such as pepper, or herbs like tarragon, parsley, or chives. A fresh cheese, and hence rindless, a Boulette de Cambrai is 3⅛–3½ in. high by 3½ in. wide, and weighs approximately 7 ounces.

Serving suggestions
This cheese is chiefly sold locally, in Cambraisis. Boulette de Cambrai is a farmhouse or artisanally produced cheese. It should be enjoyed at the end of a meal with a round white country loaf and a glass of fresh Beaujolais. Some lovers of local products, such as andouillette, sample it with a suitably bitter local beer.

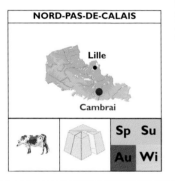

NORD-PAS-DE-CALAIS

Lille

Cambrai

Sp Su
Au Wi

BOURSIN À L'AIL ET AUX FINES HERBES

INVENTED IN 1963 BY A CHEESE DAIRY WITHIN THE NORMANDY AND ÎLE-DE-FRANCE BORDERS, THIS CHEESE, SEASONED WITH GARLIC AND HERBS, APPEALS BOTH TO CHILDREN AND TO ADULT CONNOISSEURS OF FRESH CHEESES. THE ADVERTISING SLOGAN THAT LAUNCHED IT IN 1968 HAS REMAINED IN THE COLLECTIVE FRENCH MEMORY: "DU PAIN, DU VIN, DU BOURSIN!" (SOME BREAD, SOME WINE, SOME BOURSIN!)

Method of production
Factory-produced, Boursin with garlic and herbs is a small, cylindrically shaped, rindless cheese. It comes in foil packaging ridged at the sides, which preserves its freshness effectively. Produced at 59°F, Boursin is still firm enough to be molded in its famous aluminum foil. Different varieties, such as Boursin au Poivre, have been created. Made in the same manner as Boursin with garlic, it is enriched with bits of peppercorn. Its flavor is stronger, but with the same savory mellowness. Boursin à la Ciboulette, for its part, is flavored with chopped chives.

Serving suggestions
The different varieties of Boursin, creamy and easily spread, are delicious on fresh bread and perfect for a picnic. Many wines are possible accompaniments, such as a Bordeaux or a red wine from the Loire.

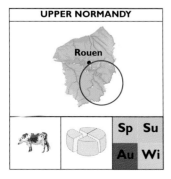

UPPER NORMANDY

Rouen

Sp Su
Au Wi

Fresh Cheeses

THE SIMPLEST AND MOST ANCIENT FORM OF CHEESEMAKING IS THE PRODUCTION OF FRESH WHITE CHEESES. EVEN OUR ANCESTORS ENJOYED THESE SMOOTH AND CREAMY PREPARATIONS BASED SIMPLY ON COAGULATED MILK, WHICH THEY EMBELLISHED WITH AROMATIC HERBS OR HONEY.

The original cheese

All cheeses start out as fresh cheeses, more commonly termed "fresh white cheeses." At this stage, they're neither fermented nor ripened. The milk has simply been curdled by the addition of rennet. Originally, this substance was extracted from the abomasum, a small pouch in the stomach of young calves. Today a synthetic rennet is used. This fermentation causes the milk to solidify and take on a slightly acid taste. After draining this preparation, we are left with curd cheese.

Fresh and delicate

This fermentation is the only step in the production of fresh white cheeses. They're called "fresh" because they're not matured in cellars like ripened cheeses. They have a high moisture content, from 60 to 85 percent. They don't keep well and must be consumed fairly quickly—their expiration date is clearly printed on the packaging. In this family, the cheeses are usually skimmed, but sometimes, cream will have been added to them. Fat content may be as high as 75 percent.

How should we eat them?

Fromage frais ("fresh cheese") packed in its own strainer is the best example of these fresh cheeses that have simply been drained, and of which Jonchée, Caillebotte, and Crémet are tasty regional variants. To make them smoother and creamier, they are sometimes whipped before being put into molds. Demi-Sels, Gournay, Neufchâtel Frais, and Fontainebleau are just a few of the cheeses in this category—as well as Charles Gervais's Petit Suisse, which is always a hit with French children—that never goes out of fashion.

It's by adding salt to certain of these cheeses that the range of fresh Carrés and Demi-Sels have developed. Finally, with honey, preserves, or fresh fruit, they make delicious desserts.

A question of terms

The term *fromage blanc* ("white cheese") applies to two different products. It may mean a young cheese, drained and molded, which has not yet been ripened. Or it can designate a future goat cheese or a Camembert in the making. As for the term *fromage frais*, it designates a cheese that has undergone little or no ripening, and can thus refer to all types of cheeses before they are ripened. Their distinctive tastes will develop only later in the dark of the ripening cellar. The term *fromage blanc* is also used to describe a cheese that has undergone only simple lactic fermentation, such as the *fromage frais* packed in its own strainer. Slightly drained, this type of cheese is sold by weight. Eaten sweet or savory, it is prized for its slightly tart aftertaste.

A few household names

Fontainebleau is said to have been created near the eponymous town in the Paris region. It's a handcrafted mixture of single cream and fresh white cheese, whipped by the cheesemaker. Light and delicate, this cheese is tasty with cubes of fruit. Cervelle des Canuts is a well-drained fresh white cheese to which fine chopped shallots, garlic, parsley, chervil, and chives are added. This cheese should be accompanied by toasted bread.

The verb *brousser* means "to mix or beat" in Provençal, and Brousse du Rove is a fresh white cheese whose curd is whipped hard before being drained. A century ago, it was called *fromage frais de corne* since it was served in a ram's horn (*corne*). This cheese is liquid and mild. Today it comes in plastic containers with curved rims, and should be eaten fairly soon after its production with fruit compote.

Gastamberra ("sheep's curds"), a Basque specialty, tastes like milk. Traditionally prepared at home, it comes packed in stoneware pots.

ROYAL RAISIN

MADE EXCLUSIVELY AT THE QUATREHOMME DAIRY ON RUE DE SÈVRES IN PARIS, THIS VERY FRESH CHEESE BOASTS A "ROYALLY" EXCEPTIONAL FLAVOR AND CONSISTENCY.

Method of production
Made from pasteurized cow's milk, Royal Raisin is a double-cream cheese (i.e., an unripened fresh white cheese). It is carefully studded all over with large golden raisins with a fine muscat flavor and few seeds.

Description
Royal Raisin is available in two forms: a large ball weighing about 7 ounces, and a ball approximately half this size. Both are properly studded all over with raisins. Like all fresh white cheeses, it contains between 55 and 60 percent fat. There is also a Royal Raisin with alcohol, in which the raisins are first marinated in a colorless spirit before being drained and stuck onto the cheese.

Serving suggestions
Royal Raisin is a delightfully creamy cheese, ideal on a cheeseboard for a sophisticated dinner in which you wish to impress your guests. Serve it with a variety of breads—country, rye, or Poilâne, and accompany it with a glass of pink champagne for its delicate bubbles!

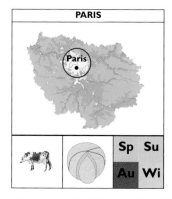

PARIS

Paris

Sp Su
Au Wi

TAUPINIÈRE

ORIGINATING IN THE ANGOULÊME REGION IN THE CHARENTES, THIS IS A FAIRLY RECENT CHEESE WHOSE SHAPE ATTEMPTS TO MIMIC THE LITTLE MOUNDS OF EARTH LEFT ON OUR LAWNS BY MOLES. HENCE ITS NAME—FRENCH FOR "MOLEHILL"—NOT TERRIBLY FLATTERING FOR A CHEESE THAT IS INCIDENTALLY QUITE DELICATE.

Description
Taupinière is shaped like a small dome, 2 inches in height by 3½ inches in diameter. It slightly resembles a Gaperon, but its natural rind, dusted in ash, sports a maze of thin, twisting furrows that recall the skin of certain melons. During the ripening period, which lasts at least two weeks, this cheese becomes covered in mold. Its very finely grained interior is tender and slightly acid, with a delicate goaty taste.

Serving suggestions
This cheese is chiefly enjoyed at the end of a meal, served with a good rye bread and some dried fruit. Try it with a Pinot Noir, which brings out the best in its character.

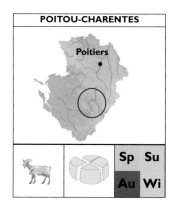

POITOU-CHARENTES

Poitiers

Sp Su
Au Wi

SOFT, BLOOMY-RIND CHEESES

PERFECTLY RIPE BRIE, RUNNY CAMEMBERT, SUBLIME SAINT-MARCELLIN . . . THESE SOFT CHEESES ARE TENDER-HEARTED WITH A UNIQUE FLAVOR.

THE BLOOM ON THE RIND

These cheeses are made from cow's, goat's, or ewe's milk, which may be raw or pasteurized. They've undergone no more than a natural ripening process, monitored by the cheesemaker in order to ensure the best quality, and helped along by simple salting. Their curd is neither pressed nor cooked. The term "bloomy rind" indicates the appearance of the light white mold that develops on the outside of the cheese in the ripening cellar. This is one of the most important families of cheeses, representing as it does about one-third of French production. Its representatives are prized for their delicate taste and their soft interior.

DOWNY MOLDS AND GOLDEN BREAD

During production, the cheese is salted, then sprayed with natural mold cultures, the Penicillium. The mold helps along the ripening process and creates the white flora, a sort of delicate felt-like down. As it ripens, this flora, which attests to the quality of the cheese, takes on the appearance of golden bread. The character of a cheese depends to a large extent on its ripening conditions, even if a prior role is played by other factors such as the type of milk and whether it is raw or pasteurized, the way in which the curd is obtained, or even the salting method.

This family includes Camembert, Brie, Coulommiers, Dreux à la Feuille, Riceys, Rigotte, Carré de l'Est, Pigouille, Chaource, Neufchâtel, Banon, Bouille, Boursault, and Saint-Marcellin, as well as the recent additions Saint-Albray, Belle-des-Champs, Caprice des Dieux, and Suprême des Ducs.

A PAINSTAKING PRODUCTION PROCESS

Making soft, bloomy-rind cheeses requires a lot of know-how and care. The production process, which is very old, has long been carried out on farms in the Île-de-France and the Rhône valley. From there, production spread throughout the whole of France.

Whatever the region, the method hardly varies at all: after the milk is coagulated, the curd is separated from the whey. The cheese is then ladled into different-shaped molds. Care is taken not to break up the curd too much, and draining is allowed to proceed slowly and without any outside help. Thus, for a Camembert whose production requires just over two quarts of milk, the draining stage lasts twenty-four hours.

THE PERIOD OF MATURATION

The cheese is then unmolded, salted all over, and sprayed with a penicillin culture. An initial maturation takes place in several days, during the course of which there forms the famous white flora, slightly bluish at the beginning. The cheese is then transferred to a humid, well-ventilated cellar for about a month. It's at this point that it develops all its flavor. The rind takes on an increasingly golden color, even becoming tinged orange-red in places.

THE FINAL RIPENING PERIOD DETERMINES THE QUALITY

The cheeses are then turned every second day under the auspices of the cheesemaker. It's on the walls, say the cheesemakers, that the cultures providing for perfect ripening are established. First, it was the cheese that spread the cultures to the walls; now, it's the walls that spread the cultures to the cheese: it's a natural cycle that mustn't be destroyed. The cheese ages for several weeks before it is ready to be sold.

Soft, bloomy-rind cheeses won't keep for much more than three to four days when stored in a well-ventilated place.

AISY CENDRÉ OR CENDRÉ D'AISY

THIS CHEESE COMES FROM THE AUXOIS REGION, FROM MONTBARD AND AISY-SUR-ARMENÇON. A HANDCRAFTED, UNCOOKED SOFT CHEESE, AISY CENDRÉ IS RIPENED IN OAK-, BEECH-, OR EVEN VINE-SHOOT ASH, WHICH SLOWS DOWN THE MATURATION PROCESS. IT IS MADE FROM RAW COW'S MILK.

In the beginning
Stored in a box, Aisy Cendré was formerly reserved for the consumption of winegrowers or farmers at grape-picking or harvesttime. It was ripened for two months. Blackened and burnished by the aging process, this powerful, strong-tasting rustic cheese can certainly whet one's thirst. Disk-shaped, measuring 4–4¾ inches in diameter by 1¼–2⅜ inches thick, it weighs about 7 to 9 ounces.

Serving suggestions
The Aisy Cendré that is marketed today is no longer as old and swarthy as it was fifty years ago, when one had to cut hard into the rind to enjoy it. The creamy interior often still has a chalky core, but even so remains strong-flavored. Powerful, spicy wines are the ideal accompaniment for this cheese. Serve it as your last course, so as not to overpower the taste of the other courses, with a crusty baguette.

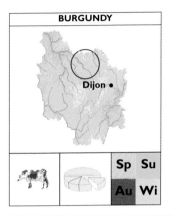

BURGUNDY

Dijon •

		Sp	Su
		Au	Wi

BOURSAULT

SMOOTH, CREAMY, AND MILD, THIS CHEESE BEARS THE NAME OF ITS INVENTOR, MONSIEUR BOURSAULT, AN IMPASSIONED CHEESEMAKER WHO IN 1951 HIT ON THE IDEA OF ENRICHING HIS RAW MILK WITH FRESH CREAM IN ORDER TO PRODUCE A "TRIPLE-CREAM" CHEESE. BOURSAULT COMES UNDER THE CATEGORY OF SOFT, UNCOOKED, UNPRESSED CHEESES.

Description
Cylindrically shaped, this cheese is 1¾ inches high by 3¼ inches in diameter, and weighs 7 ounces. Factory-produced, Boursault is ripened for twelve days in an *hâloir*, or drying room, long enough for its rind to develop a light white down and its interior to firm up. It is then left to mature in its packaging for another twenty-five days. By the time it is sold, it is golden and creamy. A very rich cheese, it contains 70 percent fat. Boursault may develop a slightly musty odor, and is all the better for it.

Serving suggestions
Enjoy it with fresh, aromatic bread from the famous Moisan bakery and with a fruity red wine from the region, such as a Bouzy.

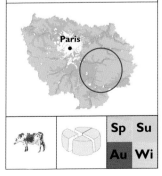

ÎLE-DE-FRANCE

Paris
•

		Sp	Su
		Au	Wi

BREBIOU

A FACTORY-PRODUCED CHEESE, BREBIOU IS MADE EXCLUSIVELY FROM EWE'S MILK. IT COMES UNDER THE CATEGORY OF SOFT CHEESES WITH A NATURAL RIND, AND HAS A FAT CONTENT OF 50 PERCENT. BREBIOU IS PRODUCED IN JURANÇON, A SMALL TOWN IN THE PYRENEES.

Description
Round, 3¾ inches in diameter by 1 inch thick, and weighing 6⅜ ounces, Brebiou also comes in a younger, smaller version, Palet de Brebiou. The ripening period lasts two to three weeks, during the course of which the rind of the cheese turns ivory-colored and its interior becomes supple. If the ripening period is extended by several days, the taste becomes stronger and spicier.

Serving suggestions
This cheese is mild flavored and creamy tasting. It has a dual texture with a firmer, slightly more acidic core surrounded by a smooth body. Brebiou can be served cut into cubes with predinner drinks, or at the end of a meal with raisin bread. There are also those who enjoy it with a green salad. Partner it with a red Jurançon from its locality, or a Madiran from the southwest of France.

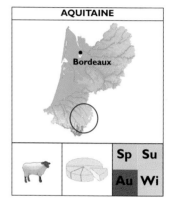

AQUITAINE

Bordeaux

Sp Su
Au Wi

BRIE DE MEAUX A.O.C.

M ADE FROM RAW COW'S MILK, BRIE DE MEAUX IS A SMOOTH, CREAMY CHEESE, HIGHLY AROMATIC WHEN RIPENED "TO THE CORE." SHAPED LIKE A FLAT CYLINDER 13¾ TO 14½ INCHES IN DIAMETER AND 1 INCH THICK, IT WEIGHS APPROXIMATELY 5¾ POUNDS.

In the beginning
Charlemagne held this cheese in high esteem. Blanche of Navarre, Countess of Champagne, was wont to send this cheese to King Philippe Auguste. Charles of Orléans would give one to the ladies of the court as a Christmas present. Henri IV ate it on buttered bread. In 1815, it was crowned "king of cheeses" by Talleyrand and the 143 negotiators gathered at the Congress of Vienna to reorganize Europe after the Napoleonic Wars.

Method of production
Brie de Meaux is made according to traditional farmhouse methods in the *département* of Seine-et-Marne, and part of the *départements* of Aube, Loiret, Marne, Haute-Marne, Meuse, and Yonne. It is ripened for a minimum of four weeks, during which time the cheese is turned several times by hand. Its downy white rind is sprinkled with reddish pigments. The interior of the cheese is straw yellow. Its consistency is supple and nonflowing. The flavor is delicate, with a subtle hazelnut taste. Marie Leczinska, wife of Louis XV, recommended it as an ingredient in *bouchées à la reine* or chicken vol-au-vents. Serve it with a sinewy, fruity red Burgundy or a Bordeaux.

ÎLE-DE-FRANCE

Paris
Meaux

Su
Au Wi

BRIE DE MEAUX A.O.C.

A WELL MAINTAINED CULT

Also called Brie de Valois, this cheese, produced from raw cow's milk, is the most famous member of the Brie family. It takes its name from the town of Meaux, located in the *département* of Seine-et-Marne, where the most prestigious cheese market was once held. Today, events organized in honor of this great cheese, such as the annual Brie de Meaux competition, still take place there each year. An organization, the Confrérie des Compagnons du Brie de Meaux, was established in 1991 with the aim of preserving many of the traditions associated with this cheese, along with a Brie de Meaux permanent exhibition hall, complete with tastings.

A LITTLE HISTORY

Around 774, Charlemagne, tasting Brie de Meaux for the first time, was said to have declared, "I've just discovered one of the most delicious dishes." Later, Brie de Meaux became a highly prized cheese at the royal court. It is important to note that Paris is only twenty-five miles from Meaux, and this proximity contributed in a large extent to the fame of the great cheese. In 1643, Condé had a great quantity of Brie delivered to celebrate the victory of Rocroi. The story of the arrest of Louis XVI is closely bound up with that of Brie de Meaux: Some allege that the king, seized by a sudden craving for Brie, made a stop at Varennes, not far from Meaux, in order to enjoy some. He was then recognized and arrested. According to other sources, the king asked the grocer, Saussejuste, for a wedge after his arrest in Varennes. We may consider this cheese to be one of the symbols of the French Revolution and equality between the classes, a revolutionary having declared, "Brie, loved by rich and poor alike, preached equality before anyone dreamed it possible."

OFFICIAL RECOGNITION

Two events occurred to bolster Brie de Meaux's success and confirm it in its role as the "king of cheeses": In 1815, after the Napoleonic Wars, thirty ambassadors met in Vienna to establish European borders. During the course of a meal, Talleyrand, the French representative, had the idea of organizing a cheese-tasting competition. Several varieties were brought from abroad: Brie de Meaux, Gouda, Parmesan, and Stilton were placed head to head . . . and it was Brie de Meaux that won the competition, hands down! Then, the awarding of the highly coveted A.O.C. label on August 18, 1980, further contributed to the establishment of its reputation.

CONTROLLED PRODUCTION

In order to lay claim to the Appellation d'Origine Contrôlée Brie de Meaux, this king of cheeses must be produced according to well-defined criteria. Thus, the milk must never be heated, in order to leave intact the microbial flora naturally present in the farm milk. Rennet—and nothing but rennet—must be added to the milk in order to bring about coagulation. The cheese is hand-ladled into molds using a Brie scoop. Dry salt is used to salt the cheeses. As for the ripening period, it lasts for at least four weeks; to achieve a product of better quality, a longer ripening period of six to eight weeks is recommended.

This soft, bloomy-rind cheese, which has made a name for the region and inhabitants of Brie, will continue to do so for years to come, delighting gastronomes the world over.

CALDEGOUSSE

SHAPED LIKE A ROUND, FLAT CAKE, THIS WHOLE-MILK SHEEP'S CHEESE LOOKS LIKE A LARGE WHEEL OF PÉRAIL. WHETHER FARMHOUSE OR ARTISANAL, IT IS MADE IN AVEYRON; ITS PRODUCTION IS ESSENTIALLY LIMITED TO THE REGION.

Description
Disk-shaped and about 3¼ inches in diameter, Caldegousse is ¾ to 1¼ inches thick. It is ripened for about ten days in a well-ventilated cellar, during which time it becomes as creamy as a Reblochon. Its rind, covered with natural mold, is ivory-colored. Its off-white, very smooth and creamy interior gives off an ewe's-milk scent. This cheese contains 45 to 50 percent fat.

Serving suggestions
In order to better appreciate its texture, eat Caldegousse at room temperature. Its mild, velvety taste and creamy consistency make it a delicious cheese. Partner it with some toasted country bread or with some crispbread. Serve this rather unusual cheese with, for example, a red Bordeaux.

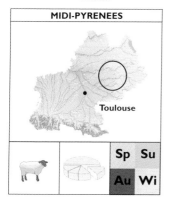

MIDI-PYRENEES

Toulouse

		Sp	Su
		Au	Wi

CAMEMBERT A.O.C.

THIS WORLD-FAMOUS BLOOMY-RIND CHEESE IS MADE FROM RAW COW'S MILK. SHAPED LIKE A SMALL DISK 4⅜ INCHES IN DIAMETER BY 1¼ INCHES THICK, AND WEIGHING 9 OUNCES, CAMEMBERT CONTAINS 45 PERCENT FAT. ITS AREA OF PRODUCTION IS LIMITED EXCLUSIVELY TO THE FIVE *DÉPARTEMENTS* OF NORMANDY.

In the beginning
Although the cheeses of the town of Camembert are mentioned as far back as 1702, Camembert itself is reputed to have been invented in 1791 by Marie Harel, a farmer's wife who ostensibly perfected an original cheese. It went down well, and production grew throughout the nineteenth century. In 1880, an engineer by the name of Ridel hit upon the idea of packing Camembert in a thin wooden box, which then also enabled it to be shipped abroad.

Method of production
Over two quarts of milk are used to manufacture a Camembert. The ripening period must last for at least twenty-one days, sixteen of which must be in the area of production. To the eye, the downy white rind is striated and tinged with red. The interior is a light yellow. To the nose, there is an unmistakeable scent of place. To the palate, the flavor is fruity.

Serving suggestions
An ending to a meal that's fit for a king, Camembert is sometimes made into croquettes and fried. Serve it with a bottled Normandy cider, a supple Bordeaux, or a generous Côtes-du-Rhône.

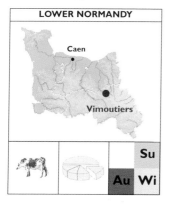

LOWER NORMANDY

Caen

Vimoutiers

		Su
		Au	Wi

CAMEMBERT AU CALVADOS

THE RIND IS REMOVED FROM A CAMEMBERT AND THE CHEESE IS THEN STEEPED IN CALVADOS TO FLAVOR IT. THIS MARRIAGE OF TWO SPECIALTIES FROM THE NORMANDY AREA YIELDS A SURPRISINGLY FRAGRANT CHEESE, IDEALLY SAMPLED WITH A GLASS OF CALVADOS.

In the beginning
Camembert au Calvados requires the same amount of milk for its production as ordinary Camembert. It also requires the same ripening time as the original.

Method of production
Camembert is an A.O.C. cheese before it is treated with Calvados. Once it has been flavored, it loses its A.O.C. label. Its rind is striated, downy with white mold, and spotted with red. Its light yellow interior, highly scented with Calvados, gives it a sustained flavor.

Serving suggestions
Sublime at the end of a meal, Camembert au Calvados is an unusual delight that should be served with country bread and a glass of water.

LOWER NORMANDY

Caen

Su
Au Wi

CAMEMBERT AU CIDRE

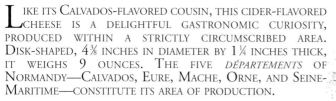

LIKE ITS CALVADOS-FLAVORED COUSIN, THIS CIDER-FLAVORED CHEESE IS A DELIGHTFUL GASTRONOMIC CURIOSITY, PRODUCED WITHIN A STRICTLY CIRCUMSCRIBED AREA. DISK-SHAPED, 4⅜ INCHES IN DIAMETER BY 1¼ INCHES THICK, IT WEIGHS 9 OUNCES. THE FIVE *DÉPARTEMENTS* OF NORMANDY—CALVADOS, EURE, MACHE, ORNE, AND SEINE-MARITIME—CONSTITUTE ITS AREA OF PRODUCTION.

Method of production
Selected young, this Camembert is left to macerate in cider for two weeks. Its rind, already formed, absorbs the taste of the liquid, developing the scent of apples. Its flavor is fruitier and more piquant than that of plain Camembert. Once flavored with cider, this Camembert loses its A.O.C. label.

LOWER NORMANDY

Caen

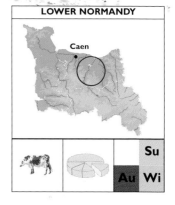

Su
Au Wi

Camembert A.O.C.

A WORLD-RENOWNED DELIGHT

Of all French cheeses, Camembert is certainly the most famous. Its reputation extends far beyond the borders of its native land. Moreover, it is exported to, and enjoyed in, numerous countries throughout the world. According to the legend, an American by the name of Joseph Knirim arrived in Normandy to pay his respects to the memory of Marie Harel, considered to be the "mother" of Camembert. According to Knirim's own words, his stomach troubles were alleviated by daily consumption of the heavenly cheese. He made a gift toward the erection of a statue of the great Marie Harel. Many local producers, aware of the commercial potential of the project, devoted a portion of their budget to it. The statue was erected and dedicated several years later.

BIRTH OF A CHEESE

The first accounts of the existence of a famous cheese produced in Camembert (Orne) go back to 1680. Marie Christine Harel, called Marie Harel, born in Crouttes in 1761, became famous in 1791. The young farmer's wife harbored the Abbot Charles Jean Bonvoust, a Catholic priest seeking to escape pressure from the authorities to swear allegiance to the new republic. The priest, a native of the Brie area, entrusted her with the secret of Camembert production. She passed on her knowledge to her daughter, Marie Harel Paynel, who settled with her husband in Champosoult. One hundred years after the birth of Camembert, an engineer by the name of Ridel perfected the "Camembert box," made from poplar wood. This process made it possible to dispatch the cheese to the four corners of France, then of the world. Camembert is a rapidly growing success story.

A VICTIM OF ITS OWN SUCCESS

Demand for the cheese became greater and greater. Camembert began to be produced outside of Normandy. Anxious to offer a product of consistent quality, Norman producers created the Assemblée Constitutive du Syndicat des Fabricants du Véritable Camembert de Normandie (Constitutive Assembly of the Association of Producers of Genuine Camembert of Normandy) on July 31, 1909. The following decree was issued: "Norman Camembert is a soft cheese, spontaneously draining, and neither cooked, nor pressed, nor kneaded; nor is the coagulum cut up; lightly salted, with surface mold, round in shape, weighing 350 grams (12 ounces), with a maximum diameter of 10 to 11 centimeters (4 to 4⅜ inches), produced from pure Normandy milk." A waste of time and effort! In 1926, the Orléans appellate court states that the term "Camembert" has fallen into the public domain. The manufacture of "Camembert" became increasingly industrialized, both in France and abroad (Switzerland, Italy, the U.S.). In order to protect the traditionally made cheese, small-scale producers requested and obtained in 1968 the words "Label Rouge." On August 31, 1983, genuine raw cow's-milk Camembert de Normandie, hand-ladled into molds, received the A.O.C. label, renewed on December 29, 1986; since 1996, it also has had European protection in the form of the official Protected Designation of Origin issued by the European Commission. Both ensure respect for traditional production methods at the stages of coagulation, hand-ladling into molds, evening out the curd, draining, turning, salting, and ripening, all the way through to packing.

THE HOUSE OF CAMEMBERT

In the village of Camembert, you can visit the Maison du Camembert, which opened in 1992. This vast building in the form of a huge, half-open Camembert box houses an exhibition tracing the history of the cheese and explaining how it is made.

Pasteurized Camembert

To meet the high demand, producers of factory-made Camembert use pasteurized milk. This makes them less dependent on milk yields. However, pasteurization also renders the cheese ineligible for the A.O.C. label, which holds producers to specific requirements. Nevertheless, the wording "Fabriqué en Normandie" (Made in Normandy) can be used for those Norman cheeses not entitled to the A.O.C. label. The ripening period does not exceed twenty days.

Description
This little wheel 4⅜ inches in diameter by 1¼ inches high and weighing 9 ounces has a fat content of 45 percent. It is factory-produced all year round.

Serving suggestions
The taste of a pasteurized Camembert is much less strong and more neutral than that of an A.O.C. cheese. Serve it with a bottled Normandy cider, a supple Bordeaux, or a generous Côtes-du-Rhône.

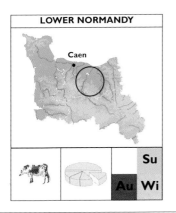

LOWER NORMANDY

Caen

Su

Au Wi

Castagniccia

This is a true typical Corsican cheese. It was "reinvented" by Ange Santoni of the Fromagerie Isula cheese dairy in Linguezetta, on the east coast of Corsica. The forerunner of this cheese was highly prized in the nineteenth century before fading into obscurity. After the recent discovery of an old recipe, production of a raw ewe's-milk Castagniccia was restarted.

Description
Flat and oblong, this cheese measures 4 inches in diameter by 1¼ to 1½ inches in height, and has a fat content of 48 percent. It is ripened for about thirty days in oak crates filled with organic chestnut flour. These chestnuts come from the Castagniccia region, hence the name of the cheese. Its rind, dusted with this flour, encloses an ivory-colored interior, soft and fairly supple.

Serving suggestions
The cheese gives off a milky scent, and has a luscious, delicate flavor. The rind should be eaten. "It's delicious, with an unmistakable chestnut flavor," says Ange Santoni. Serve Castagniccia with some country bread and a heady red Corsican wine.

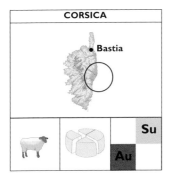

CORSICA

Bastia

Su

Au

CHAOURCE A.O.C.

CHAOURCE TAKES ITS NAME FROM A GALLIC MARKET TOWN IN THE CHAMPAGNE REGION BORDERING BURGUNDY AND AUXERROIS, TO THE SOUTH OF TROYES. FOR A LONG TIME IT WAS SOLD FRESH BY THE *COSSONIERS*, OR LOCAL DAIRY FARMERS, AT THE TROYES MARKET.

Description
Chaource d'Avril (April Chaource) is a cheese whose taste is initially sourish, then creamy. It's made from cow's milk in two formats: a big cylinder 4⅜ inches in diameter, 2⅜ inches tall, and weighing 1 pound; and a small form 3¼ inches in diameter, 2⅜ inches tall, and weighing 7 ounces. Its A.O.C. area covers the *départements* of Aube and Yonne. Its ripening period lasts for fourteen days. Some cheeses are kept in a cellar for one month, which reinforces their flavor.

Serving suggestions
The regular white rind exhibits a slight reddish pigmentation. The interior is smooth and creamy without being soft. Its aroma has affinities with mushrooms and cream. As for taste, its fruity flavor is enhanced by a touch of acidity. Chaource can be served in cubes with predinner drinks, or can accompany an old port wine. It makes a perfect ending for a celebratory meal, with a rosé des Riceys, a Santena, or a pink champagne.

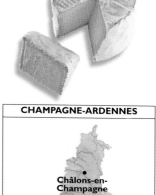

CHAMPAGNE-ARDENNES

Châlons-en-Champagne

Su
Au

COULOMMIERS FERMIER

PRODUCED IN ÎLE-DE-FRANCE, THIS CHEESE RESEMBLES A SMALL BRIE. MADE IN THE FARMHOUSE STYLE FROM RAW COW'S MILK, IT CONTAINS 40 TO 45 PERCENT FAT.

Description
There are those who say that Coulommiers Fermier is the forerunner of Brie. Although it is indeed found in Champagne and Lorraine, it originated in Île-de-France. Measuring 5 to 6 inches in diameter, this cheese is 1¼ to 1½ inches high and weighs between 14 and 17½ ounces. It is ripened for eight days.

Serving suggestions
Coulommiers Fermier can be recognized by its downy white rind, marked with the odd trace of red. Soft and tender, its light-yellow interior gives off a wholesome, grassy scent. It has a strong flavor and leaves a taste of sweet almonds in the mouth. This cheese is generally enjoyed with a fresh baguette or some country bread. Match it with a Côtes-du-Rhône or a Bordeaux.

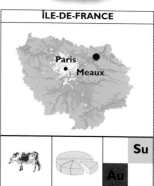

ÎLE-DE-FRANCE

Paris
Meaux

Su
Au

COULOMMIERS LAITIER

THIS "FACTORY CHEESE" IS OFTEN MADE FROM PASTEURIZED COW'S MILK. IN CONTRAST TO COULOMMIERS FERMIER, IT IS SMOOTH AND CREAMY, WITH A FAIRLY UNASSERTIVE TASTE. IT IS APPRECIATED FOR ITS MILD FLAVOR.

Description
Coulommiers Laitier is said to have the very same roots as its farmhouse cousin. Although indeed found in Champagne and Lorraine, it originated in Île-de-France. Measuring 5 to 6 inches in diameter, this cheese is 1¼ to 1½ inches high and weighs between 14 and 17½ ounces. Factory-made from pasteurized milk, Coulommiers Laitier is ripened for four weeks before it is marketed.

Choosing wisely
This cheese has a downy white rind with no traces of red flora. Soft and tender, its light-yellow interior gives off a wholesome, grassy scent. Nevertheless, factory-made Coulommiers reveals a fairly neutral flavor in the mouth.

Serving suggestions
Sample it on a Viennese baguette with some brut cider, or perhaps a Corbières.

ÎLE-DE-FRANCE

Paris

Coulommiers

Su

Au

CROQUIN DE LA MAYENNE

CROQUIN DE LA MAYENNE IS A GASTRONOMIC CURIOSITY THAT DESERVES TO BE FAR MORE WIDELY KNOWN AND AVAILABLE, GIVEN ITS DELICIOUS TASTE!

Description
This cylindrical cheese is made from the milk of cows grazing freely on the luxuriant grasslands of Mayenne, which give the milk its richness. Croquin de la Mayenne is ripened for two to three weeks, the time necessary for the cheese to firm up and for its aroma to develop. Reddish dots are scattered over the bloomy rind of the cheese, which bears the grooves of the shelves on which it was ripened.

Serving suggestions
The soft interior of this cheese is supple, creamy, and highly aromatic. It is chiefly enjoyed at the end of a meal, with a selection of breads such as multigrain and raisin. Remove it from the refrigerator at least one hour before you intend to eat it. Serve it with a slightly fresh Saint-Nicolas-de-Bourgueil or a Saumur-Champigny.

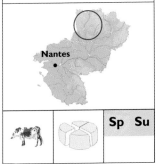

PAYS-DE-LOIRE

Nantes

Sp Su

EXPLORATEUR

EXPLORATEUR IS FACTORY-MADE IN ÎLE-DE-FRANCE. A REGISTERED TRADEMARK PRODUCT, IT WAS CREATED AFTER THE SECOND WORLD WAR BY MONSIEUR DUQUESNE, A CHEESEMAKER FROM SEINE-ET-MARNE.

Method of production
A triple-cream cheese made from raw cow's milk enriched with fresh cream, Explorateur contains no less than 75 percent fat! The rind of the cheese develops its characteristic layer of flora during the two- or three-week ripening period. Cylindrically shaped, it measures 3¼ inches in diameter and 2⅜ inches in height, and generally weighs just over 9 ounces. Explorateur does come in different shapes and sizes, however.

Serving suggestions
The very creamy interior is soft and unctuous, and gives off a slightly musty odor, tempered by the milky scent. Extremely delicious, Explorateur should be savored at the end of a meal on a Viennese baguette, accompanied by a few dried fruits or thin slices of apple. Include it on a cheeseboard and serve it with a personable Côtes-de-Bourg to enhance its slightly fatty flavor.

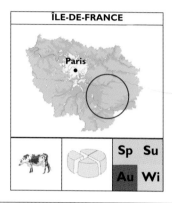

ÎLE-DE-FRANCE

Paris

| | | Sp | Su |
| | | Au | Wi |

FEUILLE DE DREUX OR DREUX À LA FEUILLE

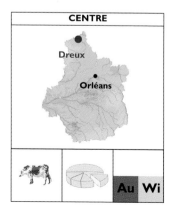

ORIGINATING IN THE TOWN OF DREUX IN EURE-ET-LOIRE, FEUILLE DE DREUX IS MADE FROM SLIGHTLY SKIMMED, RAW OR PASTEURIZED COW'S MILK. A RUSTIC CHEESE, IT HAS A LOW FAT CONTENT.

In the beginning
In bygone days, Feuille de Dreux, made just outside Normandy, would age slowly under a chestnut leaf. This leaf (*feuille*) prevented the stacked cheeses from sticking to one another—hence the cheese's name. In those days, Feuille de Dreux was a great favorite of farmers working in the fields.

Description
Shaped like a round, flat cake ¾ to 1¼ inches high, Feuille de Dreux measures 5½ to 6¼ inches in diameter and weighs between 10½ and 12 ounces. The cheese gives off a faint leafy odor. At the end of the ripening period, the rind turns brown or red and encloses a strong-flavored, fruity interior. A delicious, slight vegetal taste persists after eating the cheese. The Feuilles de Dreux most appreciated by turophiles are made in Marsauceux in Eure-et-Loire, and bear the name of the village where they are produced.

Serving suggestions
This distinctive-tasting cheese may be eaten accompanied by a green salad sprinkled with shallots, or offered on a cheeseboard at the end of a meal. Serve it with an Anjou wine or a Saumur-Champigny.

CENTRE

Dreux

Orléans

| | | Au | Wi |

FOUGERU

THIS CHEESE FROM THE BRIE FAMILY IS HANDCRAFTED IN THE TRADITIONAL MANNER. ITS PRODUCTION METHOD IS SIMILAR TO THAT OF COULOMMIERS, WITH WHICH IT SHARES CERTAIN SIMILARITIES IN TASTE.

In the beginning
When it was first created, Fougeru was produced at the farm and intended to be eaten on the spot. The fern leaf from which it takes its name (*fougère*, fern) both decorated it and scented it agreeably. Its original manufacturer, Monsieur Rouzaire, nowadays gives precedence to industrial methods in his cheese factory in Tournan-en-Brie. Fougeru is ripened for four weeks in a well-ventilated cellar. Larger than Coulommiers, it measures 6¼ inches in diameter by 1½ inches in height, and weighs approximately 23 ounces.

Serving suggestions
Fougeru's supple, smooth, and creamy interior is not very salty. The scent of the fern combined with that of the mold on the rind makes this an unusual cheese. It deserves a place on a cheeseboard, and harmonizes well with raisin bread. Serve it with a Bordeaux.

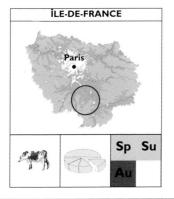

ÎLE-DE-FRANCE

Paris

Sp Su

Au

GRATTE-PAILLE

FROM THE TRIPLE-CREAM FAMILY, THIS RICH, UNCTUOUS CHEESE DELIGHTS LOVERS OF CREAM. MADE IN SEINE-ET-MARNE FROM COW'S MILK, IT CONTAINS NO LESS THAN 70 PERCENT FAT!

Choosing wisely
Oily and unctuous, Gratte-Paille has a rich taste of cream. It melts on the palate and leaves a pleasant, mild taste in the mouth. Log-shaped, it measures 3¼ to 4 inches long by 2⅜ inches high, and weighs between 10½ and 12 ounces.

Serving suggestions
Triple-cream cheeses are currently much in demand owing to their smooth, creamy texture. They add pleasant variety to a cheeseboard and can be strewn with herbs such as chives or minced parsley to enhance their flavor. Ideal after a light meal, Gratte-Paille spreads easily on a crusty loaf, whole-wheat bread, or nut bread. Serve it with a Loire wine or a Côtes-du-Rhône.

ÎLE-DE-FRANCE

Paris

Sp Su

Au Wi

LACANDOU

Made by Monsieur Lacan, this sheep's cheese is produced in Rouergue, north of Aveyron. The producer still uses traditional artisan methods—thus, the milk comes from ewes that are never fed on silage, but rather are left to graze in the mountains in absolute freedom.

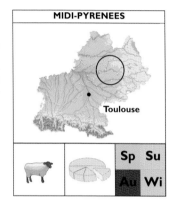

Description
Made from raw milk, this cheese has a fat content of 45 percent. Disk-shaped, it measures 4 inches in diameter by ½ inch in height, and weighs 7 ounces. Lacandou is ripened for three weeks in an *hâloir*, or drying room.

Serving suggestions
This cheese boasts a strong flavor, owing to the richness of the ewe's milk from which it is made. The sheep graze on vegetation rich in grass and a wide variety of flowers. Lacandou should be eaten accompanied by a crisp green salad or presented on a cheeseboard at the end of a meal. It harmonizes perfectly with very fresh country bread. Sample it with a Côtes-du-Roussillon.

MIDI-PYRENEES

Toulouse

		Sp	Su
🐑		Au	Wi

LAVORT

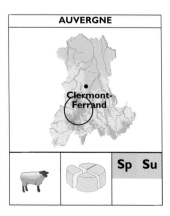

Lavort was created in the 1990s by the cheesemaker Patrick Beaumont. "This medieval-looking cheese surprises us with its shape and seduces us with its taste," explains the famous godfather of Lavort, Pierre Troisgros.

Method of production
The cheese's creator, Patrick Beaumont, found the mold that gives Lavort its craterlike shape in Spain. The raw milk used in its production comes from ewes of the Lacaune breed, raised by several producers in the Dore valley in the Auvergne. During the hundred-day ripening period, the rind of the cheese becomes colonized with flora and its interior softens.

Description
Disk-shaped, Lavort measures 8 inches in diameter by 4¾ inches in height, and weighs just under 4½ pounds.

Serving suggestions
The golden, supple interior of a Lavort gives off a slightly woodsy aroma. The longer the cheese has ripened, the more pronounced its fruity flavor. This rather unusual cheese is a genuine delicacy. Offer it on a cheeseboard with whole-wheat bread or raisin bread, and accompany it with a dry Jurançon.

AUVERGNE

Clermont-Ferrand

		Sp	Su
🐑			

NEUFCHÂTEL A.O.C.

MADE FROM COW'S MILK, NEUFCHÂTEL ORIGINATED IN THE GREEN PASTURES OF THE BRAY AREA IN NORMANDY. IT'S A SMOOTH, CREAMY CHEESE, JUST PERFECT FOR GOURMANDS.

Description
Neufchâtel is produced like Camembert, but unlike its famous neighbor, may be made in a variety of shapes: heart, square, briquette, bung (a cylindrical shape that recalls the stopper of a barrel). Whatever its shape, though, it always weighs around 3½ ounces. The most highly prized version of this cheese is made in Neufchâtel-en-Bray.

In the beginning
This cheese is said to date from the tenth century. From 1050, the Abbey of Sigy was granted the right to levy a tithe on the *frometons* (cheeses), as Neufchâtels were then referred to. In 1802, Napoleon was given a basketful of cheeses, including plenty of Neufchâtels, by way of homage, but it wasn't until the nineteenth century that Parisians were at last able to sample this marvel, whose merits were extolled by the *Almanach des gourmands* (1803–1812).

Serving suggestions
The dry, velvety rind, which cracks when pinched, hides a supple, unctuous interior of a lovely golden yellow. It has a forthright yet delicate flavor. True cheese-lovers prefer it when the interior is darker and the rind wine-colored, when it harmonizes perfectly with powerful, tannic reds. Some also sample it when very fresh, eating it like a fresh white cheese, or spiced with aromatic herbs, salt, and pepper.

UPPER NORMANDY

Rouen ● Neufchâtel-en-Bray

Su Au Wi

OLIVET FOIN

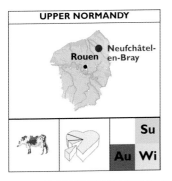

MANUFACTURED IN OLIVET ON THE BANKS OF THE LOIRET, IN THE INNER SUBURB OF ORLÉANS, THIS IS A DELICIOUS, SOFT, COW'S-MILK CHEESE. BALZAC, WHO WAS CRAZY ABOUT IT, WOULD ENJOY IT WITH WALNUTS AND A FRESH WINE.

Method of production
This artisanal cheese is made in May and June, when the cows produce a very rich milk. Formerly ripened in vine or plane leaves, today it is stored for at least one month in straw, in chests where it matures slowly.

Description
Olivet measures approximately 3¼ inches in diameter by 1 inch in height, and weighs 9 ounces. Delicately salty, it has a lovely light-yellow interior. It should be fairly firm and give off a slightly musty odor.

Serving suggestions
In bygone days, farmers and day laborers would eat it as a snack during the harvests, then during grape-picking time. When young, Olivet is preferably sampled in summer. It is best served at the end of a meal with nut bread. Accompany it with a red Sancerre or a white Touraine.

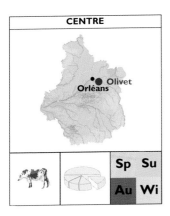

CENTRE

●Olivet
Orléans

Sp Su Au Wi

OLIVET CENDRÉ

JUST LIKE ITS COUSIN, THIS EXCELLENT CHEESE IS PRODUCED IN OLIVET, ON THE BANKS OF THE LOIRET, AND IS ALSO A SOFT, COW'S-MILK CHEESE.

In the beginning
The ash in which these cheeses were first rolled was that of the burned vine shoots. Olivet Cendré is also made in May and June, with the same very rich milk. It's a cheese that should therefore mature slowly. Olivet Cendré is generally drier than Olivet Foin.

Description
The ash-rolled version of Olivet also measures 3¼ inches in diameter by 1 inch in height, and weighs 9 ounces. Slightly salty, its interior is also a lovely light yellow, and should be fairly firm and give off a slight musty odor.

Serving suggestions
Olivet Cendré is more flavorful from November to August. It should be served at the end of the meal, on nut bread. Partner it with a red Sancerre or a white Touraine.

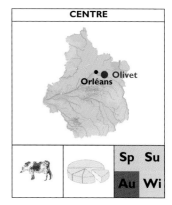

CENTRE

Olivet
Orléans

Sp Su
Au Wi

PÉRAIL DE BREBIS

A FARMHOUSE CHEESE, THIS NATIVE OF THE LARZAC, THOUGH LESS WELL RENOWNED THAN ROQUEFORT, ALSO DELIGHTS CONNOISSEURS AND FANS OF SHEEP CHEESES.

Description
This cheese is produced by coagulation with rennet only, and is hence nonacid. It can contain up to 50 percent fat. Round and flat, 3¼ inches in diameter, it weighs between 2¾ and 3½ ounces. One of the few sheep cheeses belonging to the bloomy-rind family, it is often made with milk from the last milkings, which is not rich enough for making Roqueforts.

Choosing wisely
Pérail de Brebis must be ripened for at least one week. It's a soft cheese whose consistency should be very supple. Light in color, it has a wholesome ewe's-milk scent and a mild, velvety flavor.

Serving suggestions
Should be eaten when fresh and creamy on crusty bread or toasted slices of country-style bread. Can be served with a Saint-Chinian.

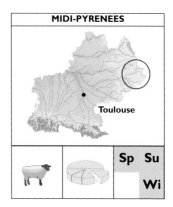

MIDI-PYRENEES

Toulouse

Sp Su
Wi

Neufchâtel A.O.C.

A cheese over 1,000 years old

The history of this delicious cheese dates back over ten centuries. Eleventh-century documents contain words to the effect that in 1050, Hugues I of Gournay granted the Abbey of Sigy the right to tithe the *frometons* (the word by which the present-day Neufchâtel was then known). At that time, it was produced by the monks of the Abbey of Sigy. It was in 1543, however, that the monks of the Abbey of Saint-Armand de Rouen officially acknowledged Neufchâtel by its present-day name.

In the nineteenth century it began to be recognized throughout Paris, and to take society dinners by storm. Its fame and reputation were probably due in part to the fact that Napoleon III, who in 1802 received a basket of cheeses, including Neufchâtel, appreciated this subtle-tasting cheese for what it was worth.

Neufchâtel and Saint Valentine

This delicacy, prized throughout the world, draws its originality from the variety of shapes it comes in, which vary according to the methods and materials available to the producers. Without a doubt, the most famous is Neufchâtel that has been molded in the shape of a heart. Moreover, an interesting legend is attached to this particular shape. During the Hundred Years' War, Norman peasants apparently had no other way of showing their appreciation to the English soldiers than to offer them Neufchâtel cheeses in the shape of a heart. The clergy, for its part, preferred to see the cheese shaped like an angel's wings. It hardly matters who's right—today Neufchâtel is the cheese of all lovers, and of Saint Valentine; what's more, the *confrérie du fromage Neufchâtel* has chosen Saint Valentine as its patron saint.

One cheese, many shapes

Besides the famous heart, Neufchâtel comes in different shapes that are recognized by the official authorities: a cylindrical bung (3½ ounces), square (3½ ounces), briquette (3½ ounces), double bung (7 ounces), and parallelepiped (2¼ pounds). Choose your shape according to personal taste or momentary fancy—Neufchâtel can humor any whim!

All about its manufacture

Neufchâtel is made from raw cow's milk poured into Norman vats. The milk is kept at a temperature of about 68°F, and rennet is added. The curd is drained in suspended cloths for about twelve hours. These cloths are then placed in a press for another twelve hours and the resulting preparation is kneaded. It is sprayed with *Penicillium candidum*, then pressed in a mold arranged over racks. The cheeses are then hand-salted before being ripened in cellars at a temperature of 54°–57°F for at least ten days.

It can be eaten young at the end of this period, or more matured if the ripening period is prolonged; the cheese then becomes delightfully runny and its flavor spicier.

Regulated production

The *syndicat du label du fromage de Neufchâtel*, an association for the protection of Neufchâtel, was created in 1957. Since May 3, 1969, Neufchâtel has been designated an A.O.C. cheese, as recognized by the amended decree of December 29, 1986.

Neufchâtel's territory of production extends throughout the area in Upper Normandy known as the Boutonnière du Pays de Bray, a plain bordered by limestone cliffs and sheltered from the winds.

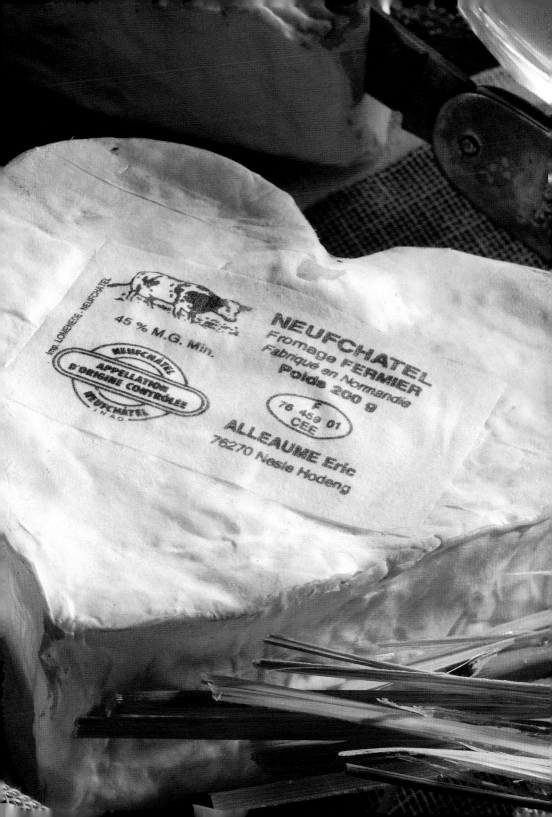

PETIT SÉNONAIS

UNDER ITS BLUISH RIND, THIS DELICIOUS COW'S-MILK CHEESE HARBORS OCEANS OF FLAVORS RANGING FROM TENDERNESS TO ACIDITY. A PITY, THEN, THAT IT ISN'T BETTER KNOWN AND MORE WIDELY AVAILABLE. LOVERS OF GENUINE CHEESES WILL WANT TO INDULGE THEMSELVES IF THEY SHOULD EVER FIND THIS CHEESE SOMEWHERE OFF THE BEATEN TRACK.

Description
This cheese is cylinder-shaped, measuring 2⅜ inches high by 2¾ inches in diameter. A lightweight, it tilts the scales at 5¼ ounces or less. At the end of a twelve-day ripening period, its rind develops a thin layer of flora covered with light patches of pretty, bluish-shaded mold. Its interior is tender, with a very pronounced milky taste. The flavor of the interior becomes more acid as time goes on, with delightful accents. It should be sampled after about twenty days of ripening to appreciate the delicious nuances to the hilt. Petit Sénonais has a fat content of between 45 and 50 percent.

Serving suggestions
Petit Sénonais should be appreciated fully at the end of a meal, with an assortment of fancy breads: raisin, nut, multigrain, olive. This farmhouse cheese will impress gourmets with its intriguing, regrettably little-known flavor. Match it with a red Burgundy or a Bordeaux served at room temperature.

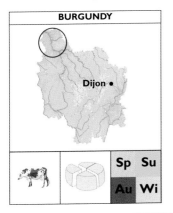

BURGUNDY

Dijon •

Sp Su
Au Wi

PITHIVIERS AU FOIN

PRODUCED IN THE LOIRET, IN BONDAROY, NEAR PITHIVIERS, THIS COW'S-MILK CHEESE ACTUALLY BEARS THE NAME OF BOTH TOWNS SO AS NOT TO CREATE JEALOUSY—EVEN THOUGH IT IS BETTER KNOWN AS PITHIVIERS AU FOIN THAN BONDAROY AU FOIN.

In the beginning
In the past, this cheese was made only in summer, when the cows were producing plenty of milk. It was stored in hay, to be eaten in the fall or winter. Grape-pickers and seasonal laborers stocked their lunch bags with it in times of heavy work in the fields and vineyards.

Description
Disk-shaped with a 4–4¾-inch diameter, Pithiviers weighs around 10½ ounces. It has a white rind, strewn with blades of hay. It gives off a delicate musty odor. Its soft, uncooked interior is very light yellow.

Serving suggestions
Now made from pasteurized milk, this cheese is eaten year-round. Unfortunately, it has lost some of its former delicacy and aroma. Its unobtrusive flavor thus goes well with a slightly acid, sourdough-type bread or a Poilâne loaf. Serve it at the end of a meal with an assortment of local cheeses and accompany it with a Chinon or a Saint-Nicolas-de-Bourgeuil.

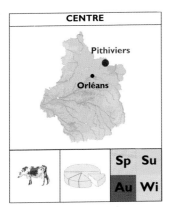

CENTRE

Pithiviers

•
Orléans

Sp Su
Au Wi

PITHIVIERS SAUGE

Also produced in the Loiret, near Pithiviers, this cow's-milk cheese is the twin of Pithiviers au Foin. Only its coat is different...

Description
Disk-like, 4–4¾-inches in diameter, Pithiviers Sauge weighs about 10½ ounces. It has a white rind covered with sage leaves that impart a pleasant aroma. It also gives off a characteristic musty scent. A soft, uncooked cheese, it has a very light-yellow interior.

Serving suggestions
To enhance its flavor, accompany it with a country-style loaf and serve it at the end of the meal with a Chinon or a Saint-Nicolas-de-Bourgeuil.

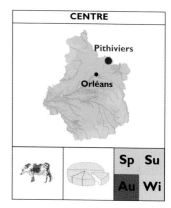

CENTRE

Pithiviers

Orléans

		Sp	Su
		Au	Wi

RIGOTTE DE VACHE

This typical cow's-milk cheese of the Lyonnais and Dauphiné is not the slightest bit like Italian ricotta, from which it nevertheless seems to have borrowed its name.

In the beginning
Production of this cheese dates back to Roman times. In the past, goat's-milk Rigottes could be found, but they are becoming increasingly rare.

Description
Whether shaped like little disks or cylindrical, Rigotte is always round, 1½ to 2 inches in diameter, and varies between 1 and 2 inches in height. It weighs anywhere between 1 and 2¾ ounces. With the passage of time, its natural rind becomes covered with orange spots. Its interior has a rather fine consistency and gives off a delicate honey aroma. Rigottes are ripened for two to three weeks.

Serving suggestions
The taste of this cheese varies according to its region of origin. Drier and slightly acid, Rigottes from the Lyonnais would be very good as an appetizer, in little cubes or in thin, rolled-up slices to be paired, for example, with a white Burgundy. At the end of a meal, offer a soft, melting Rigotte from the Dauphiné instead, which should be served with rye bread and a dry, fruity white.

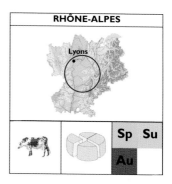

RHÔNE-ALPES

Lyons

		Sp	Su
		Au	

SAINT-FÉLICIEN

THIS VERY CREAMY CHEESE, PRODUCED IN THE VERCORS, IS MADE FROM COW'S, AND SOMETIMES GOAT'S, MILK, EITHER RAW OR PASTEURIZED. THE STORY GOES THAT IT WAS DEVELOPED FROM THE RESEARCH OF A CHEESEMAKER LIVING ON THE SLOPES OF THE CROIX-ROUSSE IN LYONS. ESPECIALLY SMOOTH AND CREAMY, IT GIVES THE IMPRESSION OF BEING HIGH IN FAT, ALTHOUGH ITS FAT CONTENT IS ONLY 50 PERCENT!

Description
Close to Saint-Marcellin in both taste and method of production, Saint-Félicien is disk-shaped, approximately 4⅜ inches in diameter by ½ inch in height. It weighs between 4¼ and 5¼ ounces. Saint-Félicien is ripened for twenty-one days, during which time its rind develops an attractive floral coating and its interior becomes off-white. The cheese gives off a scent of cream and milk.

Serving suggestions
Gourmets fond of ultra-creamy tastes will love this sort of cheese. Ripened for around thirty days, the taste sensation is slightly bitter. Sample it with whole-wheat bread at the end of a meal. The company of a Côtes-du-Ventoux or a Saint-Nicolas-de-Bourgueil should bring out its full flavor.

RHÔNE-ALPES

Lyons

Sp	Su
Au	

SAINT-MARCELLIN BLANC

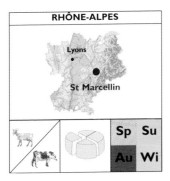

GOAT- OR COW'S-MILK CHEESE? SAINT-MARCELLIN REFUSES TO MAKE UP ITS MIND. PURE GOAT'S MILK OR COW'S MILK, SOMETIMES EVEN A MIXTURE OF THE TWO—THE RESULT IS A DELICIOUS LITTLE CHEESE THAT'S FULL OF SURPRISES.

Method of production
Originally a pure goat's-milk cheese, Saint-Marcellin is today also made with cow's milk or a mixture of the two. An unpressed, uncooked soft cheese, it is preferably made with raw milk.

In the beginning
In the past, there were a large number of goat flocks in the region of Saint-Marcellin in the Dauphiné, and this cheese is mentioned as early as the fifteenth century. It is said that while hunting in the forest of Lente, at the edge of the Vercors and Diois massifs, the future Louis XI fell off his horse. He was sheltered by two woodcutters who offered him some bread and their famous Saint-Marcellin. Once he became king, he introduced this cheese to the royal table.

Description
Measuring 2¾ inches in diameter by 1 inch in height, Saint-Marcellin weighs 2¾ ounces. Its natural rind is white when fresh.

Serving suggestions
This cheese is best when it's runny, so serve it exclusively on a cheeseboard or with a salad dressed with walnut oil. It should be eaten with a crusty loaf, accompanied by a light, fruity red wine, or red or white Savoie wines.

RHÔNE-ALPES

Lyons

St Marcellin

Sp	Su
Au	Wi

Saint-Marcellin aux Gênes

Pure goat's or pure cow's milk, sometimes even a mixture of the two, here's a delicious artisanal cheese that's full of surprises.

Method of production
Originally 100 percent goat's milk, Saint-Marcellin aux Gênes is today made with cow's milk or a mixture of the two. It is an unpressed, uncooked soft cheese made from raw milk.

Description
Measuring 2¾ inches in diameter by 1 inch in height, Saint-Marcellin aux Gênes weighs 2¾ ounces. Its natural rind, white when the cheese is fresh, becomes covered in blue dots. After two weeks' ripening, its interior becomes soft, then quite obviously creamy. When just right for eating, it is deliciously flowing—it's then sold in a little dish. This cheese is sometimes ripened in old marc brandy and and covered with pressed grape stalks.

Serving suggestions
Its flavor, reminiscent of hazelnut and with more of a lactic tang than Saint-Marcellin Blanc, harmonizes very well with a rye loaf. You can enjoy it at the end of a meal or with a salad dressed in walnut oil. Serve it with a red or white Côtes-du-Rhône.

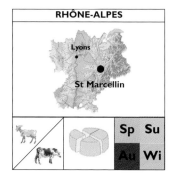

RHÔNE-ALPES

Lyons

St Marcellin

Sp Su
Au Wi

Soft, Washed-Rind Cheeses

ORANGE, BRICK, STRAIGHT-UP RED . . . THESE CHEESES HAVE A VERY FORTHRIGHT, ALMOST BRILLIANT COLOR. THEIR HIGHLY ASSERTIVE CHARACTER, AS POWERFUL AS IT IS AROMATIC, INSPIRES ANYTHING BUT INDIFFERENCE.

A BRICK WITH A HEART OF GOLD

Larger than soft, bloomy-rind cheeses, these washed-rind cheeses are made from either raw or pasteurized milk.

Their production requires a lot of handling. They undergo a mixed coagulation—both lactic ferments and a little rennet are added to the milk.

To speed up the draining of soft, washed-rind cheeses, the curd is cut up, stirred, and sometimes kneaded to extract the whey. After they are removed from the molds, the cheeses are hand-salted. They are placed on boards, then tinted with annatto, a natural coloring extracted from the seeds of the annatto tree. This stage gives them a brick-colored tint, so one can identify them easily.

A BOOZY RIPENING PERIOD

Next comes the ripening period in the *hâloir*, which lasts three to six months. During this stage, the cheeses are washed with salt water, or brine, to which alcohol is sometimes added—beer in the North, cider in Normandy, wine or marc brandy in Burgundy. At the end of this long period of careful tending, their rinds are smooth, supple, shiny, and a bit tacky.

Their interiors, smooth, creamy, and soft, are quite assertive tasting. And underneath this very strong taste, the true cheese-lover can discern highly subtle aromas. Examples of this family are Époisses, Livarot, Vacherin du Mont d'Or, Langres, Muenster, Pont-l'Évêque, and Maroilles.

MONKS AND CHEESE

Washed-rind cheeses came into being around the year A.D. 1000, aided and abetted by the troubled times of the Middle Ages.

Uneasy about their redemption and anxious to put themselves under the protection of the church, lords and their subjects took refuge in the monasteries. Benedictine monks, at the head of vast agricultural estates and large herds, organized the economic side of life and began manufacturing dairy products, which provided them with a long-lasting food resource.

It was in the heart of the Middle Ages that Cistercian and Benedictine monks invented Pont-l'Évêque, Maroilles, and Muenster (which means "monastery" in the German-speaking regions).

In 1836, boxes made of fir and beech came on the scene. With this packaging, washed-rind cheeses began to travel throughout Europe, expanding their sales area and winning over a multitude of new markets.

WHERE ARE THEY FOUND?

Washed-rind cheeses are produced throughout most of France. In Normandy, two acknowledged celebrities rub elbows: Pont-l'Évêque and Livarot, with its characteristic belt of rushes. In the north of France, the Coeur d'Arras, Boulette d'Avesnes, Dauphin du Hainaut, Gris de Lille, and Rollot Picard make a harmonious team.

In the east of France, Muenster is universally prized. In Burgundy, Chambertin and Maroilles cheeses are often flavored with marc brandy.

In Franche-Comté, the Abondance, Bauges, and Mont d'Or massifs claim Vacherin as their own.

Finally, in Corsica, a washed-rind sheep's cheese is produced—the only exception among this family of cheeses, which is normally made from cow's milk.

Soft, washed-rind cheeses can be kept for a maximum of three to four days in a well-ventilated place, at a constant temperature of 53.6°F.

Opposite: Muenster is placed on the shelves to ripen. It's during this stage that it develops its characteristic brick color. Muenster is delicious with a beer from the same region.

AFFIDÉLICE OR AFFIDÉLIS

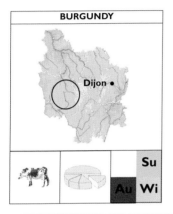

BURGUNDY

Dijon •

		Su
		Wi
	Au	

THIS BURGUNDIAN CHEESE HAS A DISTINCTIVE CHARACTERISTIC: IT IS RIPENED WITH CHABLIS. THE HEADY WHITE WINE GIVES IT A UNIQUE FLAVOR, MORE SUBTLE AND LESS STRONG THAN THAT OF ÉPOISSES, ITS NEIGHBOR RIPENED WITH BURGUNDIAN MARC BRANDY.

Method of production
Affidélice is made from cow's milk. Its ripening period lasts for a minimum of one month; its washed rind is rubbed two to three times a week with a mixture of salt water and Chablis. In the beginning, there is a higher proportion of water to wine, whereas at the end of the ripening period the reverse is true, with the Chablis impregnating the interior of the cheese with its aroma and taste. Soft, smooth, and creamy in texture, it leaves a delicious taste in the mouth. Sold in a wooden box, Affidélice measures 6¼ to 7½ inches in diameter and 1¼ to 1¾ inches thick, and weighs between 1½ and 2½ pounds. It is produced in dairy plants.

Serving suggestions
Affidélice is a good cheese to serve at the end of a meal, on country or rye bread. It should be enjoyed with a Santenay, a Chablis, or a finger of Burgundian marc brandy.

AMI DU CHAMBERTIN

BURGUNDY

Dijon •

Gevrey-
Chambertin

		Su
	Au	

RAYMOND GAUDRY, A CHEESEMAKER OF RENOWN IN BURGUNDY, CREATED THIS ARTISANAL CHEESE IN 1950. LIKE ÉPOISSES, IT IS PRODUCED IN GEVREY-CHAMBERTIN. ITS AROMA, STRONG AND PERSISTENT, IS THE HALLMARK OF A GREAT CHEESE INVITING IMMEDIATE CLOSER ACQUAINTANCE, AND IT WILL SURPRISE AND DELIGHT THE PALATE.

Method of production
Ami du Chambertin is made from cow's milk. During its ripening period, which lasts for at least one month, its moist rind, washed every two or three days with a mixture of salt water and Burgundian marc brandy, acquires a reddish hue. Disk-shaped, measuring 3½ inches across by 1½ inches in height, it weighs about 9 ounces.

Serving suggestions
Its delicate interior is smooth and creamy. Nevertheless, its powerful, penetrating taste is less strong than Époisse's. It should be sampled with a crusty baguette. Wines such as Pouilly-Fuissé or else a sweet white such as a Loupiac, a Barsac, or a Bonnezeaux, will set this cheese off magnificently.

BERGUES

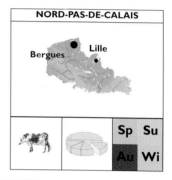

Bergues, a farmhouse or artisanal cheese, comes from the Flemish town of the same name, just under eight miles from the Belgian border. "A slightly soft cheese, produced by hardworking farmers using all of the byproducts of their milk, it is as chalk-white as the gables of the old dovecots in this area," wrote Léon Moreel, a writer from this region.

Description
Measuring 8 to 8¾ inches across by 1½ to 2⅜ inches thick, this slightly hardened soft cheese is made from partially skimmed cow's milk. It has long sought to imitate eighteenth-century Dutch cheeses. Heading toward extinction twenty or so years ago, this cheese is today made by some forty producers.

Serving suggestions
Bergues should be enjoyed fresh. Its ripening period lasts only twenty days; it has a very light-colored interior, and a fairly unpronounced taste. When ripening is extended, its rind takes on a warmer tone. Partner it with some local beer, fresh with a hint of bitterness. It may also be served with a white Rully.

BOULETTE D'AVESNES

A native of Flanders, this farmhouse or factory-produced soft, washed-rind cheese bears the name of the village where it is produced, close to the Belgian border. In spite of an unmerited reputation for strength, this cheese has a mild, pleasant, and rather unusual flavor.

Method of production
In the past, this cheese was made with scraps of various cheeses that had been damaged when removed from their molds, such as Maroilles. Now it is made from buttermilk or from fresh, white Maroilles, to which herbs, pepper, or cloves are then added according to the various cheesemakers' recipes. Boulette d'Avesnes is handcrafted, and is shaped like a pointy pear. It is ripened for three months, the rinds of certain of the artisanally produced cheeses being washed with beer. It is then reddened with annatto or rolled in paprika.

Serving suggestions
When choosing, look for a moist rind, a fine dark-red color, and a mild, delicious taste. It should be enjoyed at the end of a meal with some crispbread. Serve it with a "sunny" wine such as a Corbières or a Cahors. It is also not averse to the company of a small glass of Genever (juniper spirits).

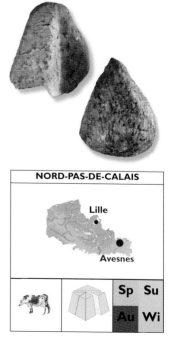

CHAUMES

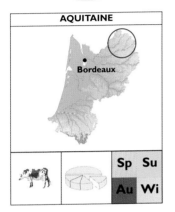

C REATED IN 1972, THIS CHEESE IS SHAPED LIKE A FLATTENED
CAKE AND HAS A RATHER CHARACTERISTIC FLAVOR. THE
FROMAGERIE DES CHAUMES PRODUCES THIS SOFT, WASHED-
RIND CHEESE MADE FROM PASTEURIZED COW'S MILK IN THE
DORDOGNE REGION.

Description
Chaumes is in the shape of a convex-sided disk 7 inches across by
1½ inches thick, and weighs 4¼ pounds. It used to be sold loose only,
until success caught up with it and it began to be marketed in prepacked
portions. During the ripening stage, it is regularly scratched and washed
for a month. This is what gives it its light-yellow rind, the color of
wheat—hence its evocative name, which means "stubble" or "thatch"
in French.

Serving suggestionss
The interior of this cheese is tender and straw-colored; its taste, rather
close to Saint-Paulin's, is mild. Nevertheless it has more character than
a number of industrial cheeses. Eat it with *fougasse,* or perhaps
olive bread, and accompany it with a Bordeaux or a Saint-Nicolas-
de-Bourgueil.

AQUITAINE

Bordeaux

		Sp	Su
		Au	Wi

COEUR D'ÉPOISSES

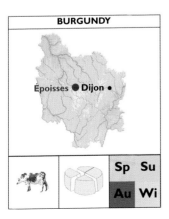

T HIS LITTLE ÉPOISSES, CALLED TROU DU CRU BY SOME
CHEESE SPECIALISTS, IS A PARTICULARLY AROMATIC WASHED-
RIND CHEESE. IT IS PRODUCED IN BURGUNDY FROM WHOLE
COW'S MILK.

Description
Tall and cone-shaped, measuring 1¼ to 1½ inches across at its base,
this cheese weighs approximately 3½ ounces. Like its big brother
Époisses, its moist, highly aromatic rind boasts a fine orange hue.
During ripening, this cheese is washed with Burgundian marc, which
imparts a bouquet of flavors to its interior.

Serving suggestions
The delicate interior of a Coeur d'Époisses develops a cow's-milk taste,
mixed with that of the marc. Its clear-cut flavor and creamy-to-soft
texture make it one of the best French cheeses. It's an ideal addition
to an "enlightened" cheeseboard, since it is neither well known
nor widely available. Serve it with a crusty baguette and a glass of
Chablis or Santenay. Fans of this cheese partner it with a finger of
Burgundian marc.

BURGUNDY

Époisses ● Dijon ●

		Sp	Su
		Au	Wi

Cœur de Thiérache

Made from pasteurized cow's milk, this artisanal cheese is a member of the washed-rind family. During its ripening period, which lasts three to four weeks, it is turned, brushed, and washed on a regular basis. Produced for the most part in Picardy, it has a mild taste.

Description
As its name indicates, Cœur de Thiérache is heart-shaped. Measuring 4 inches wide by 3¼ inches long, it is 1⅜ inches thick and weighs about 7 ounces. This typically Picardian cheese has a fat content of 45 percent and slightly resembles Maroilles.

Serving suggestions
The orange rind is tacky and a bit moist to the touch. Light yellow in color, the interior reveals a supple paste strewn with a few holes. In the mouth, Cœur de Thiérache melts on the palate, leaving behind a slightly sweet aftertaste. Serve it on a cheeseboard at the end of a meal with some cumin bread, accompanied by a Côtes-de-Blaye or a bitter beer—a drink from its own region.

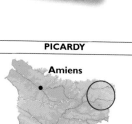

PICARDY

Amiens

Sp Su
Au Wi

Craquegnon ripened with La Gauloise beer

A typical northern French cheese, the creamy, strong-tasting Craquegnon is the ancestor of Maroilles. Don't let yourself be discouraged by its powerful aroma—this indicates that the Craquegnon is perfect for eating!

Description
Made from cow's milk, Craquegnon is marinated for forty-eight or seventy-two hours in La Gauloise beer—the best, according to Philippe Olivier, a *maître-fromager* in Boulogne-sur-Mer. The cheese is then ripened for between eighty and a hundred days. Regularly washed during the ripening period, the rind acquires an orange hue and the smooth, creamy interior develops a powerful aroma. In the shape of a 5-inch square, Craquegnon weighs approximately 1 pound 10 ounces.

Serving suggestions
Highly aromatic, this cheese has a persistent taste in the mouth. It should be eaten plain on a crusty baguette, accompanied by a slightly bitter beer.

NORD-PAS-DE-CALAIS

Lille

Boulogne-
sur-Mer

Sp Su
Au

DAUPHIN POISSON

THIS CHEESE, MADE FROM RAW OR PASTEURIZED COW'S MILK, IS MOLDED IN THE SHAPE OF A DOLPHIN, HENCE ITS NAME.

In the beginning
This cheese owes its personality first and foremost to its shape. According to the most widely accepted legend, Louis XIV and his son, traveling in the north of the country on the occasion of the signing of the Treaty of Nimègue in 1678, were particularly taken by this spicy-tasting cheese. Following the royal visit, cheesemakers were granted exemption from the taxes they had had to pay to bring their delivery wagons into the town of Cambrai. As a token of gratitude toward the royal family, they chose a mold in the shape of a dolphin (*dauphin* means both "dolphin" and "heir apparent" in French). This tradition was nearly lost in the 1950s.

Description
Less than 2 inches tall, Dauphin weighs between 10½ and 17½ ounces. Its orange rind is moist; its interior, which gives off an aroma of Maroilles, is tacky.

Serving suggestions
Dauphin is produced like Maroilles, but its interior is flavored with parsley, tarragon, pepper, and cloves. These seasonings intensify an already spicy flavor. The longer the ripening period (two or three months), the stronger the taste of the cheese. Open-textured country bread is a marvelous accompaniment to Dauphin. Serve this cheese with a Corbières.

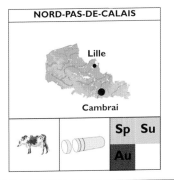

NORD-PAS-DE-CALAIS		
Lille •		
Cambrai		
🐄	◗▭	**Sp** **Su** **Au**

ÉPOISSES A.O.C.

MADE FROM WHOLE COW'S MILK, ÉPOISSES BELONGS TO THE WASHED-RIND FAMILY OF CHEESES. ORIGINALLY LIMITED TO THE CÔTE-D'OR, ITS PRODUCTION TODAY EXTENDS FROM YONNE TO HAUTE MARNE.

In the beginning
The origins of this cheese are shrouded in mystery. Some say that Époisses was invented at the beginning of the sixteenth century by Cistercian monks; others maintain that the recipe was discovered by farmers' wives, then passed down from mother to daughter in the traditional manner. Ripened for a minimum of four weeks, this cheese is regularly washed with salt water, then with Burgundian marc. Époisses has acquired great renown down through the ages. The famous gastronome Brillat-Savarin consolidated its reputation in his writings, calling it the "king of cheeses"; not to mention Napoleon I's infatuation with this cheese, which he would enjoy with a glass of Chambertin.

Choosing wisely
Smooth or slightly furrowed, Époisses has a shiny orange or straight-up brick-red rind. Its color comes from the natural pigmentation of its flora. Its smooth, creamy interior melts agreeably on the palate. Its clear-cut aroma is fairly spicy. Cylinder-shaped, Époisses is available in two sizes. Turophiles will appreciate this cheese at the end of a meal, accompanied by Poilâne-type bread and a white Burgundy.

BURGUNDY		
Époisses ● Dijon •		
🐄	🧀	**Sp** **Su** **Au** **Wi**

Fleur de Bière

Produced in Meurthe-et-Moselle, this unusual cheese is regularly washed with Val de Weiss beer during ripening. It has a fat content of 50 percent.

Description
The size of a large Camembert but thicker, Fleur de Bière measures approximately 6¾ inches across. Its washed rind is slightly moist. During ripening, which lasts a minimum of three weeks, this cheese is regularly washed with beer, then turned. The beer is not chosen at random—Val de Weiss is a local specialty. As a result, the pale yellow interior of the cheese gives off a characteristic aroma.

Serving suggestions
Fleur de Bière is not a cheese that passes unnoticed. Highly aromatic, it has a spicy taste, in which a delicate scent of cinnamon can be detected. Its flavor is best complemented by a slice of fresh bread and a green salad as an accompaniment. Naturally, it should be enjoyed with a bitter beer.

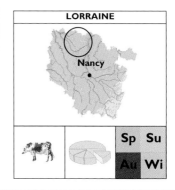

LORRAINE
Nancy

Sp Su Au Wi

Langres A.O.C.

Made from whole cow's milk, Langres is a washed-rind cheese. Its area of production extends over part of the *départements* of Côtes-d'Or, Haute-Marne, and Vosges.

Method of production
Langres is produced on the farm in the traditional manner. After the milking, the still-warm milk is poured into terra-cotta *fromottes*, or cheese molds. Once removed from the molds, the cheeses are dried on plane leaves, then ripened on oat straw for a period of fifteen to twenty-one days. Langres is cylinder-shaped, with a concave top. It comes in two sizes: a large 1¾-pound cheese measuring 6¼ to 8 inches across by 2 to 2¾ inches thick; and a small one weighing about 5 ounces and measuring 3 inches across by 1½ inches thick. Its fat content is 50 percent.

Choosing wisely
Langres can be recognized by its slightly tacky, light-yellow or orange-brown rind. The dip in its top, barely noticeable when the cheese is young, is accentuated during ripening. The supple interior of this cheese gives off a penetrating, characteristic aroma. Less strong than Époisses, Langres has a pleasant flavor, sustained without being aggressive, and fairly salty. Langres is used as an ingredient in soufflés and savory pies. Gourmets love to pour a drop of Burgundian marc or champagne in its "fountain" or dip before sampling it. Serve this cheese with sturdy wines such as Mercurey or Nuits-Saint-Georges.

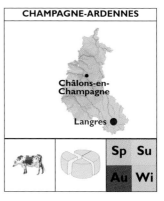

CHAMPAGNE-ARDENNES
Châlons-en-Champagne
Langres

Sp Su Au Wi

Livarot A.O.C.

Angelot and Livarot

The forerunner of Livarot, Angelot is a round or square cheese (the latter being the forerunner of Pont-l'Évêque) that is mentioned in the *Roman de la Rose* as well as by the poet Guillaume de Lorris in the thirteenth century. What's certain is that Angelot became Livarot in the seventeenth century. In one of his 1693 writings, Jean Baptiste Pommereu de la Bretesche asserts that Livarot is a highly prized delicacy in Paris. In 1708, Thomas Corneille mentioned it in his *Dictionnaire uni- versel géographique et historique*: "Every Monday at Vim- outiers, a big market is held to which the excellent cheeses from the Camembert and Livarot areas are brought." This native of the Auge area became phenomenally successful in the nineteenth century, and was nicknamed "poor man's meat" on account of its nutritional value.

A roaring success

Livarot gets its name from the eponymous town in Calvados from which it hails. It would be a pity to go to Livarot without visiting the museum dedicated to the cheese. There you will find the reconstruction of both a traditional dairy and an old-style cheese factory. A permanent exhibition of labels is also on display. The museum is open from April to October. In Livarot, you can also visit an authentic cheese factory, the Fromagerie Graindorge.

Production and packaging

The cow's milk obtained—nonpasteurized and never heated above 98.6°F—is renneted. The curds obtained are then cut up into large cubes. These are left to rest before being cut up again and stirred, and the resulting preparation is poured into a mold. The cheese is turned several times before being removed from the mold and salted. It is then left to drain for twenty-four hours before being placed in a cellar to ripen. The ripening stage lasts four weeks, during which time the cheese's rind is colored with annatto, the seeds of a plant native to South America; this is what gives it its lovely orange color.

Livarot produced from milk collected in the spring and the beginning of the summer is of better quality; these cheeses are on the market in fall and winter.

In the past, Livarot was a leaner cheese. In order to keep its shape, it was cinched with five strips of sedge— *Tipha latifolia*, a kind of aquatic rush—similar to military stripes; this is how it earned its nick- name of "Colonel." Nowadays Livarot has a higher fat content, 40 percent.

Official recognition

Since December 17, 1975, Livarot has been a member of the very exclusive circle of cheeses bearing an A.O.C. label. This A.O.C. is controlled by the amended decree of December 29, 1986. The area of production of Livarot is fairly circumscribed—to be entitled to the initials A.O.C., the cheese must have been produced in an area straddling Orne and Calvados. Today it is mainly produced in the Viette and Vie valleys.

Other cheeses may be considered to be the "younger brothers" of Livarot—here, we are thinking in particular of Petit Lisieux and Mignot, whose flavor is similar to Livarot's.

Which wine?

Although Livarot is traditionally sampled with a bottled cider or a glass of Calvados, it may also be enjoyed accompanied by a sturdy, tannic red wine with plenty of body: Corbières, Pommard, Morgon, Hermittage, or Pomerol, to name but a few.

LIVAROT A.O.C.

LOWER NORMANDY

Caen

Livarot

Au Wi

Presenting one of the more aromatic Normandy cheeses! Made from raw cow's milk, Livarot is a member of the washed-rind family of cheeses. Its production is limited to the Auge area, covering part of the *départements* of Calvados and Orne.

In the beginning
Livarot is one of the earliest Normandy cheeses. In one of the writings of the intendant Pommereu de la Bretesche, we learn that it was commonly consumed in Paris in 1693. It was not until the nineteenth century, however, that it reached its peak of popularity. Chroniclers nicknamed it "poor man's meat" because of its nutritional value. In 1877 Livarot beat the record for cheese production in Normandy, with no fewer than two hundred *affineurs* ripening four million Livarots per year! This cheese comes in four sizes, ranging from the *quart* Livarot measuring 2¾ inches across, to the *grand* Livarot 4¾ inches in diameter.

Choosing wisely
The ripening period lasts between three weeks and two months. At the end of three weeks, Livarot yields to thumb pressure. The rind is tacky, with shiny glints. The interior of the cheese weighs on the tongue before melting, and its fairly spicy flavor remains for a long time in the mouth. This cheese is generally offered on a cheeseboard. Livarot is best in fall and winter, when it has been made with spring milk. It should be enjoyed plain with country bread, accompanied by a bottled cider or Calvados.

RIPER LIVAROT

LOWER NORMANDY

Caen

Livarot

Au Wi

Made from raw cow's milk, Livarot is a member of the washed-rind family of cheeses. Its production is limited to the Auge area, covering part of the *départements* of Calvados and Orne. It contains 40 percent fat or higher.

Method of production
Thomas Corneille, brother of the more famous playwright Pierre, devoted an article to this, one of the oldest Normandy cheeses, in his *Dictionnaire universel géographique et historique*, published in 1708. Chroniclers also nicknamed it "poor man's meat." In 1877 this twin Livarot beat the cheese-production records of the time—in some two hundred cellars, four million Livarots per year were ripened! This cheese also comes in four sizes, ranging from the *quart* Livarot measuring 2¾ inches across, to the *grand* Livarot 4¾ inches in diameter.

Serving suggestions
This Livarot is ripened for a period of four to five weeks. Even so, it doesn't give off the whiff of ammonia that indicates an overripe cheese. Its smooth, shiny rind yields to thumb pressure. Its flavor is spicy and more pronounced than that of its less-ripe brother. This cheese should be enjoyed with Viennese bread and a glass of Calvados.

MAROILLES OR MAROLLES A.O.C.

INDISPUTABLY, MAROILLES IS THE CHOICEST OF THE STRONG CHEESES. MADE FROM COW'S MILK, IT BELONGS TO THE FAMILY OF SOFT, WASHED-RIND CHEESES. MAROILLES IS PRODUCED IN THE *DÉPARTEMENTS* OF NORD AND AISNE.

Description
This cheese is said to have been invented in 960 by a Benedictine monk of the Abbey of Maroilles. It takes its name from the Gallic village in the Avesnes area, also called Maro Lalo, which means "large clearing." Quickly gaining fame, it delighted numerous kings (Philippe Auguste, Saint Louis, Charles VI, Charles the Fifth of Spain, François I) and personalities (the prelate and writer Fénelon and the marshal Turenne). A farmhouse or factory-produced cheese, Maroilles is ripened for a period of five weeks to four months, during which time its yellow rind turns orange, then red. In the shape of a square block, it measures 5 inches across and 2⅜ inches thick and weighs approximately 25 ounces. It also comes in several smaller sizes: *sorbais* (19 ounces), *mignon* (just over 12 ounces), and *quart* (6⅜ ounces).

Serving suggestions
The orange-colored rind houses a golden interior, supple to the touch. Maroilles gives off a persistent aroma and leaves a spicy taste in the mouth. This famous cheese takes the place of honor on a cheeseboard. In cooking, it is used in traditional recipes like *flamiche*, a vegetable and cheese pie, or *goyère*, a sort of cheesy quiche. Accompany it with a sturdy red wine, a bitter beer, or a local cider.

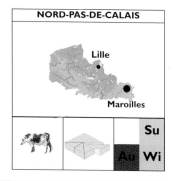

NORD-PAS-DE-CALAIS

Lille

Maroilles

Su
Au Wi

MONTS DE JOUX

A RELATIVE OF VACHERIN OR MONT-D'OR, THIS CREAMY CHEESE IS FIT FOR A KING. IT IS EATEN IN THE HEART OF WINTER, SCOOPED WITH A LITTLE SPOON. MADE IN DAIRY PLANTS FROM COW'S MILK, IT HAS A FAT CONTENT OF 45 PERCENT.

Description
Monts de Joux is ripened for three weeks in a cellar at a temperature of 59°F. Regularly washed, its wrinkled, reddish rind develops spots of orange mold. This cheese is sold in a fir-bark box whose scent impregnates the interior of the cheese, giving it a very pleasant aroma. Monts de Joux measures 4¾ to 12 inches across by 1½ to 2 inches thick, and weighs between 17½ ounces and 2¼ pounds, including its circle of bark.

Serving suggestions
This cheese is a genuine delight. Salty without being sharp, it can be enjoyed plain, on bread, or in cooked dishes. Gourmands can't resist its creamy interior, and eat it with a small spoon. Some people prefer to spread it on fresh bread or toast. Others use it to top hot potato dishes and prefer to melt this runny cheese. Serve it with a Beaujolais or a Mâcon, two wines produced near its region of origin.

FRANCHE-COMTÉ

Besançon

Sp
Wi

MUENSTER FERMIER A.O.C.

A KING AMONG CHEESES, MUENSTER IS ONE OF THE SUCCESS STORIES OF FRENCH GASTRONOMY. IT IS PRODUCED IN SEVEN *DÉPARTEMENTS*: BAS-RHIN, HAUT-RHIN, VOSGES, MEURTHE-ET-MOSELLE, MOSELLE, HAUTE-SAÔNE, AND THE TERRITORY OF BELFORT. ITS STRONG AROMA IS ON A PAR WITH ITS FAME.

In the beginning
Invented by monks, Muenster first appeared in 855 to the south of the Vosges massif, in the Fecht or Munster valleys. It is ripened for at least twenty-one days in a well-ventilated cellar, during which time it is turned and washed every other day. Cylinder-shaped, Muenster measures 5 to 7½ inches across by 1 to 3¼ inches thick, and weighs between 1 and 3¼ pounds.

Choosing wisely
Muenster is best in summer and fall, the time of year when the pastures are covered with green vegetation and flowers that enrich the cows' milk. Muenster's smooth, moist rind changes from orange-yellow to orange-red as ripening progresses. Inside, the cheese is supple and creamy-to-soft to the touch. Its strong aroma and clear-cut, spicy flavor are characteristic of the washed-rind cheeses. It can be eaten at the end of a meal, with a few cumin seeds. Alsatians eat it without bread, on top of hot potato dishes. Some people embellish their quiches and omelettes with thin slices of Muenster. Serve it with a powerful red such as Haut-Médoc, or with some beer.

LORRAINE

Strasbourg

Munster

Su

Au

MUENSTER FERMIER AU CUMIN

T HIS MUENSTER IS STUDDED WITH CUMIN SEEDS—A DELICIOUS LITTLE REFINEMENT. IT IS PRODUCED IN SEVEN *DÉPARTEMENTS*: BAS-RHIN, HAUT-RHIN, VOSGES, MEURTHE-ET-MOSELLE, MOSELLE, HAUTE-SAÔNE, AND THE TERRITORY OF BELFORT. LIKE ALL MUENSTERS, IT HAS A PERSISTENT AROMA.

Description
Invented by monks, Muenster first appeared in 855 to the south of the Vosges massif, in the Fecht or Muenster valleys. It is ripened for at least twenty-one days in a well-ventilated cellar, during which time it is turned and washed every other day. Cylinder-shaped, Muenster measures 5 to 7½ inches across by 1 to 3¼ inches thick, and weighs between 1 and 3¼ pounds. This farmhouse Muenster is studded with cumin seeds.

Serving suggestions
Cumin enhances the flavor of Muenster. Quite delicious and persistent on the palate, this cheese should be served with nut bread or raisin bread. Sample it with a glass of Tokay.

LORRAINE

Strasbourg

Munster

Su

Au

MUENSTER LAITIER

THIS CHEESE IS PRODUCED IN SEVEN *DÉPARTEMENTS*: BAS-RHIN, HAUT-RHIN, VOSGES, MEURTHE-ET-MOSELLE, MOSELLE, HAUTE-SAÔNE, AND THE TERRITORY OF BELFORT. PRODUCED IN DAIRY PLANTS, THIS CHEESE HAS A MILDER AROMA THAN MUENSTER FERMIER.

Description
Like its cousins, Muenster Laitier first appeared in 855 to the south of the Vosges massif, in the Fecht or Munster valleys. It is ripened for at least twenty-one days in a well-ventilated cellar, during which time it is turned and washed every other day. Cylinder-shaped, Muenster measures 5 to 7½ inches across by 1 to 3¼ inches thick, and weighs between 1 and 3¼ pounds.

Serving suggestions
Muenster Laitier's smooth, moist rind changes from orange-yellow to orange-red as ripening progresses. Inside, the cheese is supple and creamy-to-soft to the touch. Its strong aroma and clear-cut, spicy flavor are characteristic of the washed-rind cheeses. This cheese should be enjoyed at the end of a meal on country-style bread. Serve it with beer or a Pinot Noir.

LORRAINE

Strasbourg

Munster

Su
Au

HANSI AFFINÉ AU MARC DE GEWURZTRAMINER

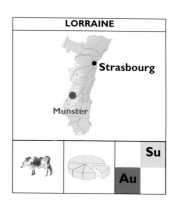

A RECENT CREATION, THIS CHEESE IS A MEMBER OF THE SOFT, WASHED-RIND FAMILY OF CHEESES. IT IS PRODUCED YEAR-ROUND IN THE *DÉPARTEMENT* OF BAS-RHIN, NEAR ROSHEIM, BY THE FROMAGERIE SIFFERT.

Description
Hansi, made from pasteurized cow's milk according to the same process as Muenster, is ripened with a Gewurztraminer marc specially selected for its cheese-compatible taste. Cylinder-shaped, it comes in two formats: one weighs 7 ounces and measures 4 to 4⅜ inches across by approximately 1¼ inches thick; the other weighs between 1 pound and 1 pound 12 ounces and is sold loose in dairies.

Serving suggestions
Sample it with an Alsatian wine, such as—what else?—a Gewurztraminer. A crusty country-style bread with a fine crumb makes the ideal accompaniment.

LORRAINE

Strasbourg

Munster

Su
Au

MUENSTER A.O.C.

IN A NUTSHELL

Muenster was created by Benedictine monks from Italy who, in the Middle Ages, made their way up the Fecht valley before founding, south of the Vosges massif in 855, a monastery in honor of Saint Gregory, which they called *Monasterium confluentes.* Several villages grew up around this monastery, including the market town of Munster—from the Latin for "monastery"—which gave its name to the cheese. The monks' objective was to perfect a process that would avoid the wasting of milk and that would provide food year-round for the area's inhabitants. In addition, the philosophy of this congregation was to avoid the consumption of meat in favor of dairy products and their derivatives. Thus, they created a cheese that they called Muenster Kaes. From the thirteenth century onward, Muenster Kaes took the name Muenster-Gérome, from the name of the town of Gérome (Gérardmer), where this cheese was sold. Petit Muenster is a scaled-down version of Muenster. Even in this format, though, it must weigh at least 4¼ ounces and measure 2¾ to 4¾ inches across by ¾ to 2⅜ inches thick, to meet the requirements of its A.O.C. label.

AGE-OLD PRODUCTION METHODS

Since its creation, Muenster has been made according to the same time-honored rituals. The curd obtained after the addition of rennet is broken up, then poured into molds before being drained to eliminate the whey. After this the cheese is salted by hand, then ripened in cellars for a three-week minimum for Muenster or Muenster-Gérome, and for a two-week minimum for Petit Muenster or Petit Muenster-Gérome.

The cheeses are washed in warm water from the Vosges massifs and turned every second day. This process aims to develop the characteristic red flora that keeps the cheeses sound during the ripening period.

A SUPERVISED PRODUCTION PROCESS

Production of Muenster Fermier A.O.C. is also strictly controlled and subject to numerous checks. To protect production of Muenster, the authorities have awarded an A.O.C. label to this strong tasting, colorful cheese as a token of product quality. This A.O.C. was recognized by the decree of May 21, 1969, and is currently governed by the amended decree of December 29, 1969.

Its area of production extends over the Vosgian slopes of Alsace and Lorraine, a territory encompassing seven *départements* in eastern France.

A GASTRONOME'S DELIGHT

Its strong aroma and taste tend to scare off those with sensitive palates—children aren't always its biggest fans—and delight genuine gastronomes. Muenster is traditionally savored with a powerful red wine such as a Corton or Haut-Médoc. Nevertheless, the aroma of a Gewurztraminer, a Pinot Noir, or even a good Alsatian beer has a refining effect on the taste of this cheese.

Eat it at the end of a meal, plain and without bread, or else sprinkled with cumin. Bear in mind, though, that it features in many specialties of the Alsace: Muenster omelette or quiche, Alsatian meat stew with Muenster, potato pie with Muenster. As a main dish, it harmonizes superbly with potatoes boiled in their skins.

MUROL

M ADE FROM PASTEURIZED COW'S MILK, THIS FACTORY-PRODUCED CHEESE ORIGINATED IN THE VILLAGE OF MUROL IN THE AUVERGNE.

Description
Murol comes in the shape of a wheel 4¾ inches in diameter, with a central hole 1¼ inches across. Measuring 1⅛ to 1¾ inches tall, it weighs between 16 and 17½ ounces and contains 45 percent fat. Its orange-colored, washed rind may bear traces of cloth. The scooped-out center, which enabled the producer to reduce the ripening period, is "salvaged": Shaped into a cone, it is enclosed in red paraffin and sold under the name of Murolait—so nothing is wasted!

Choosing wisely
Murol resembles a Saint-Nectaire with its center scooped out. Its interior turns light yellow after ripening. This cheese gives off an unobtrusive aroma. Its taste, too, is fairly neutral. Murol should be included in a cheeseboard at the end of a meal. For an ideal match, opt for a light wine such as a Saumur-Champigny, or a red Touraine.

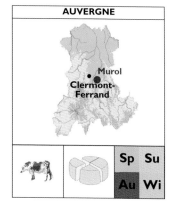

MUROLAIT

T HIS COW'S-MILK CHEESE IS MADE FROM THE SCOOPED-OUT CENTRAL PORTION OF A MUROL. THE CHOICEST, MOST SUPPLE PART, AND THE GENUINE "HEART" OF THE CHEESE, IT WAS BAPTIZED MUROLAIT.

Description
Shaped like a small cork or stopper, Murolait measures 1⅜ inches across by 1¾ inches high, and weighs 1¾ ounces. Lacking a rind, it is enveloped in red paraffin to protect its interior. A semihard, uncooked, pressed cheese, its fairly elastic curd recalls that of Saint-Nectaire. This is a delicate cheese with an unobtrusive taste.

Serving suggestions
This gastronomic oddity is eaten as an appetizer, with a finger of port or a whiskey on the rocks. You can also sliver it into a salad or cut it into thin slices to flavor a quiche or a savory tart. Use it to decorate the top of a gratin—it's wonderful baked or gratinéed. Enjoy it with a salad, accompanied by a lively little local wine, or with a Saint-Pourçain from its own area.

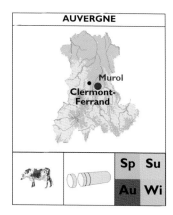

Plaisir au Chablis

THIS COMPACT NEW ARRIVAL, FIRST PRODUCED IN 1999 IN THE CÔTE-D'OR DAIRY IN BROCHON NEAR DIJON, CELEBRATES THE ALLIANCE BETWEEN WINE AND CHEESE WITH CONVICTION.

Description
Sold in a wooden box, Plaisir au Chablis measures 3½ inches across by 1⅜ inches thick and weighs approximately 7 ounces. It is ripened in a cellar for one month, during which time its rind is washed every three days with a mixture of brine and Chablis, a very highly regarded white Burgundy. The proportion of wine increases as ripening progresses. The rind, moist and smooth, takes on an attractive orange hue, and its aroma becomes stronger. The cheese's interior, supple and light yellow, melts in the mouth and is highly flavorful, although not as strong as Époisses.

Serving suggestions
Plaisir au Chablis is at its best at the end of the fifth week, when its taste gains in intensity. This cheese goes well with an open-textured country bread. Naturally, it should be accompanied by a fresh Chablis or a dry, fruity white wine.

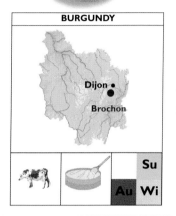

BURGUNDY

Dijon ●

Brochon

Su

Au Wi

Pont-l'Évêque A.O.C.

HAILING FROM A VILLAGE NEAR LISIEUX, THIS CHEESE, ONCE NICKNAMED ANGELOT (CHERUB), IS INDISPUTABLY ONE OF THE GASTRONOMIC WONDERS OF NORMANDY.

In the beginning
It's thought that this cheese was first created by monks in the twelfth century, then exported to the French capital from the sixteenth century onward. It was not until 1600 that it assumed the name Pont-l'Évêque.

Method of production
This is a soft cheese with an uncooked curd. It is salted the fifth day after production and ripened for two months. Some maintain that its rind should be washed several times during the ripening period; others insist that it develops its full range of flavors only as it dries. Assuming that the latter is true, it would be best to remove the mold-covered rind.

Description
Square-shaped, 4 to 4⅜ inches across, Pont-l'Évêque weighs about 12 ounces. There's also a small Pont-l'Évêque (2 inches across) and a "giant" version (8 inches across), for gourmands or large gatherings. As time passes, its golden-yellow to orange rind turns red and becomes tackier. Its interior is tender and creamy, with a pronounced flavor.

Serving suggestions
Pont-l'Évêque cheeses from the Auge area are among the most flavorful. This cheese should be served at the end of a meal. Sample it plain with fresh bread, accompanied by a spicy, generous-tasting red, or, for a rustic touch, with a good bottled cider.

LOWER NORMANDY

Caen ●

Pont-
l'Évêque ●

Su

Au Wi

ROUCOULONS

Two birds cooing inside a red heart on a black background announce a cheese designed to seduce lovers of novelty and fans of the sweet and mild . . . Factory-produced Roucoulons is a good way for the newly initiated to discover cheese.

Description
Disk-shaped, measuring 4 inches across by 1¼ inches thick, Roucoulons weighs approximately 9 ounces. From a distance it resembles a Camembert, minus the tradition and taste. Created in 1987, it was conceived as a combination bloomy-rind/washed-rind cheese.

Method of production
During the three-week ripening period the rind is washed regularly, which preserves its light bloom. Supple and golden yellow, the interior has the time to develop quite a delicate taste that's fairly long lasting in the mouth.

Serving suggestions
Roucoulons should be sampled at the end of a meal with fresh bread and walnuts. It's also an ideal cheese for picnics, since it slices easily. A red Bandol or a Corbières would be the perfect partner.

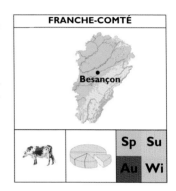

FRANCHE-COMTÉ

Besançon

		Sp	Su
		Au	Wi

ROUY

This factory-produced cheese, created at the turn of the century by a certain Monsieur Rouy, is on the way to becoming a great classic among the non-traditionals . . . Its personality is proof that even a factory-produced cheese can be a success.

Description
Its square shape imitates that of a small Pont-l'Évêque. Rouy measures 3¾ inches across by 1 inch thick. Its slightly orange rind encloses a soft interior whose fairly strong taste is reminiscent of Muenster. Between Alsace and Normandy, it has its share of devotees.

Choosing wisely
This cheese from the Dijon region has a fairly pronounced aroma. It should be enjoyed at the end of a meal, accompanied by an open-textured baguette and a handful of black grapes, along with a red Touraine.

BURGUNDY

Dijon

		Sp	Su
			Wi

PONT-L'ÉVÊQUE A.O.C.

AN AGE-OLD CHEESE

Pont-l'Évêque has a very old pedigree. It is said to have been invented by the monks of an abbey in the Auge area, sometime in the twelfth century. In the Middle Ages, it was sold in the markets of the region under the name of Angelot. Guillaume de Lorris refers to Angelons in his thirteenth-century work, *The Romance of the Rose.*
From the sixteenth century onward, the forerunner of Pont-l'Évêque is enjoyed in Paris. In the seventeenth century, in 1660 to be precise, Hélie le Cordier dedicated a poem to the cheese, to the effect that "Augelot is made there with such artistry, that, young or old, it is pure cream."
It's not known whether the term first used to describe this cheese is *augelot* (literally, from the Auge area) or *angelot* (cherub, and clearly a deformation of *augelot*). In any case, the two terms are found in different texts. It's during this century, though, that Angelot takes the name of Pont-l'Évêque, a little market town in the *département* of Calvados, between Trouville and Lisieux. In 1722, Masseville declared that "the cheeses of the Pont-l'Évêque area are highly prized, and transported to various lands."

THE CHEESEMAKING PROCESS

This characteristic soft, washed-rind cheese is made from cow's milk from Normandy or Mayenne, which, once obtained, is dispatched to the cheese dairy, then heated to under 104°F before rennet is added to bring about coagulation. Over three quarts of milk are needed to make one Pont-l'Évêque.

Next, this nonacid curd is cut up, stirred, kneaded, and poured into square molds before being placed on racks in a very warm room (72°F), then turned frequently to encourage draining. After removal from their molds, the cheeses are transferred to an *hâloir*, or drying room, to rest for five days, where they are turned daily. Next, they are salted, washed, and brushed. Finally they are moved to a ripening room, generally for two weeks, but up to a maximum of six weeks. It's during this period that the rind of the Pont-l'Évêque develops its orange color.

STRICTLY CONTROLLED PRODUCTION

Each year, over 3,500 tons of Pont-l'Évêque are produced in France, courtesy of twelve factories, six farmhouses, and 900 milk producers. Its area of production extends over the old province of Normandy.

This production process is strictly controlled; Pont-l'Évêque was awarded an A.O.C. on August 19, 1970, governed by the amended decree of December 29, 1986.

A team of specialists ensures that production quality is maintained. Like other A.O.C. products, Pont-l'Évêque undergoes numerous analytical and organoleptic checks. Every two months, a committee of experts meets to test and grade the cheeses. After two warnings, the committee can withdraw a producer's right to use the initials "A.O.C." on their cheeses—"fakes" are rapidly unmasked.

DIFFERENT FORMATS

Pont-l'Évêque cheeses are sold in different shapes and sizes:

The large *(grand)* Pont-l'Évêque, square, 8 inches across;

Pont-l'Évêque, also square, measuring just under 4½ inches across;

The small *(petit)* Pont-l'Évêque, likewise square, measuring 3½ inches across;

The half *(demi)* Pont-l'Évêque, in the form of a rectangle approximately 4½ inches by 2¼ inches.

VACHERIN A.O.C.

A BRIEF HISTORY

In the fourteenth century *fruitières*, or rustic dairies, sprung up in the mountain pastures of the high plains of the Jura. There, a succulent but nonetheless fragile cheese was produced, particularly in the dairies located on the Mont d'Or, a peak reaching 4,800 feet at its highest point. Vacherin, still called Vacherin du Mont d'Or in honor of its origins, or sometimes Vacherin du Haut Doubs, is made from the raw milk of cows of the Montbéliard or Pierouge de l'Est breeds.

At the time of Louis XV, Vacherin was known as *fromage de boëtte* (box cheese) because it was sold in a spruce box that helped it maintain its original shape and travel without mishap. It was also dubbed *fromage de crème* (cream cheese), owing to its creamy consistency. Vacherin is a fragile cheese that for many years could only be enjoyed on the spot. Several centuries elapsed before the means of transportation were perfected that enabled the cheese to be dispatched to the four corners of France, as well as to numerous foreign countries.

PRODUCTION DOWN THROUGH THE CENTURIES

Vacherin is a handcrafted cheese, made according to ancestral methods. In order to receive the A.O.C. label, it must be made between August 15th and March 31st, which is why cheesemakers and sellers generally call it a "winter cheese."

The raw cow's milk is renneted. The curds obtained are poured into molds, where the cheeses acquire their rough form. To help them keep their shape, they're encircled with a strip of spruce or fir, which imparts balsamic aromas to the cheese.

Next comes the ripening period: This takes place in a cellar at a temperature of about 59°F, on a spruce board, for a minimum of three weeks. During this stage, the Vacherin is regularly washed with salt water and turned. The last part of the ripening takes place in a spruce box.

STRICTLY DELIMITED PRODUCTION

To be awarded the A.O.C., Vacherin must be made from raw cow's milk from a herd grazing on pastures located at an altitude of about 2,300 feet, in the *cantons* of Montbéliard and Pontarlier. The ribbon of the Haut Doubs, situated along the Swiss border, in the region of the Mont d'Or massif and the base of the Doubs, constitutes the area where Vacherin A.O.C. can be produced.

Every year more than 3,000 metric tons of Vacherin are produced in this region, thanks to eighteen factory producers and cooperatives.

Since the decree of March 24, 1981, Vacherin has held an A.O.C., governed by the modified decree of December 29, 1986.

CULINARY CUSTOMS

Vacherin is a cheese that is both rich in fat and moist. Its spruce "belt" helps keep its stoutness firmly under control. A very runny cheese, it is traditionally eaten at the end of a meal, with a small spoon, but it is also a key ingredient in a number of authentic dishes. Hollowed out in its center, which is then filled with white Jura wine or champagne, the Vacherin is baked in a warm oven to create an unusual fondue, delicious accompanied by potatoes in their skins.

A red or white Jura (Côtes-du-Jura) or Arbois wine is generally suggested as an accompaniment to a Vacherin tasting. White Savoie and dry Jurançon wines are also recommended.

PRESSED, UNCOOKED CHEESES

THE PRESSED, UNCOOKED CHEESES MAKE UP A VERY OLD, LARGE, AND DIVERSE FAMILY, INCLUDING CANTAL, REBLOCHON, AND SALERS. THEIR CURD IS SUPPLE AND AROMATIC, LIKE A SPRING PASTURE.

FROM MILK VAT TO CELLAR

Rennet is added to heated cow's or ewe's milk. The milk coagulates, producing a homogeneous, elastic curd. The draining stage, however, doesn't happen auto-matically: the curds must be cut and stirred so that they acquire a granular consistency. Next, after the whey is eliminated, this paste is once again stirred and washed before being placed in a press—this is the way Saint-Paulin, Saint-Nectaire, and Tomme are made.

For Laguiole, Salers, or Cantal, the curds are first pressed, then the paste is broken up and resalted before being pressed again.

The cheeses are then placed in an *hâloir*, a cool, damp cellar, where they are brushed, washed, and turned every day—this ripening period can last anywhere from two weeks to over a year.

VARIABLE RIPENING PERIODS AND FLAVORS

Saint-Paulin, for example, is ripened for two weeks, Cantal or Morbier, three to four months, and Mimolette Étuvée, a minimum of one year. The flavor varies according to the length of the ripening period. Young, pasteurized-milk cheeses will have a mild, delicate flavor, while other raw-milk cheeses will develop a more lactic or fruity taste. Certain "old cheeses" acquire a strong flavor much prized by connoisseurs.

Numerous great cheeses belong to the pressed-curd family: the various Tommes, Saint-Nectaire, Cantal, Saint-Paulin, Morbier, Abondance, Reblochon, Ossau-Iraty, and Laguiole. Mimolette is also a member of this family—it is French by birth, even if it is most often associated with the Netherlands.

DIFFERENT ORIGINS

Monks, especially Trappists, perfected these pressed, uncooked cheeses; in particular, they fine-tuned the pressing system with a view to manufacturing cheeses that would keep for a long time.

For their part, the cattle breeders of the Massif Central, no doubt moti-vated by similar concerns, created the oldest known pressed-curd cheeses: Cantal and Saint-Nectaire.

Today these cheeses are produced on the plains as well as in the mountains, from cow's or ewe's milk. They vary greatly in shape and size, with the 7-ounce Curé Nantais and the 110-pound Laguiole both being members of this family.

THE A.O.C. CHAMPIONS

Six A.O.C. cheeses form part of this family.

First, there's Abondance, which resembles a Tomme: this cheese, produced by the Abbey of Abondance since the fifteenth century, was highly regarded by the popes during their stay in Avignon. Cantal, produced since time immemorial in the Auvergne mountains, is still made according to the same process. Laguiole, produced on the high plateaus of the Aubrac, must be made from the milk of cows of the Aubrac breed. Ossau-Iraty is made in the Basque Country from whole ewe's milk. Saint-Nectaire, produced on Mont Dore in the Auvergne, was presented at the table of Louis XIV by Marshal de Senneterre. The king was so taken with the cheese that he christened it with the Marshal's name. High-mountain Salers is nothing other than the original Farmhouse Cantal. To earn its A.O.C., it must be made from only the whole milk of cows of the Salers breed during the move from mountain to lowland pastures.

ABBAYE DE CÎTEAUX

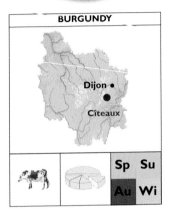

BURGUNDY

Dijon •

Cîteaux

Sp Su
Au Wi

CERTAIN ABBEYS, LIKE THAT OF THE CISTERCIAN ORDER, DREW PART OF THEIR INCOME FROM THE MANUFACTURE OF LIQUEURS, SWEETMEATS, BEERS, AND DAIRY PRODUCTS. THIS FAR-TOO-LITTLE-KNOWN CHEESE HAS BEEN MADE SINCE 1925 IN THE CISTERCIAN ABBEY OF CÎTEAUX, FOUNDED IN 1098.

Description

From the family of semihard, washed-rind cheeses, Abbaye de Cîteaux is a farmhouse cheese. It doesn't have the strong aroma of the latter, but develops a delicate, perfumed flavor. Made from whole, nonpasteurized cow's milk, it is ripened for a period of three to six weeks. Shaped like a large wheel 7 inches across by 1⅜ inches thick, it weighs 1½ pounds. Its smooth, thin rind may vary from gray to orange in color.

Serving suggestions

Its supple, golden-yellow, elastic interior gives off a subtle scent. Rich in fat and creamy-to-soft, it has a distinctive character, very much of its native Burgundy. Its fruity flavor harmonizes deliciously with rye or Poilâne bread. This is a typical local cheese, essentially found in the region of Dijon, Nuits-Saint-Georges, and Beaune. A Burgundy wine, or fruity wines such as Beaujolais or Côtes-du-Rhône, make the ideal accompaniment.

ABBAYE DE NOTRE-DAME DE BELVAL AND MONASTÈRE DE TROISVAUX

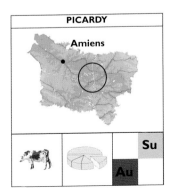

PICARDY

Amiens

Su
Au

THESE TWO RAW-COW'S-MILK CHEESES ARE MADE IN EXACTLY THE SAME MANNER; ONLY THEIR RIPENING METHODS DIFFER. BELVAL IS RIPENED LIKE ITS ANCESTOR, PORT-DU-SALUT, FOR FIVE TO SIX WEEKS; TROISVAUX FOR EIGHT WEEKS. THE EXTERIOR OF BOTH CHEESES IS BRUSHED REGULARLY WITH AMBER BEER, GIVING THEIR RINDS A BROWN HUE. THE INTERIOR RIPENS AND DEVELOPS A STRONG TASTE.

Description

Both cheeses have a supple, golden-yellow interior that won't give way under thumb pressure. They give off a sustained aroma that cheese-lovers find very agreeable. Wheel-shaped, these two pressed, uncooked cheeses have a characteristic small-hole formation.

Serving suggestions

Offer them on a cheeseboard at the end of a meal, with a local beer such as Angélus. If you're lucky enough to find either of these cheeses, don't pass up the chance to try them. Likewise, wines like Chinon or Bourgueil perfectly support their very "present" taste. Serve them with country-style bread or a dark German loaf.

ABBAYE SAINTE-MARIE DU MONT-DES-CATS

THIS ARTISANAL CHEESE WAS CREATED IN 1890 BY THE TRAPPIST MONKS OF THE ABBEY OF MONT-DES-CATS NEAR GODEWAERSVELDE IN FLANDERS. THEY USED THE RECIPE FOR PORT-DU-SALUT, INVENTED IN 1830 AT ENTRAMMES, NEAR MAYENNE, IN AN ABBEY THAT PASSED ON ITS KNOW-HOW TO OTHER CONGREGATIONS. THE CHEESE IS STILL MADE BY THE MONKS OF THE ABBEY.

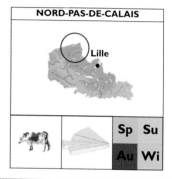

Description
Made from raw cow's milk, Abbaye du Mont-des-Cats is a disk-shaped cheese measuring 8 to 10 inches across by about 1½ inches thick. Its weight varies from 3¼ to 4½ pounds. Its brine-washed rind turns orange after one month's ripening. Its supple, golden-yellow interior is elastic in texture.

Serving suggestions
Abbaye du Mont-des-Cats gives off an unobtrusive scent of its native heath, and melts deliciously in the mouth. Enjoy this cheese in the morning, like the locals, on bread and butter dunked French-style in a bowl of coffee. At the end of a meal, it should be accompanied by a red Bordeaux.

NORD-PAS-DE-CALAIS

Lille

Sp Su
Au Wi

BAROUSSE FERMIER

IN THE CENTRAL PYRENEES, THIS ARTISANAL CHEESE BEARS THE NAME OF THE VALLEY OF BAROUSSE DE L'OURSE. A HANDFUL OF PRODUCERS STILL MAKE BAROUSSE FROM RAW COW'S MILK. ITS TASTE VARIES FROM ONE SEASON TO ANOTHER, ACCORDING TO WHETHER THE COWS HAVE BEEN FED ON DRY FODDER IN WINTER OR FRESH GRASS IN SPRING AND SUMMER.

Description
Farmhouse Barousse is a wheel-shaped cheese measuring about 7½ inches across by 2¾ inches thick, and weighing about 4½ pounds. It is ripened for at least 1½ months; according to the traditional method, it is washed, dried, and turned every day for the first two weeks. This farmhouse cheese gives off a pronounced aroma, and its supple interior is riddled with numerous small holes. It is less sweet-tasting than other cow's-milk cheeses from this region.

Serving suggestions
The springy texture of this cheese is best appreciated with a *Campagrain*, a five-grain tin loaf. Farmhouse Barousse is practical to take on a picnic or to serve diced with an apéritif. It can also be served at the end of a meal with a fruity Irouléguy.

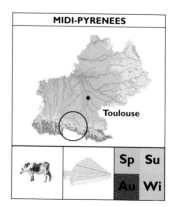

MIDI-PYRENEES

Toulouse

Sp Su
Au Wi

BETHMALE OR OUSTET

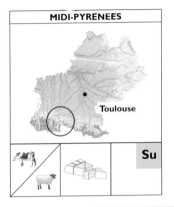

MADE FROM COW'S OR EWE'S MILK, BETHMALE IS A VERY TYPICAL CHEESE OF THE ARIÈGE PYRENEES. RESEMBLING A SMALL, STRAIGHT-HEELED GRUYÈRE WITH A GRAY RIND, IT'S PRODUCED IN THE COUNTY OF FOIX, AN ENCLAVE IN THE PYRENEES.

Description
A pressed-curd cheese, Bethmale is wheel-shaped, measuring 10 to 16 inches across by 3¼ to 4 inches thick, and weighing 7¾ to 13¼ pounds. Bethmale cheeses are made from October to the end of May, when the cows or the sheep are stabled.

Serving suggestions
This cheese is consumed after a three- or four-month ripening period, by which time the interior has become aromatic and delightfully tender. A fairly high-fat cheese with 45 to 50 percent fat, its flavor is pronounced and almost piquant. Some people like to grate it when it has been matured for several months. Available in the shape of a "millstone," or wheel, weighing 11 to 15½ pounds, they are sold locally. The Bethmale produced near the Spanish border at Orrys is larger, with a strong, aromatic flavor. One of the best of the region, it is particularly prized by connoisseurs. Bethmale should be enjoyed at the end of a meal with brown bread, accompanied by a varietal wine, a Collioure, or a Corbières.

MIDI-PYRENEES

Toulouse

Su

CANTAL DE MONTAGNE A.O.C.

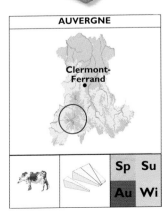

A SEMIHARD CHEESE MADE FROM RAW OR PASTEURIZED COW'S MILK, CANTAL DE MONTAGNE CONTAINS 45 PERCENT FAT.

Description
Cantal de Montagne is made in a large cylinder 15¾ inches across by 17¾ inches tall and tilts the scales at 95 pounds. A 44-pound version, Petit Cantal, and a 22-pound version, Cantalet, are also produced. Each piece bears an aluminum plate confirming the origin of the cheese and attesting to its authenticity. Its area of production is restricted to the *département* of Cantal and to forty-one *communes* of the neighboring *départements*. The *fourmes* are ripened in a cellar for a minimum of thirty days to yield the "young" Cantal Jeune. Cantal Entre Deux is cellar-ripened for four to six months; the mature Cantal Vieux is ripened for over six months.

Serving suggestions
When young, Cantal has a tender, pale yellow interior with the aroma and taste of hazelnuts and fresh milk. This cheese is used to make *truffade*, a dish of fried potatoes with cheese, bacon, and garlic. At the end of a meal, it makes a fine course accompanied by grapes, apples, berries, or walnuts. Serve it with a Côtes-d'Auvergne, a Saint-Pourçain, a Beaujolais, or a Corbières.

AUVERGNE

Clermont-Ferrand

Sp   Su

Au   Wi

CANTAL VIEUX

Made with either raw or pasteurized milk, Cantal Vieux is ripened in a cellar for over six months. Its area of production is restricted to the *département* of Cantal and the forty-one *communes* of the neighboring *départements*.

In the beginning
The legend of Cantal goes back two thousand years: In his *Historia Naturalis,* Pliny the Elder praised the qualities of the cheeses "from the land of the Arvernes and the Gévaudan" at the beginning of the Christian Era.

Description
Cantal is a large cylindrical cheese 15¾ inches across by 17¾ inches in height, weighing 95 pounds. Each cheese bears an aluminum plate confirming its origin and attesting to its name. Its natural rind thickens and becomes bumpy during ripening. From gray, it takes on golden glints of buttercup yellow while the fruity aromas of its interior become concentrated.

Serving suggestions
Cantal Vieux will appeal to those fond of slightly tart flavors, with echoes of hay and mountain grasses. Inside its rind peppered with reddish mold, its body has a more concentrated, almost piquant flavor. Its aromatic palette is also richer. Serve it with an assortment of bread and a Châteauneuf-du-Pape.

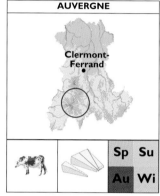

AUVERGNE

Clermont-Ferrand

		Sp	Su
		Au	Wi

CAPITOUL, FROMAGE DES PYRÉNÉES

Increasingly, the designation *Pyrénées* refers to factory cheeses made from cow's milk in the Pyrenees region. Capitoul is the exact copy of a cheese from the Ariège.

Description
Capitoul is enveloped in a thin black rind with an elastic texture. Its interior is supple and golden yellow. To the nose, it gives off an unobtrusive, fairly neutral smell. Precut into portions, it is sold in plastic packaging in supermarkets.

Serving suggestions
This Pyrenean cheese is anything but aggressive in flavor. Fairly mild, it can be eaten in thin slices as an hors d'oeuvre, accompanied by a glass of whiskey or port. It can also embellish a composed salad. On a cheeseboard, serve it with a light wine such as a Côtes-de-Provence or a fruity Beaujolais.

MIDI-PYRENEES

Toulouse

		Sp	Su
		Au	Wi

CANTAL A.O.C.

THE MOST ANCIENT OF THE AUVERGNE CHEESES

The best-known cheese of the Auvergne is also the oldest. In his *Historia Naturalis*, Pliny the Elder (A.D. 23–79) evoked the taste of the cheeses "from the land of Arvernes and the Gévaudan." Later, it was Saint Gregory of Tours (538–594), Frankish prelate and historian, who cited it in his *Historia Francorum* at the end of the sixth century. Diderot (1713–1784) described its production in his *Grand Encyclopedia*.

The name "Cantal" was long synonymous with the word *fourme* ("form") because of its drumlike appearance. It was created by the bourrée dancers of Guévaudan and Aubrac in their *burons*, or mountain huts, where Cantal is produced.

HOW CANTAL IS MADE

The cow's milk obtained from the milking is renneted and the resulting curds are pressed twice. They are then broken up into little pieces to encourage the elimination of the whey. The curds are then pressed once more before being left to rest for the first time. They are then ground into nut-sized pieces before being salted en masse. This preparation is then poured into molds that will be wrapped in unbleached canvas cloths. Next comes the ripening period, which takes place in deep, humid, and cool cellars at a constant temperature of about 59°F. During this stage, which can last from two to six months, the cheeses are turned and brushed several times, which encourages the formation of its characteristic thick, gray rind.

Once the production process is finished, an aluminum plate is affixed to each cheese. This serves to identify the cheese's origin, and constitutes a guarantee of quality.

Cantal is produced in several sizes: "genuine" Cantal tilts the scales at 95 pounds, Petit Cantal weighs 33 to 44 pounds, and Cantalet ranges between 17½ and 22 pounds.

PRODUCTION FIGURES

Every year, more than 17 million tons of Cantal are manufactured by thirty-one producers, both factory and cooperative, thanks to sixty-two farm producers and 4,000 milk producers.

The legally delimited area of origin of Cantal includes the *département* of Cantal itself, as well as forty-one *communes* of many surrounding *départements*: Aveyron, Corrèze, Haute-Loire, and Puy-de-Dôme. This zone actually extends around the volcanic Massif of the Upper Auvergne, at altitudes between 2,297 and 3,281 feet.

Cantal holds an A.O.C., obtained by the ruling of May 17, 1956, confirmed in 1980, and governed by the modified decree of December 29, 1986.

Like all products worthy of such a label, its production is subject to stringent regulations and checks.

CULINARY CUSTOMS

Cantal can be served any time of the year, accompanied by a light, fruity wine such as Côtes-d'Auvergne, Côtes-du-Rhône, Saint-Pourçain, Beaujolais, or Corbières, to name a few. Its woodsy aroma, hazelnut flavor, and mountain scent will delight the most delicate palates.

This cheese can be sampled at different stages of ripeness: Cantal Vieux (mature or aged) in particular is highly prized by connoisseurs.

Cantal is served at the end of a meal; it is also used as an ingredient in dishes typical of the Auvergne—crêpes with Cantal, puff pastry with Cantal, Cantal salad, Cantal pie . . .

GAPERON

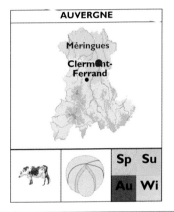

AUVERGNE

Méringues

Clermont-Ferrand

Sp	Su
Au	Wi

IN THE AUVERGNE, THIS CHEESE IS NICKNAMED "MOTHER-IN-LAW'S BREAST." GAPERON IS AN ARTISANAL FARMHOUSE CHEESE MADE FROM RAW OR PASTEURIZED, WHOLE OR PART-SKIM COW'S MILK.

In the beginning
The name *Gaperon* is said to come from the Auvergne dialect word for "buttermilk," the liquid residue left over from butter-making. In the past, buttermilk was mixed with fresh milk to produce Gaperon. It was therefore a "recovered" cheese, ripened at the fireside, hanging in a braided string from a hook, or arranged on rye straw. It is said that at one time, a girl's potential dowry could be estimated by the number of Gaperons hung up to dry in the family dining room.

Method of production
Shaped like a ball flattened on one side and often tied with a yellow ribbon, Gaperon measures about 3½ inches across and weighs between 9 and 12 ounces. During ripening, it's washed down with buttermilk and seasoned with pepper and garlic. After a period of drying, the cheese's interior becomes elastic while the rind turns hard and dry.

Serving suggestions
Although its aroma is fairly unassertive, Gaperon's coarse, piquant flavor comes as a surprise on a first tasting. Eat this unusual cheese on its own, as its strong, lingering aftertaste renders any food that follows insipid. Enjoy it with a fairly neutral-tasting country bread, accompanied by a Côtes-d'Auvergne, a Cahors, or a Corbières.

GAPERONNAIS FRAIS

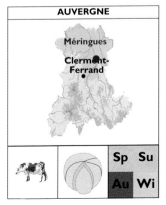

AUVERGNE

Méringues

Clermont-Ferrand

Sp	Su
Au	Wi

THIS HANDCRAFTED FARMHOUSE CHEESE IS MADE FROM RAW OR PASTEURIZED, WHOLE OR PART-SKIM COW'S MILK. BEARING THE SAME EARTHY NICKNAME AS ITS COUSIN, GAPERON, THIS CHEESE IS SMALLER AND IS EATEN FRESH.

In the beginning
The word *gaperon* might come from the word *gape*, which in the Auvergne dialect means "buttermilk," the liquid residue left over from the churning of the milk during butter making. In the past, buttermilk was mixed with fresh milk to produce Gaperon. It was therefore a "recovered" cheese, ripened at the fireside, either hanging in a braided string from a hook, or arranged on rye straw. As a matter of interest, it's said that in the past, a girl's potential dowry could be estimated by the number of Gaperons hung up to dry in the family dining room.

Choosing wisely
Shaped like a ball flattened on one side, this cheese is smaller than Gaperon. Seasoned with pepper and kneaded with garlic during its production, Gaperonnais Frais is eaten fresh. Its ripening period is very short. The body of this cheese is supple and creamy-to-soft. It should be sampled with fresh fruit or preserves and accompanied by a Côtes-d'Auvergne, a Cahors, or a Corbières.

Fromage de Gouda Français

ORIGINALLY FROM THE NETHERLANDS, GOUDA BEGAN TO BE PRODUCED IN FRANCE, WHERE IT WAS MARKETED UNDER THE NAME FROMAGE DE GOUDA.

In the beginning
In 1806 when Napoleon I mounted a blockade of all European ports, Gouda manufacturers expanded production to feed the Dutch population. Subsequently, the cheese was widely exported. Made from pasteurized cow's milk, French Gouda is today produced in factory dairies. It is ripened for a minimum of two or three months. At the end of one year, a dry Gouda, referred to as *étuvé* (mature), is obtained.

Description
French Gouda differs from its Dutch forebear in both taste and appearance. Its yellow paraffin "rind" encloses a pale-yellow interior, supple and firm. It also differs in size: French Gouda is much smaller, measuring 10 to 12 inches across by 2¾ inches thick, and weighs between 4½ and 11 pounds.

Serving suggestions
Its hazelnut taste is appreciated by connoisseurs. French Gouda is eaten in cubes with an apéritif or in a salad, and thinly sliced in a sandwich. When the cheese is aged and dry, some like to grate it and mix it with Emmental. Serve this cheese with a light wine that will bring out its flavor without overwhelming it.

THE NETHERLANDS		
🐄	🧀	Sp / Su — Au / Wi

Gouda

FIRST APPEARING IN THE NETHERLANDS IN THE SIXTEENTH CENTURY, GOUDA WAS PRODUCED ON FARMS NEAR THE VILLAGE OF THE SAME NAME, ABOUT FIFTEEN MILES FROM ROTTERDAM. THANKS TO THE PORT OF GOUDA, THE CHEESE WAS SOON EXPORTED IN GREAT QUANTITIES. ITS PRODUCTION INCREASED WITH THE OPENING OF FACTORY DAIRIES AT THE BEGINNING OF THE TWENTIETH CENTURY.

In the beginning
In the past, Gouda was handcrafted on the farm. The milk used was very fresh. It was collected immediately after the twice-daily milking and the first stage of transformation began the same day. Today the milk is stored overnight at a temperature of approximately 46°F and mixed the following day with the fresh morning milk.

Description
Cylinder-shaped, Gouda generally weighs between 5½ and 33 pounds, but sometimes tilts the scales at 66 pounds. It contains 48 percent fat. Firm, indeed at times very hard, its interior is light yellow or ocher, depending on the length of the ripening period. To determine its quality, connoisseurs "sound" it by tapping it with a bent index finger. If the Gouda sounds "full," that means that it's good, and can take its place on a cheeseboard. Sample it with a slightly sour bread, like a Poilâne loaf, and serve it with a fruity wine such as a Beaujolais.

THE NETHERLANDS		
🐄	🧀	Sp / Su — Au / Wi

MUSTARD GOUDA

FIRST DISCOVERED IN THE NETHERLANDS IN THE SIXTEENTH CENTURY, GOUDA WAS PRODUCED ON FARMS NEAR THE VILLAGE OF THE SAME NAME, ABOUT FIFTEEN MILES FROM ROTTERDAM. THANKS TO THE PORT OF GOUDA, THE CHEESE WAS SOON EXPORTED IN GREAT QUANTITIES. ITS PRODUCTION INCREASED WITH THE OPENING OF FACTORY DAIRIES AT THE BEGINNING OF THE TWENTIETH CENTURY.

In the beginning
In bygone days, fresh milk was used to make Gouda. When it was collected twice daily after the milking, the first stage of the transformation would begin. Now the milk is stored overnight at a temperature of approximately 46°F and mixed the next day with the fresh morning milk.

Description
To make Mustard Gouda, mustard seeds are added to the milk in strictly defined proportions. The body of the cheese then turns orange-yellow and takes on the taste of the seeds. Like the other types of Gouda, the Mustard variant is cylindrical and generally weighs between 5½ and 33 pounds. It contains 48 percent fat. Sample it with a slightly sour bread, like a Poilâne loaf, and serve it with a fruity wine such as a Beaujolais.

THE NETHERLANDS			
🐄		Sp	Su
		Au	Wi

MATURE GOUDA

MADE IN THE NETHERLANDS, GOUDA WAS CRAFTED ON FARMS NEAR THE VILLAGE OF THE SAME NAME, FIFTEEN MILES FROM ROTTERDAM. PRODUCTION INCREASED WITH THE OPENING OF FACTORY DAIRIES AT THE BEGINNING OF THE TWENTIETH CENTURY.

In the beginning
For a long time, fresh milk was used to manufacture Gouda. It was collected immediately after the twice-daily milking and the first stage of the transformation began the same day. Manufacturers aren't quite so demanding these days. The milk is stored overnight at a temperature of approximately 46°F and mixed the next day with the fresh morning milk.

Description
Most Goudas are ripened for a period of one to six months. An "old" or "mature" Gouda is obtained from at least six months' ripening. Like the other Goudas, mature Gouda is cylindrical in shape and generally weighs between 5½ and 33 pounds. It too contains 48 percent fat. As it ages, Gouda becomes hard and tends to develop cracks. Its taste becomes pleasantly spicy. Presented on a platter surrounded by other cheeses, Gouda should be sampled with a soft bread, such as Viennese bread. Accompany it with a particularly tannic wine, such as a Bordeaux or a Madiran.

THE NETHERLANDS			
🐄		Sp	Su
		Au	Wi

LAGUIOLE A.O.C.

THIS CHEESE BEARS THE NAME OF A TOWN ON THE AUBRAC PLATEAU. ITS DELIMITED PRODUCTION AREA COVERS THIRTY *COMMUNES* IN THE AUBRAC, STRADDLING THREE *DÉPARTEMENTS*: AVEYRON, CANTAL, AND LOZÈRE. THE PICTURE OF A BULL AND THE NAME PRINTED ON ITS RIND ARE A GUARANTEE OF AUTHENTICITY.

In the beginning
The origins of this cheese stretch far back in time. Pliny refers to cheesemaking in the Aubrac region, confirmed in the fourth century by ancient writings. Laguiole, as it's now known, however, wouldn't have been invented until the twelfth century in an Aubrac monastery. In bygone days, it replaced the meat or dessert course in peasant homes.

Method of production
The best Laguioles are produced from the summer grazing on high pastures, between May and October, when Aubrac cows graze on lush vegetation, mainly gentians and violets, increasing the richness of the milk. Laguiole is a cylindrical cheese measuring 15¾ inches across by 15¾ inches in height and weighing between 99 and 106 pounds.

Serving suggestions
Laguiole can be recognized by its thick, light-orange rind. The body of the cheese is pale yellow and smooth to the touch. Supple and unctuous, it melts on the palate and has a clear-cut, slightly sour flavor. Laguiole should be enjoyed at the end of a meal, with a Corbières, a Costière-de-Nîmes, or a Marcillac.

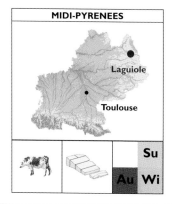

MIDI-PYRENEES

Laguiole

Toulouse

Su | Au | Wi

MANCHEGO

ORIGINALLY MADE ON THE PLAINS OF LA MANCHA TO THE SOUTH OF MADRID, THIS BEST KNOWN OF SPANISH CHEESES, PRODUCED FROM THE RICH MILK OF EWES GRAZING ON VARIED FLORA, BOASTS HIGHLY PRIZED FLORAL AROMAS.

Description
Manchego is produced exclusively in certain parts of the provinces of Alicante, Ciudad Real, Cuenca, and Toledo. It is generally ripened for between three and thirteen weeks, but sometimes up to five months, when its rind turns brown and it becomes more assertive-tasting. Shaped like a disk, Manchego weighs a scant 6½ pounds. Its straw-yellow rind encloses a hard, white curd riddled with small holes.

Serving suggestions
A fairly fatty cheese with 50 percent fat, Manchego changes in line with the length of its ripening period. *Fresco*, it has the slightly sour taste of a fresh sheep's cheese. *Tierno*, after ten days' ripening, its freshness is still intact. *Curado*, after three months, the cheese becomes assertive, with a stronger aroma, and is eaten with quince paste. Referred to as *Duro*, then *Viejo* between three and five months, it turns hard, almost cured. Manchego is sometimes preserved in olive oil for up to two years. Used a great deal in cooking, Manchego can be grated over pasta. The Spanish cube this cheese and fry it in oil. Ripened for between four weeks and two months, it earns its place on a cheeseboard. Enjoy it with a dry Jurançon wine.

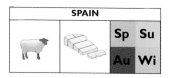

SPAIN

Sp | Su | Au | Wi

MIMOLETTE FRANÇAISE OR BOULE DE LILLE

THIS SEMIHARD, PRESSED-CURD CHEESE IS MADE FROM PASTEURIZED COW'S MILK. MIMOLETTE FRANÇAISE, ALSO CALLED BOULE DE LILLE, HAS A CHARACTERISTIC HARD, BRITTLE RIND AND ORANGE INTERIOR.

Description
The Lille region is renowned for its know-how in ripening cheeses. For this reason Mimolette Française is essentially produced in the dairies of the Meuse or Normandy. It is eaten at four different stages of ripeness: *jeune* (young), after approximately three months; *demi-vieille* (semiaged), between six and eight months; *vieille* (aged), between twelve and fourteen months; and last, *extra-vieille* (extra-aged), after twenty or twenty-two months. The natural rind of the cheese is brushed regularly and sounded with a wooden mallet—the producer's way of checking quality. The interior changes color during ripening, from orange to light brown. Microscopic mites live on the rind and bore tiny holes into it, allowing the cheese to "breathe." Boule de Lille measures 8 inches in diameter by 6 inches in height, and weighs between 4½ and 6½ pounds.

Serving suggestions
Connoisseurs prize the hazelnut taste of this cheese, which should be served on a cheeseboard at the end of a meal. Aged or extra-aged, it's used in cooking, grated over vegetable gratins, or in soufflés. Serve it with a sweet, aged wine, such as Banyuls or Rivesaltes.

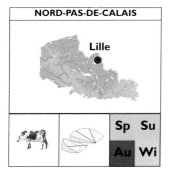

NORD-PAS-DE-CALAIS

Lille

Sp Su
Au Wi

MIMOLETTE VIEILLE

MADE FROM PASTEURIZED COW'S MILK, THIS IS A SEMIHARD, PRESSED-CURD CHEESE. MIMOLETTE VIEILLE HAS A CHARACTERISTIC HARD, BRITTLE RIND AND ORANGE INTERIOR.

Description
The Lille region is renowned for its know-how in ripening cheeses. For this reason Mimolette Vieille is essentially produced in the dairies of the Meuse or Normandy. Brushed regularly, the natural rind is sounded with a wooden mallet—the producer's way of checking quality. The interior changes color during ripening, from orange to light brown. Mimolette is eaten at different stages of ripeness. Between twelve and fourteen months, it is described as *vieille*, or aged. Mimolette Vieille measures 8 inches in diameter by 6 inches in height, and weighs between 4½ and 6½ pounds.

Serving suggestions
Mimolette is particularly prized by connoisseurs when it has been aged for a year, at which point its now-hard interior gives off a highly perfumed aroma. Partner it with a Cahors or a Châteauneuf-du-Pape.

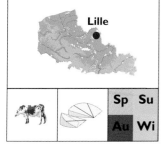

NORD-PAS-DE-CALAIS

Lille

Sp Su
Au Wi

MORBIER FERMIER A.O.C.

PRODUCED IN FRANCHE-COMTÉ, MORBIER IS MADE FROM RAW OR PASTEURIZED COW'S MILK. ENVELOPED IN A NATURAL RIND, THIS CHEESE CAN BE RECOGNIZED BY THE BLACK LINE RUNNING THROUGH ITS LIGHT YELLOW INTERIOR.

In the beginning

In the nineteenth century, Morbier was made in two stages. In order to protect them from insects during the night, the curds were sprinkled with soot. In the morning, the blackened mass of the night before was covered with a new, fresh cheese. Morbier was eaten exclusively by the families of Comté producers. Now the black line running through the interior of the cheese has no reason to be there. Nevertheless, the producers have kept it, since it is decorative—and above all, recognizable. During the ripening period, which lasts one or two months, Morbier develops a fairly thin natural rind. Light gray or beige in color, this rind is brushed regularly. Wheel-shaped, Morbier measures 12 to 15¾ inches across by 2⅜ to 3¼ inches thick.

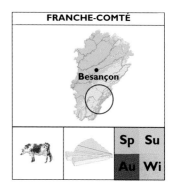

FRANCHE-COMTÉ

Besançon

Sp Su Au Wi

Serving suggestions

This unobtrusive cheese gives off a faint aroma. Its flavor, neither mild nor strong, won't attack the palate. The light-yellow interior is supple and creamy-to-soft to the touch, simultaneously dry and tacky. Morbier is eaten at the end of a meal, usually with country bread. Enjoy it with a Crépy or a Seyssel.

NAPOLÉON

THE NAME OF THE MOST ILLUSTRIOUS OF CORSICA'S FAMOUS SONS IS ALSO BORNE BY AN EWE'S-MILK CHEESE THAT LIKES TO THINK OF ITSELF AS "IMPERIALLY" GOOD. THIS MAY, FOR THAT MATTER, BE NO IDLE BOAST, THANKS TO THE PARTICULARLY RICH, CONCENTRATED MILK WHICH, AS CERTAIN LOCAL PRODUCERS ASSERT, COMES FROM EWES THAT ARE "DIFFERENT" FROM THOSE ON THE MAINLAND.

Description

The size of a small Brin d'Amour, another cheese produced on the "Isle of Beauty," Napoléon measures 3 to 4 inches across and weighs approximately 9 ounces. The natural rind of this cheese is covered with orange and white mold. Its interior is golden yellow, elastic, and supple. Napoléon is ripened for four to six weeks in a well-ventilated cellar.

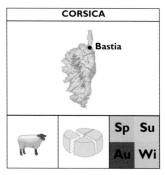

CORSICA

Bastia

Sp Su Au Wi

Serving suggestions

Napoléon should be sampled in cubes with an apéritif under an arbor, with a glass of fresh local wine, of course! It can also be enjoyed at the end of a meal, quite simply with a good, fresh country loaf, in which case it should be accompanied by a Corsican wine.

Ossau-Iraty A.O.C.

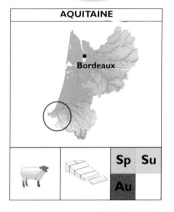

THIS SHEEP'S CHEESE HAS BECOME A SYMBOL OF THE BASQUE COUNTRY. ITS FLAVOR, DEVELOPED IN THE SUMMER-GRAZING HUTS, CELEBRATES THE RICHES OF ITS NATIVE SOIL.

Method of production
Made from ewe's milk, this cheese is pressed, then stored in a cool room and turned every day for three weeks. Ripening lasts at least five months. The best cheeses are those made by the shepherds in their mountain huts or on the farm, with the milk from ewes that have grazed all summer long on the lush, tender grass of the high pastures.

Description
Ossau-Iraty is a large, straight-sided wheel 10 inches across by 6 inches in height, and weighing 11 pounds on average (raw-milk cheeses weigh up to 15½ pounds).

In the beginning
Ossau-Iraty is the fruit of a successful alliance between two regions, Béarn and the Basque Country, which at one time manufactured a very similar cheese called Ossau in Béarn and Iraty in the Basque Country. It has been an A.O.C. cheese since 1980.

Serving suggestions
Enveloped in a thick rind whose color varies from orange-yellow to ash gray, the interior of this cheese is white, supple, and creamy-to-soft. If made artisanally, the curd may contain small holes and should not stick to the palate. The cheese may become firmer-textured if ripened for longer. Enjoy it plain with rye bread and a Madiran or an Irouléguy wine.

Ourliou

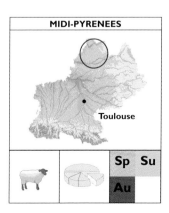

THE FORMER NAME OF THIS CHEESE, CAZELLOU, COMES FROM THE WORD *CAZELLE*, WHICH MEANS "SHEPHERD'S HUT" IN THE HILLS OF THE LOT. THIS SOFT, WASHED-RIND CHEESE IS MADE FROM WHOLE EWE'S MILK. OURLIOU IS ALWAYS MADE IN THE LOT. ITS PRODUCTION PROCESS IS INSPIRED BY THE OLD METHOD THAT IS TRADITIONALLY FOLLOWED.

Description
This disk-shaped cheese measures about 4 inches across by ½ to ¾ inch thick, and weighs just under 6 ounces. During the ripening period, which lasts for at least one month, Ourliou's rind is washed in brine. The cheese develops a supple, runny interior. Its texture is close to that of Reblochon or Saint-Nectaire, unctuous and creamy. Ourliou has a subtle aroma, quite unlike that of a sheep's cheese.

Serving suggestions
Ourliou should be enjoyed on a cheeseboard at the end of a meal with a crusty baguette, or with a round country loaf. Offer it to lovers of farmhouse cheeses with a white Bergerac wine or a dry white Jurançon chilled to 54°F.

AQUITAINE

Bordeaux

Sp Su Au

MIDI-PYRENEES

Toulouse

Sp Su Au

PAVIN

P RODUCED IN THE FOREZ MOUNTAINS IN THE AUVERGNE, THIS COW'S-MILK CHEESE IS A CLOSE COUSIN OF SAINT-NECTAIRE.

Description
Smaller than its famous cousin at only 17½ ounces, this pressed, uncooked cheese is also shaped like a flat disk and made according to the same process. Its natural rind becomes covered with white, yellow, or red mold (or flora), according to its degree of ripeness. Its light-yellow interior is supple but firm.

Serving suggestions
Ripened to the core, Pavin gives off a delicate aroma of mushrooms or damp soil. It too has a gentle hazelnut flavor. Cut into thin slices, this cheese makes a delicious alternative to overly salty peanuts! It can also be served before the dessert course, with a Côtes-de-Bourg or a Côtes-de-Blaye, two robust, sturdy red wines from the Médoc. Just like Saint-Nectaire, Pavin is a key ingredient in numerous regional specialties.

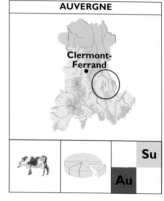

AUVERGNE

Clermont-Ferrand

Su
Au

PECORINO

P ECORINO IS SURELY THE MOST ANCIENT OF ALL ITALIAN CHEESES, WITH PLINY THE ELDER SINGING ITS PRAISES BACK IN THE FIRST CENTURY A.D. IT'S MADE IN ARID REGIONS, WHERE THE VINE AND THE OLIVE TREE GROW.

In the beginning
Some claim that Romulus made this cheese with the milk of his goats, but genuine Pecorino is produced from ewe's milk. Handcrafted by shepherds, this cheese only began to be exported outside Italy at the end of the nineteenth century.

Description
Originally, the term *Pecorino* referred to all Italian cheeses made from ewe's milk. There are therefore several varieties of this cheese. The most famous is Pecorino Romano, a large cylinder weighing between 13 and 49 pounds, ripened for a minimum of eight months, and produced from October to June. The smaller Pecorino Siciliano weighs between 9 and 27 pounds. It can be eaten fresh, before it is salted, or with the addition of black pepper, in which case it is dubbed Pecorino Pepato. Sardinian Pecorino is an imitation of Pecorino Romano, and is chiefly intended for export.

Serving suggestions
This cheese with its compact, white curd is eaten fairly young. It is delicious with fresh bread and a robust red. When aged, it acquires a piquant flavor, and is then served grated over pasta or vegetables. Try it shaved thinly over raw ribbons of zucchini, seasoned with lemon juice and olive oil.

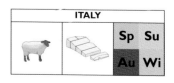

ITALY

Sp Su
Au Wi

Ossau-Iraty A.O.C.

A little history

Back in the first century B.C., a cheese strongly resembling modern-day Ossau-Iraty was being purveyed in the market squares of Toulouse. In the Middle Ages, numerous shepherds' families settled in the Ossau valley.

A native of two regions, Béarn and the Basque Country, this nutty-flavored cheese has borne several names before securing its A.O.C., successively called Laruns, from the name of the market town in the Ossau valley; Esbareich-Tardets, native of the Basque Country; Oloron (Ardignasa); Iraty; or Amou Landais. According to some sources, this cheese was made by the monks of the Abbey of Bellocq three hundred years ago; other experts maintain that Ossau-Iraty (still called by the name of certain sheep of the Pyrenees) was created by Pyrenean farmers who had thus hit on a prudent, not to mention delicious, way of using their ewes' milk by manufacturing a product that had the added advantage of keeping for a long time.

Production

Ossau-Iraty is made from whole ewe's milk. Two breeds are mainly raised for the production of this cheese: the Manech and Basco-Béarnaise sheep, which are black- or russet-faced. About 2,000 tons of this cheese are produced annually in France by eight manufacturers working with sixty-five farms and 2,045 diaries. Highly digestible, Ossau-Iraty is recommended by dieticians, as are all sheep's cheeses; the fat contained in ewe's milk is rich in alphalinoleic acid, which protects the heart and the arteries.

Where is it found?

Ossau-Iraty A.O.C. is produced in a region combining the *département* of Pyrénées-Atlantiques and a small area of the Hautes-Pyrénées, over a territory extending from the Basque coast up to the Col d'Aubisque.

Ossau-Iraty A.O.C. is traditionally made in mountain huts: the *cujalas* of the Béarn or the *cayolars* of the Basque Country. Since recent times, it has also been produced on farms or in dairies according to the traditional methods.

The cheesemaking process

For centuries, local shepherds have practiced what is known as "transhumance"; starting in June, they lead their flocks from the lowlands to the high mountain pastures, or *estives,* and live all summer long in their dry-stone cabins, where they make Ossau-Iraty. In September, they make their way down the valley again. The cheese is thus finished from December to August on the farm.

Ossau-Iraty is made from ewe's milk that has been heated to between 82.4°–95°F and renneted. The resulting curds are cut up, then stirred and heated to 100.4°F. The purpose of the second heating operation is to separate the whey from the curds. Next the curds are placed in perforated molds and pressed, drained, and strewn with coarse salt.

Ossau-Iraty is ripened in cool (53.6°F) cellars for the relatively long period of three months.

Ossau-Iraty has held an A.O.C. since March 6, 1980, governed by the amended decree of December 29, 1986.

Choosing a wine

To set off to perfection the flavor of this choice cheese, serve a wine from the region: sweet Jurançon, Madiran, Béarn, or Irouléguy. Bordeaux Graves also enhances its slightly piquant taste.

PETITE TOMME BEULET

THIS LITTLE FACTORY-PRODUCED TOMME IS MADE IN HAUTE-SAVOIE, IN BEULET. SMOOTH, CREAMY, AND DELICIOUS, THIS WHOLE-COW'S-MILK CHEESE ACHIEVES ITS AIM: TO PLEASE THE GREATEST NUMBER OF PEOPLE, THANKS TO ITS SOFT TEXTURE.

Description
Measuring 2⅜ to 2¾ inches across, Petite Tomme Beulet weighs approximately 10½ ounces and contains 50 percent fat. During its ripening period, which lasts for at least one month, the cheese develops patches of gray, black, and white mold on its rind, which hardens and gives off a slightly acrid odor. Golden yellow and dotted with small holes, the cheese's semihard curd has a mild lactic aroma.

Serving suggestions
This little Tomme is fresh to the palate—its delicate flavor harmonizes well with figs or a few hazelnuts. Cut it into cubes and sample it with a glass of port or Banyuls for an apéritif in the company of friends. Slivered thinly, Tomme Beulet is good melted over potatoes. This cheese holds its own served with brunch or on a cheeseboard, accompanied by olive or bacon bread. Offer it with a red Saint-Joseph or a white Savoie wine.

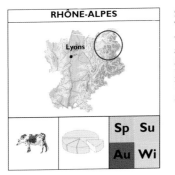

RHÔNE-ALPES

Lyons

Sp | Su
Au | Wi

RACLETTE

COMMONLY CALLED FROMAGE À RACLETTE, FROM THE FRENCH WORD *RACLER*, "TO SCRAPE," ITS NAME DERIVES FROM A TYPICAL SWISS DISH OF THE SAME NAME, A SPECIALTY OF THE VALAIS CANTON.

In the beginning
Raclette is a Swiss recipe that combines several high-fat, aromatic cheeses that are melted and eaten with air-cured beef (*viande des Grisons*) and potatoes boiled in their skins.

Description
Originating in Savoie, Fromage à Raclette is a pressed, uncooked cheese made from raw or pasteurized cow's milk. Handcrafted cheeses should be chosen over factory-produced Raclette, made under perfectly sterile conditions with little risk, but for the most part without much taste either. Round or square, Raclette measures 11 to 14 inches across by 2¾ inches thick and weighs between 9 and 15½ pounds. Its golden yellow rind encloses a lighter yellow or white curd.

Serving suggestions
This is a fairly hard cheese that's rarely served on a cheeseboard. It should be eaten according to tradition—melted and accompanied by boiled potatoes and smoked or cured meats. As with fondue, it's not a good idea to drink much when eating Raclette. Serve it with a fresh white Savoie wine, or better, a glass of eau-de-vie.

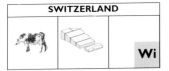

SWITZERLAND

Wi

REBLOCHON A.O.C.

THIS CHEESE MADE ITS APPEARANCE IN THE SIXTEENTH CENTURY. AT ONE TIME NICKNAMED "THE CHEESE OF DEVOTION," IT WAS OFFERED TO THE CARTHUSIANS OF THE THÔNES VALLEY AS THANKS FOR THEIR BLESSING OF THE PEASANTS' COTTAGES.

In the beginning
The word *reblochon* doubtless comes from *reblocher* ("to milk a second time"). In bygone days, farmers owed the landowner a rent proportional to the quantity of milk produced. On the day when payment was to be made, the farmer would carry out a partial milking, which he would finish off after the landowner's departure. Reblochon was made with the milk from this second milking.

Method of production
This is a pressed-curd cheese with a washed rind. The cheeses are shaped in cloth-lined molds, then ripened in a cellar for two weeks.

Choosing wisely
Farmhouse Reblochons bear a green casein label. Disk-shaped, they measure 5½ inches across by 1⅜ inches high and weigh about a pound. The rind is a lovely saffron-yellow hue, while the cream-colored interior has a supple, fatty consistency.

Serving suggestions
Serve Reblochon at the end of a meal with a Mondeuse or Roussette de Savoie. It is also used to make *tartiflettes*, thick potato pancakes with bacon and cheese.

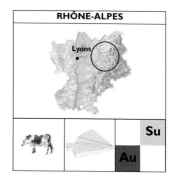

RHÔNE-ALPES

Lyons

Su

Au

SAINT-ALBRAY

FIRST CREATED IN 1977 IN THE CHAUMES CHEESE DAIRY, SAINT-ALBRAY SPORTS AN ELEGANT SIX-PETALED FLOWER SHAPE.

Description
Made from pasteurized cow's milk, this large family cheese weighs in at a surprisingly light 4 to 4½ pounds. Despite being shaped like a six-petaled flower hollowed out in the center, it resembles a Saint-Paulin. Like the latter, it has a thin, light-colored, washed rind, with hints of orange. Its creamy-white, semihard interior also has a pleasantly perfumed, though not particularly assertive, and very sparingly salted flavor.

Serving suggestions
Saint-Albray is an extremely mild cheese, guaranteed to be without health risks, as it's made with pasteurized milk. Its fairly unpronounced taste delights children and fans of neutral cheeses. Served up between two slices of bread, it makes an ideal quick meal or an instant snack for energetic kids. Serve it cut into small cubes with an apéritif, with an assortment of vegetable crudités. On a cheeseboard, accompany it with a glass of red Bordeaux.

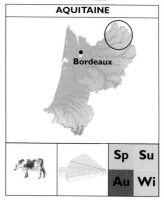

AQUITAINE

Bordeaux

Sp Su

Au Wi

SAINT-NECTAIRE A.O.C.

THIS GREAT CLASSIC OF AUVERGNE GASTRONOMY WAS INTRODUCED AT THE TABLE OF LOUIS XIV BY THE MARSHAL OF FRANCE, HENRI DE SENNECTERRE (SAINT-NECTAIRE).

In the beginning
Saint-Nectaire has been made for nearly a millennium in the region of the Dore mountains. Its native land, at an altitude of almost 3,300 feet, is a volcanic uplands with rich soil and abundant, varied flora.

Description
Saint-Nectaire is shaped like a large wheel 8¼ inches across by 2 inches high and weighs approximately 3¾ pounds. It's also made in a smaller size, 5 inches across by 1⅜ inches thick and weighing 21 ounces.

Choosing wisely
This is a semisoft, pressed, uncooked cheese. Its natural rind, which is covered with white, yellow, or red flora, depending on its degree of ripening, encloses a supple, creamy-to-soft body. Saint-Nectaire exhibits a slight acidity in the mouth and a hazelnut flavor in which a strong lactic taste can be detected. It gives off a characteristic odor of mushrooms and dead leaves.

Serving suggestions
An ideal choice for a cheeseboard, served with a country loaf and a good red Bordeaux such as Saint-Émilion or Côtes-de-Bourg. It's found in a large number of hearty, substantial regional dishes: brioche with Saint-Nectaire, *croûtes rôties*, and *soupe de Noël*, an Auvergne "Christmas soup."

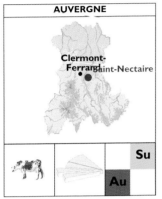

AUVERGNE

Clermont-Ferrand
Saint-Nectaire

Su

Au

SAINT-WINOC

THIS CHEESE BEARS THE NAME OF THE ABBEY IN THE NORTH OF FRANCE WHERE IT WAS FIRST MADE. IT WOULD SEEM TO BE BLESSED BY THE GODS, HAVING MANAGED TO ACQUIRE A BIT OF A REPUTATION IN LOCAL GASTRONOMY.

Description
Saint-Winoc is shaped like a small wheel 3½ to 4⅜ inches across and weighs about 10½ ounces. It's a semihard, pressed cheese made from skim cow's milk. Its beer-washed rind has an attractive, light-orange hue. The ripening period lasts three weeks, at the end of which time the cheese is covered in light patches of white mold. Saint-Winoc's supple, elastic, straw-yellow interior acquires quite a pronounced taste in which aromas of beer and lactic flavors mix.

Serving suggestions
Tender and mild at the outset, Saint-Winoc becomes devilishly tasty after four weeks' ripening in a cellar—the ideal time to sample it with some country bread and a beer or a glass of Crémant d'Alsace (a moderately sparkling wine).

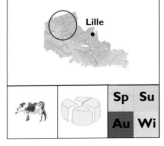

NORD-PAS-DE-CALAIS

Lille

Sp   Su

Au   Wi

SALERS A.O.C.

THE FULL NAME OF THIS CHEESE IS SALERS HAUTE MONTAGNE, A DESIGNATION OF ORIGIN RESERVED FOR A CANTAL MANUFACTURED STRICTLY BETWEEN MAY 1 AND OCTOBER 31. ITS NAME COMES FROM A MEDIEVAL VILLAGE SITUATED AT AN ALTITUDE OF 2,953 FEET IN THE HEART OF THE CANTAL MOUNTAINS.

Description
Cylindrical in shape, Salers measures 15 to 19 inches across by 12 to 15¾ inches tall and weighs between 77 and 121 pounds. Although no longer made exclusively from the milk of Salers cows, it's still produced during the grazing period between May 1 and October 31. Close to 105 gallons of milk are needed to produce a single 88-pound cheese. Ripening, which takes place in a deep cellar, lasts between three months and one year.

Choosing wisely
This is a raw, whole-cow's-milk cheese with a firm, unpressed interior. Its rind is golden and scattered with red and orange patches. Its yellow curd, both supple and firm, is highly aromatic, with a faint scent of fruit. A very delicious cheese.

Serving suggestions
A cheese with a complex, inimitable taste, Salers harmonizes with fresh walnuts, apples, or grapes. It can be sliced thinly in a salad or served at the end of the meal, accompanied by a red Sancerre or a lively Saumur.

AUVERGNE

Clermont-Ferrand

Salers

Su

Au

TAMIÉ DE SAVOIE

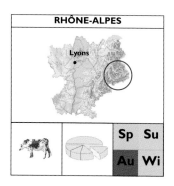

THIS MILD, TENDER CHEESE IS MADE IN SAVOIE. LESS CREAMY THAN ITS COUSIN REBLOCHON, TAMIÉ IS CONSIDERED TO BE THE BETTER OF THE TWO BY WELL-INFORMED TUROPHILES.

In the beginning
The abbey of Tamié in the Bauges was founded in 1131; it is there that this semihard, pressed, uncooked cheese originated. It is still produced by Trappist Monks, who wrap it in blue paper stamped with a white Maltese cross.

Description
Tamié de Savoie is a large round slab measuring 7 to 8 inches across by 1½ to 2 inches thick and weighing just under 3 pounds. Ripened for one month in a cellar, its washed rind is slightly moist with a pinkish tint. Its mild, elastic curd is similar to Reblochon's but less creamy; its taste, however, is more pronounced and deliciously perfumed.

Serving suggestions
This mountain cheese harmonizes perfectly with a slightly sour bread, such as a Poilâne loaf. It is a good one to sample among friends after a fine day's outing, accompanied by a Roussette de Savoie.

RHÔNE-ALPES

Lyons

Sp Su

Au Wi

Saint-Nectaire A.O.C.

A little history

Manufactured for centuries in the Dore mountains region, Saint-Nectaire owes its fame to the Marshal of France, Henri de la Ferté Sennecterre, who allowed the cheese to be served at the table of Louis XIV. At the same time, in his *History of the Auvergne*, the writer Pierre Audigier praises the qualities of the cheeses native to the region, which "in terms of quality do not lag behind those of Europe that are more famous." That's saying a mouthful!

The cheese-making process

Once it has been collected, the cow's milk is renneted under heat in a large iron basin called a *gerle* or *baste*. This stage lasts about half an hour. The resulting curds are broken up into very small pieces to facilitate the elimination of the lactoserum, then ground before being pressed. The whey is drained off, then the whole is reconstituted before being ground and pressed to yield a Tomme-style cheese. Next, the cheese is salted by hand, then wrapped in a cloth before being returned to the mold and pressed a second time.

Ripening

Ripening in a humid wine cellar, on rye straw or flush with the ground, lasts for about twenty-one days. In order to obtain a more pronounced aroma, ripening may be prolonged by two to five weeks. During this period, successive washings in salt water allow the rind to form and the cheese to develop its full range of flavors.

Only the milk from cows of the Salers breed, which graze on the flavorful grass of the Auvergne volcanic plateaus with their unique mixture of flowers, is used in the manufacture of Saint-Nectaire.

Two cheeses in one

There are two recognized sizes of Saint-Nectaire: one weighs approximately 3¾ pounds, and the other, Petit Saint-Nectaire, just under 21 ounces. Both are shaped like a flat disk. They sport a green casein label, rectangular in the case of dairy-plant-produced Saint-Nectaire, and oval for the farmhouse version.

Production

The A.O.C. held by Saint-Nectaire is quite old, having been recognized by the ruling of December 1, 1955; moreover, it is governed by the amended decree of December 29, 1986. Every year in France, nearly 14,000 tons of Saint-Nectaire are produced; this production is guaranteed by six manufacturers, both private and cooperative. A total of 350 farm producers and 910 milk producers help keep the ever-increasing number of fans of this cheese supplied.

Saint-Nectaire is produced in seventy-two *communes*, located in the southwest area of the *département* of Puy-de-Dôme, and in the northern portion of the *département* of Cantal.

Choosing a wine

You can't go wrong pairing Saint-Nectaire with a classic red Bordeaux (Saint-Émilion, Côtes-de-Bourg, Saint-Estèphe), but you could be more adventurous, enjoying it with a Pouilly-Fumé, that famous Loire wine, or again with a Montrachet. It would also be delicious with a traditional Auvergne wine such as a Coteaux-d'Auvergne.

Saint-Nectaire should be enjoyed at the end of a meal or as a snack; it is also a key ingredient in a number of recipes, in which it may be savored hot or cold.

TOMME D'AUVERGNE

LIGHT AND LOW-FAT, THIS IS THE PERFECT CHOICE FOR THOSE UNWILLING TO GIVE UP THE PLEASURES OF CHEESE WHILE STILL KEEPING AN EYE ON THEIR WAISTLINE.

Description

Tomme d'Auvergne is a middle-of-the-road cheese on all accounts: measuring 6 to 8 inches in diameter, with a fat content between 15 and 30 percent, and an unobtrusive taste. Its thick, wrinkled gray rind is scattered with patches of white mold. The ripening period lasts for at least two months, during the course of which the Tomme is turned and rubbed by hand several times a week. Tomme d'Auvergne is made from skim cow's milk.

Serving suggestions

Its golden yellow interior has an unobtrusive flavor with a slightly lactic aftertaste. This is an ideal diet cheese that can be eaten in thin slices on low-fat crackers. Although hardly bursting with flavor, it helps satisfy a craving with a healthy snack. Serve Tomme d'Auvergne on a cheeseboard with a light wine, or with water.

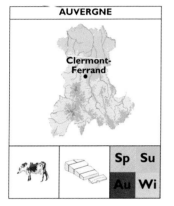

AUVERGNE

Clermont-Ferrand

Sp Su
Au Wi

TOMME DE PONT-ASTIER

PRODUCED IN THE DÔLE VALLEY, THIS COW'S-MILK TOMME DELIGHTS THE PALATE WITH ITS UNUSUAL FLAVORS. ESSENTIALLY AVAILABLE ONLY IN ITS AREA OF PRODUCTION, THIS IS A CHEESE YOU SHOULD GET BETTER ACQUAINTANTED WITH.

Description

Shaped like a large "millstone" or wheel, Tomme de Pont-Astier develops a grayish rind covered with white mold. Its light yellow interior is studded with small, irregular holes. It gives off a lovely, faint scent of milk. In the mouth, its delicate, delicious curd melts on the tongue, leaving a pleasant, fresh aftertaste.

Serving suggestions

Tomme de Pont-Astier is delicious with "fancy" breads—walnut, raisin, multigrain, or even bacon bread. Cut into cubes, it will liven up a green salad beautifully. It can be accompanied by walnuts and dried almonds. Serve Tomme de Pont-Astier with a wine from the same region, such as a Saint-Pourçain.

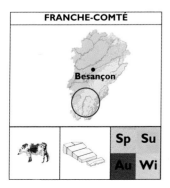

FRANCHE-COMTÉ

Besançon

Sp Su
Au Wi

TOMME DE SAVOIE D'ALPAGE

THIS GENERIC NAME COVERS A GREAT DIVERSITY OF CHEESES WHOSE FLAVORS VARY ACCORDING TO THE VALLEY OR CORNER OF THE MOUNTAIN WHERE THEY WERE FIRST MADE.

Method of production
Tomme de Savoie is a pressed, uncooked, raw-cow's-milk cheese. Its taste varies according to the quality of the grass and plants of the high mountain pastures. It is made with whole or part-skim milk. The cheeses are ripened for one month in a warm cellar, followed by several months in a cold, humid cellar.

Description
These large cheeses measuring 7 to 12 inches across weigh between 3¼ and 6½ pounds. Their rind is gray and favors the formation of yellow or red flora with the passage of time. The interior, white to light yellow in color, is studded with small holes. Tacky to the palate, they give off a strong "cellar" smell, but have a mild and delicate taste. Tomme de Savoie cheeses are protected by a regional guarantee of quality.

Serving suggestions
Plain, ripened with marc, or even flavored with fennel, Tomme de Savoie can be enjoyed at any time—with an apéritif, on a picnic in the mountains, or at the end of a meal. Accompany this cheese with walnut bread and a fruity white Savoie wine, for example a Chignin-Bergeron with highly developed aromas.

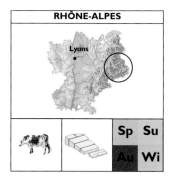

RHÔNE-ALPES

Lyons

Sp Su

Au Wi

TOMME FRAÎCHE DE L'AUBRAC

IN ITS FIRST FLUSH OF YOUTH AND WITH NARY A WRINKLE ON ITS STILL-VERY-FAIR COMPLEXION, THIS CHEESE REIGNS SUPREME OVER *ALIGOT* AND *TRUFFADE*, TWO LAVISH DISHES TYPICAL OF THE AVEYRON.

Description
Fresh Tomme comes in a large, compact 5½-pound block. At this stage, the cheese is white, unsalted, slightly spongy, and rindless. This Tomme is enjoyed in a number of dishes. Plain and melted, it stretches into strings that can reach 2 or 3 yards in length, whereupon the cheese is said to be "spinning."

In the beginning
The origin of the word *aligot* is disputed. It may be a deformation of the Latin *aliquid*, meaning "something," the word that the mendicant pilgrims of the Middle Ages repeated at the door of the monasteries when begging for food. The monks would then give them a soup made of bread and fresh Tomme.

Serving suggestions
Aligot is made by adding fresh Tomme cheese to mashed potatoes and garlic. *Truffade* is a pancake of thinly sliced potatoes, bacon, garlic, and Tomme. Fresh Tomme can also be served with a chestnut puree and with *tripous*, a highly seasoned dish of mutton tripe and sheep's feet. This cheese may be sampled with a Saint-Pourçain.

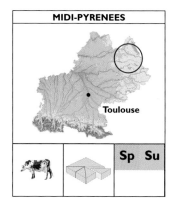

MIDI-PYRENEES

Toulouse

Sp Su

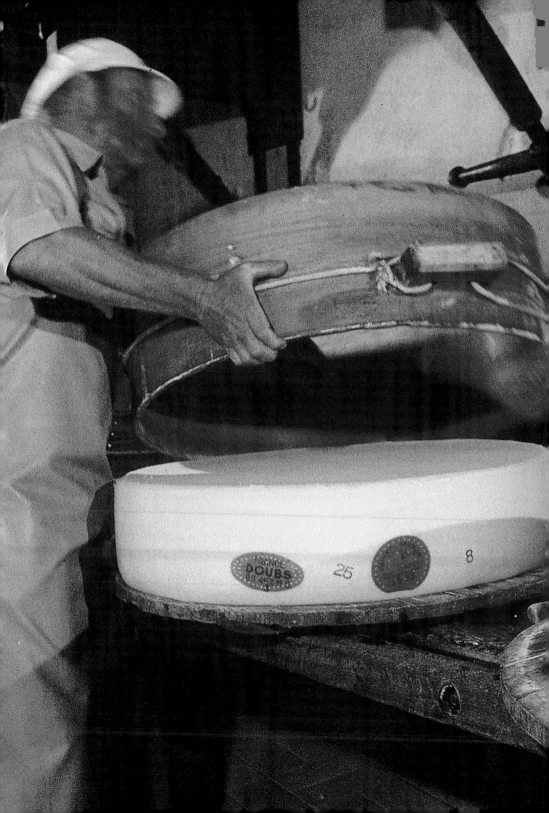

PRESSED, COOKED CHEESES

MOUNTAIN DWELLERS MADE THIS PRODUCT OF THE HIGH MOUNTAIN PASTURES BECAUSE OF ITS NUMEROUS ADVANTAGES: RICH IN PROTEIN AND CALCIUM, IT KEPT FOR A LONG TIME AND WAS EASILY EXCHANGED FOR OTHER COMMODITIES.

A RESOLUTELY HIGHLAND CHEESE

It took a lot of milk to make these large cheeses. Thus, mountain dwellers decided to organize themselves into *fruitières*, dairy cooperatives before the term was coined. All members received in turn a "batch of milk," i.e., the collection from the neighboring villages, with which they produced a large wheel of cheese that they then owned. At the end of the nineteenth century, however, pasteurization of the milk enabled the industrial production of Emmental, Comté, and Beaufort in the plains.

AN UNCHANGED PROCESS

In the first step, the cow's milk is heated to 90°F and cultured with lactic ferments to which rennet has been added. After coagulation of the milk, the firm, white curds are cut into small flakes so as to extract the whey. The resulting paste is stirred, then heated for thirty minutes to an hour. The whey is then eliminated, leaving only the curds, which will be molded and pressed for several hours. This process compresses and shapes the cheese. During this stage, the lactic ferments go to work, acidifying the curds. Once pressing is finished, the cheese is plunged in a brine bath.

RIPENING

Transferred to a cold cellar, the cheese is washed, brushed, and turned regularly for two to three weeks. Its dense rind traps the gas that forms inside the cheese, but the "eyes," or holes, will only appear after the cheeses have spent six weeks in a warm cellar. There, the bacteria will consume the lactic acid and give off the gas responsible for the characteristic hole formation.

The *affineur* follows the progress of the cheeses very closely, and when he judges them to be rounded enough, "listens" to them by "sounding" or tapping them. It is hoped that the sound will reveal a good texture, and thus a promising taste and aroma. He then takes a sample from the interior of the cheese with a cheese borer to confirm its quality, then transfers the cheese to a cold cellar to stop production of gas and end the ripening process. This family of cheeses includes Gruyère; Emmental and its two labels, Grand Cru and Savoie; and two A.O.C. cheeses, Beaufort and Comté.

HISTORY OF THE *FRUITIÈRES*

The first recognized cooperative cheese dairy was that of Desservilliers, founded in the Doubs in 1267. Thus, since the Middle Ages, collectively made cheeses called *fromages de grande forme* (large-format cheeses) were exchanged under the name of Vachelins or Abondances. These cooperatives operated without written rules until the advent of the first contracts governing them in the mid-eighteenth century. These days the cheeses are no longer produced in each member's home, but in a common central chalet. Formerly passed down from father to son, the cheesemaking trade is now taught in schools such as those opened in 1888 in Poligny or Mamirolles in the Jura.

CHEESES TO BE EATEN THROUGHOUT THE YEAR

Protected from drying out and from excessive cold, pressed, cooked cheeses can be kept for a long time. Simply wrap them in waxed paper or plastic wrap and place them in the cheese drawer in the refrigerator. They may also be stored in a cloth.

BEAUFORT A.O.C.

HISTORY AND ORIGIN

Back in the times of the Roman emperor Trajan (A.D. 53–117), a palatable cheese was consumed at court, which can safely be considered to be the ancestor of Beaufort. The writings of Pliny the Younger (A.D. 61–114) attest to it being one of the most highly regarded cheeses of its time. In the Middle Ages, its production was guaranteed and developed by numerous monastic communities and certain Savoie villages. It was in 1865 that the cheese was given its present-day name. Dubbed "Prince of the Gruyères" by Brillat-Savarin, Beaufort owes its superb flavor to the quality of the milk of the Tarine and Abondance breeds grazing the high mountain pastures between 2,625 and 6,560 feet. These cows must not produce more than 5 tons of milk per year.

ONE CHEESE, TWO FACES

You'll find two types of Beaufort grouped together under the same A.O.C.: Beaufort d'Été (Summer Beaufort), comprising "all cheeses produced from June to October inclusive, including those from high-mountain-pasture milk"; and Beaufort Chalet d'Alpage (High-Mountain-Pasture Chalet Beaufort), comprising "summer cheeses produced twice a day according to traditional methods in high-mountain-pasture chalets above 4,920 feet, comprising at the very most the milk production of a single herd in the chalet."

PRODUCTION PROCESS

The cow's milk that has been collected is heated to 91°F, then renneted with calves' vells and *recuite* (deproteinized acid whey) in the traditional manner. The resulting curds are broken up in order to eliminate the whey. The curds are then heated to between 127°–129°F.

This preparation is stirred, then poured into a linen cloth. The curd is then molded and pressed in a wooden hoop called the "Beaufort hoop," which will give the cheese its shape, especially its concave bottom, which was practical for its transportation by mules in bygone days. The pressing operation lasts twenty-four hours, at the end of which time a cheese with a homogeneous curd is obtained, and it is allowed to rest before being immersed in a brine bath to encourage rind formation. The ripening period lasts from five to twelve months. It takes place in a very humid cellar, at a temperature of 50°F. During this stage, the cheese is salted, rubbed, and turned several times.

Unlike Comté or Emmental, Beaufort should contain no holes, but just a few cracks.

PRODUCTION

The A.O.C. area comprises the high valleys of Savoie: Tarentaise, Beaufortin, Maurienne, and part of Val d'Arly. Annual production comes to nearly 4,000 tons, manufactured by seventeen cheese dairies, seven of which are cooperatives.

Beaufort has held an A.O.C. since April 4, 1968, and is governed by the decree of August 12, 1963.

DINNER'S SERVED

Beaufort is generally sampled with a local wine: Abymes, Apremont, Chignin-Bergeron for lovers of white wine, and a red Mondeuse or a Chouragne for those who prefer reds. This cheese is used as an ingredient in the famous *fondue savoyarde*, as well as in other specialties such as pies, tarts, soufflés, and gratins.

Although eaten throughout the year, luscious summer Beaufort, made from the milk of cows that have grazed on tender grass sprinkled with flowers, should be your first choice.

APPENZELL

THIS SWISS CHEESE, HAILING FROM THE CANTON OF THE SAME NAME, IS PRODUCED FROM RAW COW'S MILK IN THE TRADITIONAL MANNER, AND CONTAINS 50 PERCENT FAT. A HIGHLY AROMATIC CHEESE, IT HAS THE AUTHENTIC TASTE OF ITS NATIVE HEATH.

Description
Shaped like a millstone 12 to 13 inches across and weighing 13¼ to 17¾ pounds, Appenzell has a slightly concave heel and a smooth, firm, brownish-yellow rind, which should be moist and elastic. The method used to produce this cheese has scarcely varied for over a century. Characteristically, it is delivered very early on to finishers who wash it two or three times a week with a brine prepared from white wine, salt, pepper, and spices, which after three months' ripening imparts a typical aroma to the cheeses. Those that are ripened for six months are termed Appenzell Extra.

Choosing wisely
Appenzell has a light, perfumed aroma. Its curd exhibits regular "eyes" the size of cherries. This cheese is eaten in cubes with an apéritif. It's also good with cornichons or cocktail onions, or melted on top of boiled potatoes, Swiss-style. A sparkling little red from Lake Constance sets it off perfectly; for an apéritif, a brut cider or a fruity white Jura wine are best.

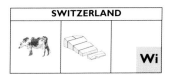

SWITZERLAND

Wi

BEAUFORT A.O.C.

MADE IN SAVOIE, THIS CHEESE IS IN THE SHAPE OF A LARGE MILLSTONE. ALONG WITH COMTÉ AND FRENCH EMMENTAL, IT'S ONE OF THE THREE "LARGE FORMAT" FRENCH CHEESES. THERE ARE TWO VERSIONS OF THIS MOUNTAIN CHEESE, "SUMMER" BEAUFORT AND "HIGH MOUNTAIN PASTURE" BEAUFORT.

In the beginning
The Romans were already enjoying a cheese from the Alpine regions, made when the herds were grazing in the high pastures of Beaufortin, Tarentaise, and Maurienne. The weight of this cheese, 99 pounds, represents the daily milk yield of a herd of forty-five cows; over three gallons of milk are needed to make 2⅛ pounds of Beaufort. This cheese is ripened for at least five months.

Choosing wisely
Wheel-shaped, Beaufort measures 13¾ by 29½ inches across by 4½ to 6¼ inches thick. The cheese has a moist, tacky rind and a pale yellow interior. The first "high mountain pasture" Beauforts in March give off a scent of milk and butter, with a floral touch. The slightly acid, salty flavor lingers in the mouth. Beaufort should be sampled with a local wine such as Mondeuse, Apremont, or a fruity white Savoie wine.

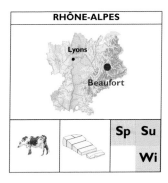

RHÔNE-ALPES

Lyons

Beaufort

Sp Su

Wi

COMTÉ A.O.C.

From the Gruyère family of cheeses, Comté is made from raw cow's milk, exclusively from the Montbéliard or Pie Rouge de l'Est breeds that graze in the pastures of this region. Comté's area of production extends over the whole of the Jura massif.

Description
Cylinder-shaped, a Comté millstone measures 3½ to 5 inches high, and weighs between 66 and 121 pounds. Over 140 gallons of milk go into the making of a single wheel of Comté. This cheese is ripened on spruce boards for a period ranging from three months to two years. The longer Comté is ripened, the stronger its flavor. The yellow or brown rind of the cheese encloses a supple, creamy-to-soft interior that gives off a wholesome scent of hay.

Choosing wisely
A grading scale is used to assess the cheeses that are marketed, and the A.O.C. is only awarded to those receiving a mark of 15/20 or higher. The cheeses that make the grade are then entitled to bear the Comté logo, a green bell. This unobtrusively flavored cheese should be enjoyed plain, or with a mixed salad. Comté is also delicious eaten in cubes along with an apéritif. Serve it with a light, fruity red or a white Jura wine.

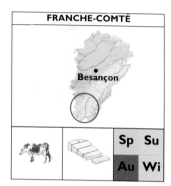

FRANCHE-COMTÉ

Besançon

Sp Su
Au Wi

COMTÉ EXTRA-VIEUX

Like all Comtés, "extra-mature" Comté is the product of an area rich in verdant pastures with a lush natural flora. It's the length of ripening that distinguishes the numerous varieties of this cheese from each other: Comté Extra-Vieux is matured for over eighteen months on spruce boards.

In the beginning
This cheese's method of production hasn't changed for over a millennium. In the twelfth and thirteenth centuries, *fructeries* or *fruitières* produced large wheels of cheese to feed the community during the snowy months of winter. Called Vachelin in the fifteenth century, then Vachelin façon Gruyère (Gruyère-style Vachelin) in the eighteenth century, it wasn't until the twentieth century that Comté received the designation of Gruyère de Comté.

Choosing wisely
During the eighteen-month ripening period, the cheese is rubbed and turned quite often. The rind gradually changes from yellow to dark brown. The firm, elastic curd becomes harder and gives off a persistent aroma. The flavor of the cheese is sustained and very powerful. Lovers of strong-tasting cheeses are particularly fond of Comté Extra-Vieux. Enjoy this cheese with, for example, a Jura vin de paille (straw wine).

FRANCHE-COMTÉ

Besançon

Sp Su
Au Wi

COMTÉ A.O.C.

HISTORY OF THE CHEESE

A member of the Gruyère family, Comté is the product of a thousand-year-old pastoral tradition. The writings of Pliny the Elder (A.D. 23–79) attest to this. Much later, in the nineteenth century, authors such as Victor Hugo cite it in their writings as a cheese of distinction. Today it is produced in 200 *fruitières* located within a delimited area in the Jura massif. This cooperative production dates from the eleventh century, when farmers of the Franche-Comté region banded together in order to collect the daily quantity of milk necessary to produce a large wheel of Comté according to traditional methods. In fact, more than 132 gallons of milk from two consecutive milkings are required to produce one millstone of Comté—proof yet again that unity makes strength!

The official quotation bulletins of the central food markets of Paris attested to its fame, since in the past its quotation differed from that of cheeses of the same family.

PRODUCTION PROCESS

Shaped like a large wheel, Comté is made from whole, fresh cow's milk collected exclusively from herds grazing the high mountain pastures of Jura. The cheesemaker coagulates the milk by adding natural fermenting agents to it. The curds are then cut up into very small pieces and stirred. The 132 gallons or so of curdled milk are heated for 30 to 40 minutes to a temperature of around 127°–131°F. This is done to facilitate the selection of thermophilic bacteria and the separation of the small bits of the coagulum and the whey. Next, the curds are decanted into a cloth that is suspended to allow draining.

This preparation is then put in a press, which is turned regularly.

Next comes the ripening stage. This may last from four to twelve months, but generally does not exceed six months. This cycle enables the cheese to develop its highly subtle aroma. Several weeks after its production, the cheese is transferred to a warm cave with a humid atmosphere to encourage the evolution of gases creating the bubbles that will form the spherical "eyes" in the curd, which are cherry-sized holes. According to a local proverb, good-quality Comté must have "eyes which are few, small, and moist." Thus, the fewer holes the cheese has, the more delicious it will be!

PRODUCTION

Comté or Gruyère de Comté is produced in the region of Franche-Comté, mainly in the *communes* of Doubs, Jura, and Haute-Saône, and in certain *communes* of the *département* of Ain, the Territory of Belfort, and the *départements* of Côte-d'Or, Haute-Marne, Saône-et-Loire, and Vosges. This extended territory constitutes the A.O.C. area of the cheese. Every year, within this area, 42,500 metric tons of Comté are produced by forty-one private and cooperative dairies. Comté's A.O.C. was awarded on July 22, 1952, and is governed by the decree of December 30, 1998.

WHICH WINE?

Besides the light, fruity red or the white Jura wines that are usually recommended, this cheese may be served with all kinds of dry white wines, or even with champagne.

Comté can be enjoyed from the appetizer course to dessert, and is a key ingredient in many original dishes such as fondue, *croûte comtoise* or *flan de comté*.

CUYALAS

BOTH BÉARN AND THE BASQUE COUNTRY CLAIM PATERNITY OF THIS FARMHOUSE SHEEP'S CHEESE, MARKETED CHIEFLY IN ITS AREA OF PRODUCTION. KNOWN AS CUYALAS IN BÉARN AND CAIOLAR IN THE BASQUE COUNTRY, ITS NAME DERIVES FROM THE SHEPHERDS' HUTS DOTTING THE HIGH MOUNTAIN PASTURES, LIKE THE *BURONS* IN THE AUVERGNE. IN THE PAST, THIS MOUNTAIN CHEESE WAS MADE BY SHEPHERDS AS A WAY OF PRESERVING MILK THROUGH THE WINTER.

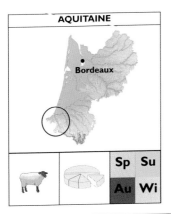

AQUITAINE

Bordeaux

Sp Su
Au Wi

Description
Cuyalas resembles Ossau-Iraty, another whole ewe's-milk cheese. Cylindrical in shape, measuring about 8 inches across by 2¾ to 3¼ inches high, it weighs between 4½ and 6½ pounds. Like its cousin Ossau-Iraty, it is ripened for at least sixty days in a cellar with a temperature of under 54°F. By this time, its interior will be white to golden-yellow and perfumed, protected by a thick, hard, and slightly furrowed rind. Cuyalas has a fat content of 50 percent.

Serving suggestions
The cheese has only a faint aroma, but the longer it is aged, the more it yields the flavor of its native soil. Cuyalas is at its best when cut up one to two hours before it is eaten. Serve it in cubes to accompany an apéritif, or as part of a fine cheeseboard. Cuyalas is delicious accompanied by olive bread or *fougasse*, and a white wine such as an Irouléguy, a dry Jurançon, or a Pacherenc du Vic-Bilh.

FRENCH EMMENTAL

PRODUCED IN SAVOIE AND HAUTE-SAVOIE, FRENCH EMMENTAL IS A COOKED, PRESSED CHEESE. UNLIKE THE TYPICAL FACTORY-PRODUCED EMMENTAL THAT IS FOUND FROM BURGUNDY TO BRITTANY, THIS CHEESE IS MADE FROM RAW MILK. IT HAS A FAT CONTENT OF 45 PERCENT.

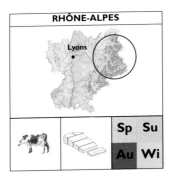

RHÔNE-ALPES

Lyons

Sp Su
Au Wi

Description
Measuring 27½ to 39½ inches across by 5 to 10 inches thick, Emmental weighs between 132 and 286 pounds. Between 185 and 264 gallons of milk are needed to produce a single wheel! A natural rind, washed and brushed regularly during ripening, encloses the curd. The interior should be studded with oval, regular holes that are also called "eyes." These are caused by the fermentation of the cheese due to a month's sojourn in a cellar heated to 64°–75°F. A good Emmental can be recognized by the frequency of its holes: three "eyes" for every 6 inches. Ripening lasts a minimum of four months.

Serving suggestions
Emmental has a firm, ivory or light yellow interior. Its aroma and flavor are fairly delicate. The "Savoie" regional label, represented by a red mark on the heel of the cheese, allows for the positive identification of French Emmental. More than any other cheese, this one lends itself to a variety of uses—in cubes in a prepared salad, sliced in a sandwich, or on a cheeseboard at the end of a meal. It is also an ingredient in hot dishes such as soufflés or vegetable gratins. Serve it with a white Savoie wine.

SWISS EMMENTAL

THE MIDDLE AGES SAW THE APPEARANCE OF SCALDED OR "COOKED" CURD CHEESES IN SWITZERLAND, IN THE BERN AND GRUYÈRE REGIONS. THESE IMPOSING MILLSTONES, OR WHEELS, OF CHEESE MEASURE UP TO 40 INCHES IN DIAMETER. EMMENTAL OWES ITS NAME TO THE VALLEY OF EMME, ITS PLACE OF ORIGIN (*TAL* MEANING "VALLEY" IN GERMAN.)

Description
Slightly convex in shape, a wheel of Emmental weighs up to 220 pounds. Ripening lasts about a year, and is carried out in a cool cellar. The label guaranteeing the name of the cheese and the name of the country of origin, Switzerland, is stamped in red on the side of the cheese. Swiss Emmental can be recognized by the size of the holes in the curd, which must be no larger than a walnut.

Serving suggestions
Under a golden or light brown rind, the pale yellow interior of this cheese is supple and tender. Slightly fruity, its flavor tends to become more assertive with longer ripening. Swiss Emmental more than merits its place on a cheeseboard. Serve it with a locally produced white wine.

SWITZERLAND			
		Sp	Su
		Au	Wi

FOL ÉPI

HAILING FROM THE REGION OF MAYENNE, FOL ÉPI IS A FACTORY-PRODUCED CHEESE MADE FROM PASTEURIZED, SKIM COW'S MILK. IN APPEARANCE, IT RESEMBLES A ROUND LOAF OF BREAD; IT SEEMS TO HAVE BEEN THE AIM OF THE PRODUCERS TO CREATE A SORT OF CHEESE/BREAD HYBRID. FOL ÉPI IS A MILD, FRUITY CHEESE, ENJOYED BY CHILDREN AND ADULTS ALIKE.

Description
Fol Épi can be easily identified at the cheese market: golden, shaped like a round loaf of bread, it is decorated with wheat ears! Its unusual rind-cum-crust is made from lightly toasted wheat flour, and envelops a soft, tender, light yellow interior studded with small, regular holes.

Serving suggestions
Cheese-lovers enjoy the mild, slightly fruity flavor of Fol Épi. "Light" tasting but perfumed, Fol Épi should be served cut into cubes along with an apéritif, or on a cheeseboard. It makes an ideal sandwich for picnics, being easy to eat. Accompany it with a slightly tannic wine, such as a Loire red.

PAYS-DE-LOIRE			
Nantes			
		Sp	Su
		Au	Wi

GRANA PADANO

THIS COOKED, PRESSED CHEESE IS PRODUCED ON THE PO PLAIN IN NORTHERN ITALY. THE WORD *GRANA* SERVES TO DESIGNATE TWO KINDS OF CHEESES: FIRST, PARMIGIANO-REGGIANO, OR PARMESAN, FROM A DELIMITED AREA AND WITH AN A.O.C.; AND SECOND, ALL OF THE CHEESES OF GRANULAR STRUCTURE MANUFACTURED IN NORTHERN ITALY, SUCH AS GRANA PADANO OR GRANA TRENTINO.

In the beginning
Grana came into being around the tenth and eleventh centuries near Piacenza, by the banks of the Po River. The word *grana* is traditionally followed by a qualifier indicating its place of production: *grana emiliano, grana veneto, grana trentino.* This cheese is ripened for between ten and eighteen months. Shaped like a millstone, it weighs between 40 and 55 pounds. A clover-shaped stamp on the rind attests to its authenticity.

Description
Measuring ⅙ to ⅓ of an inch thick, the rind of this cheese is dark and oily. Inside, the white curd has a granular, compact, and hard texture. Like Parmesan, Grana has a tendency to break into pieces when cut up. Its aroma is pronounced without being strong. Grana Padano is eaten grated over pasta or in a soufflé. It can also take its place on a cheeseboard. Serve it with an Italian wine or a red Côtes-de-Provence.

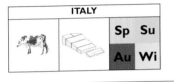

ITALY		
		Sp Su
		Au Wi

SWISS GRUYÈRE

TRADITIONAL GRUYÈRE IS PRODUCED IN THE CANTONS OF FRIBOURG, NEUCHÂTEL, AND VAUD. THE SWISS USUALLY REFER TO IT AS FRIBOURG. THIS CHEESE BELONGS TO THE FAMILY OF COOKED CHEESES WITH A BRUSHED, WASHED RIND.

In the beginning
For the Swiss, Gruyère gets its name from the Counts of Gruyère, whose coat of arms was embellished with a crane (French, *grue*). This family settled in the canton of Fribourg in the ninth century. For the French, who also call cheeses produced in Savoie, Burgundy, and Franche-Comté by the same name, "Gruyère" is said to derive from the word *gruyer,* a medieval forestry officer who collected taxes in the form of wood or cheese. Having said this, the French overuse the word *Gruyère,* applying it to all pressed, cooked cheeses made into large wheels.

Choosing wisely
Made from raw milk, Gruyère is ripened for six months. A wheel of Gruyère measures 15¾ to 25½ inches across by 3½ to 5 inches high, and weighs between 44 and 110 pounds. Genuine Swiss Gruyère has an ivory-colored interior that is slightly sticky from the brining treatment. Its flavor is more or less fruity, depending on how long it has matured in a cellar. The holes habitually found in French Gruyères are rare in the Swiss version of this cheese. This truly delicious cheese should be enjoyed at the end of a meal, either on a cheeseboard or accompanied by walnuts and slices of ripe pear. Serve it with a white Swiss wine.

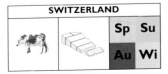

SWITZERLAND		
		Sp Su
		Au Wi

LEERDAMMER

A FAIRLY RECENT INVENTION OF THE NETHERLANDS, LEERDAMMER IS ALSO KNOWN AS MAASDAMMER. HAVING AFFINITIES WITH BOTH GOUDA AND EMMENTAL, THIS DUTCH CHEESE BOASTS A PLEASANT, UNOBTRUSIVE, FRUITY FLAVOR AND A 45 PERCENT FAT CONTENT, AND HAS NUMEROUS EUROPEAN FANS.

Description

This cow's-milk cheese is made in the shape of convex, 13¼-pound wheels that can sometimes weigh up to 31 pounds. Enclosed in a light-yellow rind, its golden-yellow curd is studded with large holes. This type of cheese is produced in several European countries.

Serving suggestions

Mild and delicate on the palate, Leerdammer has a homogeneous curd. It can be eaten at any time of day—at breakfast, lunch, or afternoon tea. It may be enjoyed sliced on buttered bread or in a sandwich, cubed with an apéritif, or on a cheeseboard. It can also be melted on top of vegetables for a delicious au gratin dish. Enjoy it with a light wine.

THE NETHERLANDS		
		Sp Su
		Au Wi

PARMIGIANO-REGGIANO

T HE ENGLISH TERM "PARMESAN" DESIGNATES A GROUP OF ITALIAN CHEESES TO WHICH THAT GREAT CLASSIC OF ITALIAN CUISINE, PARMIGIANO-REGGIANO, BELONGS.

In the beginning

Made from the thirteenth century onward, with its praises sung by Boccaccio a century later, this cheese was being served grated over pasta as early as the sixteenth century. A cheese of noble lineage, it was introduced to France by a duchess of Parma who married a grandson of Louis XV.

Method of production

Made between mid-April and mid-November, this cheese is typical of the provinces of Parma, Mantua, and Bologna. Molded in the shape of large millstones, Parmigiano-Reggiano is ripened for at least twenty-four months. A distinction is made between *nuovo* (one year), *vecchio* (two years), *stravecchio* (three years), and *stravecchione* (four years or more).

Description

This cheese has a thick rind, which may sport a blackish hue without the taste being affected. Its hard, brittle, golden-yellow interior sometimes exhibits a slight "sweat." Its very fruity flavor with a slightly piquant finish lingers for a long time in the mouth. Its granular texture has earned it the generic name *grana* in Italy.

Serving suggestions

Serve this cheese thinly shaved and rolled up as part of an apéritif, with a glass of champagne. Young, it comes into its own on a cheeseboard, to be savored with a fairly powerful red wine.

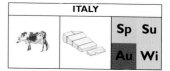

ITALY		
		Sp Su
		Au Wi

PAVÉ DE ROUBAIX

NEARLY AS HARD AS THE FAMOUS COBBLESTONES (*PAVÉS*) OF THE TOWN FROM WHICH IT TAKES ITS NAME, THIS CHEESE, AT ONE TIME THREATENED WITH EXTINCTION, HAS FINALLY EARNED ITSELF A SELECT PLACE IN THE GASTRONOMIC LANDSCAPE OF THE NORTH OF FRANCE.

Method of production
This is a pressed, semiscalded cow's-milk cheese, made from pasteurized milk. Aged on wood, it is ripened for a minimum of one year, during which time it is turned and brushed by hand at least once a month.

Description
Shaped like an elongated cobblestone measuring 10½ inches long by 5 inches wide by 3¼ inches thick, Pavé de Roubaix weighs about 6½ pounds. Its orange-brown rind encloses a hard, carrot-colored interior. Its prolonged ripening imbues it with powerful aromas and a persistent taste in the mouth.

Serving suggestions
Pavé de Roubaix harmonizes happily with sweet tastes. Its hard texture makes it an ideal cheese to serve with an apéritif. Serve it in cubes with a glass of Banyuls or a slightly sweet *vin cuit*. At the end of a meal, it goes very well with a Gewurztraminer and Viennese bread.

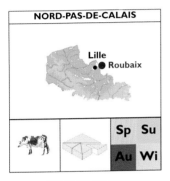

NORD-PAS-DE-CALAIS

Lille
Roubaix

		Sp	Su
		Au	Wi

PROVOLONE

IN ITS NATIVE ITALY, PROVOLONE IS SOLD IN *SALUMERIE* (DELICATESSENS), SUSPENDED FROM A ROPE THAT IMPARTS A RIBBED, BULGING SHAPE TO THE CHEESE.

Description
This Lombardian cow's- or buffalo's-milk cheese comes in a variety of forms—truncated cone, pear, large salami, even melon shaped. Handcrafted, it may weigh from 2 to 88 pounds, with the *gigante* version reaching almost 200 pounds. Provolone is a *pasta filata* or "spun curd" cheese. Its rind is smooth and shiny, and may range from golden yellow to brown; its curd is compact but soft. Provolone may also be smoked.

Serving suggestions
When ripened for between two and four months, this is a very mild-tasting cheese, good on bread or in a sandwich, or for a little snack. After six months, its flavor becomes more pronounced, indeed slightly piquant, and it should be served with an Italian red wine. Aged longer, it is ideal grated or shaved over pasta and vegetables.

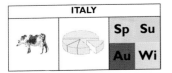

ITALY

		Sp	Su
		Au	Wi

SBRINZ

THIS 100 PERCENT SWISS CHEESE ALSO BEARS THE AMUSING ITALIAN NAME SULLE SPALLE ("ON THE SHOULDERS")—DOUBTLESS BECAUSE IT HAS LONG BEEN THE SUBJECT OF REGULAR TRADE WITH THE NORTH OF ITALY, AND HAS CROSSED THE SAINT-GOTHARD PASS ON MULEBACK ON NUMEROUS OCCASIONS!

In the beginning
A scalded-curd cheese from the cantons of Lucerne, Schwyz, Uri, and Unterwald, Sbrinz is one of the oldest Swiss cheeses, doubtless the one cited by Pliny the Elder under the name of *Caseus helveticus*. Around the fourteenth century, the Italians named this cheese Sbrinzo, having confused it with a Romanian sheep's cheese, Brinza.

Description
This cheese comes in large millstones weighing 44 to 88 pounds, stored vertically, rather than horizontally like Gruyère or Emmental. Sbrinz has a smooth, hard rind and a compact, light-yellow interior devoid of holes.

Serving suggestions
Hard and brittle in texture, Sbrinz has a pronounced flavor, with a slightly rancid taste. This cheese melts on the tongue, but may become sharp as it ages. It's used like Parmesan, grated over pasta or vegetables, or thinly shaved in a salad. In Switzerland, it's eaten with gherkins and sausage. Cut into cubes, it makes an unusual apéritif, served with a sturdy wine such as Dôle du Valais.

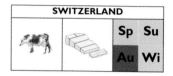

SWITZERLAND		
		Sp Su
		Au Wi

TÊTE-DE-MOINE

Round LIKE THE MONKS' HEADS, WHICH STILL HAVE PRIDE OF PLACE IN CERTAIN ADVERTISEMENTS, THIS ARTISANAL CHEESE IS MADE TO SEDUCE GOURMANDS.

In the beginning
In bygone days, the prior of the Abbey of Bellelay in Switzerland received one cheese per monk every year from his tenant farmers as a tax payment—hence the name of the cheese, which translates as "monk's head." In point of fact, at the very beginning of its history, this cheese was known more simply as *fromage à talon* (heeled cheese). It is also referred to as Bellelay.

Description
Tête-de-Moine is a tall cylinder from which the first vertical slice is removed. Although cheeses might formerly have reached weights of 9 to 13¼ pounds, smaller sizes from 2 to 4½ pounds or even less are found today. This cheese is ripened for four to five months in a cool cellar. Its brown rind is thick and granular; its yellow interior is supple. Tête-de-Moine has a spicy flavor and an aromatic scent. This cheese reddens with the passage of time.

Serving suggestions
Tête-de-Moine is ideal served with an apéritif. Rather than being cut in pieces, the top slice is removed, then the cheese is scraped with the tip of a knife in a spiral shape to create thin shavings. Its flavor can best be appreciated when it's sliced thinly. Partner it with a Côtes-du-Jura. If serving this cheese at the end of a meal, accompany it with a rustic raisin loaf.

SWITZERLAND		
		Wi

BLUE-VEINED CHEESES

MARBLED WITH BLUISH STREAKS, THESE CHEESES ARE SOMETIMES SIMPLY REFERRED TO AS "BLUES." STRONG AND PUNGENT-SMELLING, THEY HAVE AN EXTRAORDINARY PERSONALITY, INSPIRING LOVE OR LOATHING—BUT NEVER INDIFFERENCE!

MARBLED WITH PENICILLIN MOLD

The family of blue-veined cheeses groups together all cheeses with blue or green internal mold. These cow's-milk cheeses are generally known as "blue cheeses" or "blues" for short. During production, the milk is heated to 89.6°F, then cultured with lactic ferments and rennet. Once drained, the curds are broken up by hand or machine, then salted. At this stage, they are cultured with the spores of a microscopic fungus, *Penicillium roqueforti*. These spores are responsible for marbling the cheese with the blue or green veins, which give it a spicy flavor.

SALTING AND RIPENING

Salting takes place over five to six days in a cool, humid cellar. The cheeses are then removed from their molds and placed in an *hâloir*. There they are pierced all over with long, metallic needles to permit the circulation of air in the cheese, thereby encouraging the marbling process. The ripening conditions are crucial to the quality of blue cheeses. This very long stage lasts from four to six months, the time it takes for the cheese to take on the characteristic consistency and aroma that are the hallmark of blue cheeses. Ripening most often takes place in humid caves (as opposed to cellars), at a stable temperature.

Among the French blue-veined cheeses, we may cite Bleu d'Auvergne, Bleu des Causses, Bleu du Quercy, Bleu de Gex, Fourme d'Ambert, and Fourme de Montbrison. Stilton and Blue Cheshire are examples of British blues, and Gorgonzola is Italy's best-known blue.

THE CHEESE FROM THE MOUNTAIN THAT BREATHES

Roquefort is the only blue sheep's cheese, made from the milk of ewes grazing in Aveyron, Lozère,

Tarn, Gard, Hérault, Alpes-de-Hautes-Provence, as well as in Corsica and the Pyrenees. The cheese is ripened in the caves of Cambalou, which are swept by *fleurines*, naturally-occurring currents of air that balance the fermentation process. To qualify for the highly coveted A.O.C., the cheese must be ripened in the caves of Roquefort, that "breathing mountain" formed following the collapse of an underground lake some thirty or forty thousand years ago.

FRAGILE: HANDLE WITH CARE

Blues are among the most fragile of all cheeses. In order to enjoy them to the fullest, you must care for them properly. Blue-veined cheeses are sensitive to changes in atmosphere. They dry out quickly when exposed to the air, and are easily damaged by excesses of both cold and heat. Only serve on a cheeseboard the amount that is likely to be consumed. Store blue cheeses wrapped in aluminum foil at the bottom of the refrigerator. Protected from the air, they won't yellow, and their strong, yet subtle, flavor will remain intact.

THE PERFECT MATCH

Because of their pronounced flavor, these cheeses should be served at the end of a meal. Nevertheless, a fairly mild Bleu de Bresse or a fruity Fourme d'Ambert may be eaten before strong cheeses such as Puant de Lille, Boulette d'Avesnes, or Époisses. Blue-veined cheeses encourage fine alliances: slices of apple with Roquefort, walnuts and Bleu de Sassenage. You could even try an unusual touch of sweetness, such as honey with a Bleu des Causses, or a juicy pear with a Fourme d'Ambert.

BLEU D'AUVERGNE A.O.C.

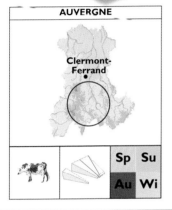

AUVERGNE

Clermont-Ferrand

Sp | Su

Au | Wi

Made from cow's milk, this blue-veined cheese is covered with a natural bloomy rind. Bleu d'Auvergne is made in the *départements* of Cantal and Puy-de-Dôme, and part of the *départements* of Haute-Loire, Aveyron, Corrèze, Lot, and Lozère.

Description
Molded in the shape of a flat cylinder, the large version measures 8 inches across by 3¼ to 4 inches high, and weighs from 4½ to 6½ pounds. The small cheese is a wheel 4 inches across, weighing 1 to 2 pounds. Bleu d'Auvergne was created in the mid-nineteenth century by an Auvergne farmer who hit on the idea of culturing his curds with a blue mold that he had seen growing on rye bread. He then pierced his cheese with a needle so that the air filtering through the holes would encourage the mold to proliferate. This blue is ripened in a humid, well-ventilated cellar. At the end of three weeks, the penicillium spores develop and marble the cheese with blue. The cheeses are ripened for three to four weeks, depending on their weight.

Serving suggestions
The regular, creamy-to-soft curd has a dark green to blue marbling. Bleu d'Auvergne has a sharp aroma attesting to its liveliness, and a strong, spicy flavor. This cheese lends itself to a thousand and one combinations in soufflés or salads, or with slices of pear. Accompany it with a Madiran, a Gaillac, or a mellow Barsac.

BLEU DE GEX

FRANCHE-COMTÉ

Besançon

Su

Au | Wi

Bleu de Gex is an unpressed, uncooked blue-veined cheese made from raw, whole cow's milk, with a minimum fat content of 50 percent. This cheese comes in the shape of a millstone 13¾ inches across by 4 inches thick, and weighing 16½ pounds. The word "Gex" is etched on one side. It hails from Haut Jura, straddling the *départements* of Ain and Jura.

Description
This cheese is said to date back to the sixteenth century, when settlers from the Dauphiné arrived in Jura after the former was ceded to the French crown in 1343 by Humbert II. Bleu de Gex was born in the highest pastures of Jura, where the varied, sweetly scented flora gives the milk of Montbéliard cows a unique flavor, so different from other blue cheeses. This cheese is produced solely in the mountains. Bleu de Gex is ripened for a minimum of three weeks in a cool, humid cellar.

Serving suggestions
The rind of this cheese is thin, dry, and yellowish. The white to ivory paste exhibits well-distributed, fairly pale blue-green marbling. The curd is creamy-to-soft, almost crumbly. Bleu de Gex has a fairly unpronounced aroma and a very characteristic hazelnut flavor. Enjoy this cheese either at the end of meal or, thanks to its delicate flavor, as an appetizer with a red or rosé Jura wine.

BLEU DE LAQUEUILLE

THIS BLUE-VEINED CHEESE ORIGINATED IN LAQUEUILLE IN THE AUVERGNE. IT WAS INVENTED IN 1850 BY A CHEESEMAKER NAMED ANTOINE ROUSSEL, WHOSE STATUE NOW GRACES THE VILLAGE SQUARE. A COW'S-MILK CHEESE, IT WAS MANUFACTURED BY ONLY TWO DAIRIES. FOR SOME THIRTY YEARS, PRODUCTION OF THIS FINE, SMOOTH, AND CREAMY CHEESE NEARLY CEASED ENTIRELY, BUT HAS PICKED UP AGAIN. BLEU DE LAQUEUILLE BELONGS TO THE SAME FAMILY OF CHEESES AS FOURME D'AMBERT AND FOURME DE MONTBRISON.

Method of production
In the beginning, this cheese was cultured with mold obtained from rye bread. Today it is for the most part factory-produced. Bleu de Laqueuille is made from pasteurized milk and ripened for one to two months in a humid atmosphere.

Description
Bleu de Laqueuille is cylindrical in shape, measuring 7 inches across by 4 inches thick, and weighing 5½ pounds. It is sometimes wrapped in foil. Its natural rind encloses an interior evenly marbled with blue, which gives off an odor of a cellar. This cheese has a penetrating, clear-cut aroma and a fat content of 45 percent.

Serving suggestions
Enjoy this cheese with multiseed bread and dried fruit, or crumbled into a green salad. Serve it with a sturdy wine or a mellow Rivesaltes.

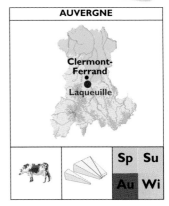

AUVERGNE
Clermont-Ferrand / Laqueuille
Sp Su / Au Wi

BLEU DE SASSENAGE

THIS TRADITIONAL MONASTIC CHEESE IS A BLUE WITH A DELICATE FLAVOR AND SUBTLE FRUITINESS. BLEU DE SASSENAGE IS NOT WIDELY AVAILABLE—IF YOU SHOULD HAPPEN TO COME ACROSS SOME IN A WELL-STOCKED DAIRY, BE SURE TO SNAP IT UP.

In the beginning
The recipe for Bleu de Sassenage is said to have been perfected by monks of the Dauphiné and Vercors regions. In 1338, Baron Albert de Sassenage published a charter authorizing the inhabitants of his estate to sell their cheeses freely, an entirely new development at the time. This blue was thus "democratized," and could be enjoyed throughout the country.

Description
Shaped like a wheel measuring 12 inches across by 3¼ to 3½ inches in height, Bleu de Sassenage weighs 11 to 13¼ pounds and is ripened for two to three months. Today this cheese is mainly factory-produced. The summer cheese captures the flavor of the milk of cows grazing in the mountain pastures, and is characterized by a rounded flavor and an aroma of mold. Enjoy it with a dark rye loaf at the end of a meal. Serve this cheese with a Banyuls or a sturdy red.

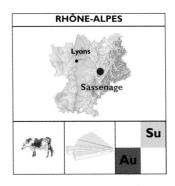

RHÔNE-ALPES
Lyons / Sassenage
Su / Au

BLEU D'AUVERGNE A.O.C.

ONE MAN'S DISCOVERY

Antoine Roussel, a cheesemaker born in Laqueuille, a small market town some twenty-five miles west of Clermont-Ferrand in the Puy-de-Dôme region, can be considered the father of Bleu d'Auvergne. After a brief stay at a pharmacist's in Rouen, he returned to his native village following the death of his father. The oldest son of the family, responsible for many brothers and sisters, he took over the running of the family farm, producing a *fourme* cheese based on a nonstirred, very lightly pressed curd, the sale of which kept the family's farm above water. One day, by chance, certain cheeses in his cellar turned blue. Roussel sampled the cheeses, finding them to have a "special, pleasant, and perfumed" flavor. He then decided to alter his production process so as to produce systematically the cheese he had obtained accidentally, and create a "proper" product. He changed his molds several times—terra-cotta, wooden, and tin molds succeeded one another in his cellar. Roussel then noticed that the rye bread near his cheeses became moldy in the same way. He then hit on the idea of depositing in the heart of his *fourmes*, with the aid of a needle placed on the end of a bit of wood, the blue powder that developed inside the cheese, imbuing it with a highly distinctive taste, which made for its success. This was in 1854, nine years after Antoine Roussel had returned to his native village.

A SMASHING SUCCESS

Success came quickly. The price of the *fourme* that was to become Bleu d'Auvergne skyrocketed, and production was unable to keep pace with demand. Small local entrepreneurs successfully launched themselves into the battle to produce their very own Bleu d'Auvergne from the milk of their herds, and bit by bit, farmhouse production was succeeded by factory production of the cheese.

In 1893 the first study touching on Bleu d'Auvergne, referred to as "Roquefort-style cheese," was conducted. In 1937 a first official decree ruled on what constituted a genuine Bleu d'Auvergne. On March 7, 1975, the cheese received the supreme recognition of admission to the noble family of A.O.C. products. Bleu d'Auvergne's A.O.C. is governed by the amended decree of December 29. At the time, seventeen dairies were producing Bleu d'Auvergne. Today, there are no more than six dairies, which every year produce over 8,000 tons of this delicious blue-veined cheese.

PRODUCTION

Cow's milk is cultured with a specific lactic ferment, *Penicillium roqueforti*, before being reheated. Next, rennet is added, and after coagulation, the mixture is stirred, an essential operation that aims to encourage the spread of the blue-green marbling.

After the whey has been drained off, the curds are placed in molds and remain like this in the draining room for two days. The molds are turned several times to allow the whey or lactoserum to drain off. Next, the cheeses are salted by hand, then mechanically pricked with needles to encourage the marbling to develop. They are then placed in humid, well-ventilated cellars for four weeks at a temperature between 44°–48°F. The cheeses are then packaged for storage and sale—wrapped in aluminum foil, they are stamped with the wording "Appellation d'Origine Contrôlée Bleu d'Auvergne," and with the highly coveted initials of the INAO, the A.O.C.-awarding institute.

Bleu des Causses A.O.C.

MADE FROM WHOLE COW'S MILK, BLEU DES CAUSSES IS A BLUE-VEINED CHEESE WITH A NATURAL BLOOMY RIND.

In the beginning
There were many artisanal dairies in this moorland, and it's from this harsh region of contrasts that Bleu des Causses draws its qualities, its milk being enriched with the scent of wild flora. The cheese is ripened in caves hollowed out in masses of fallen limestone rocks, swept by cool, moist air currents that favor the development of the mold. Ripening lasts for three to six months.

Description
Bleu des Causses contains at least 45 percent fat. Cylindrical in shape, it measures 8 inches across by 4 inches thick, and weighs between 5½ and 6½ pounds. Its production area is spread over certain *communes* of the *départements* of Aveyron, Lot, Lozère, Gard, and Hérault.

Serving suggestions
To the eye, Bleu des Causses displays a solid, creamy-to-soft, ivory-yellow paste especially shiny in summer, and whiter and less moist in winter. It has a pleasant, sustained aroma and a characterful taste. Crumble Bleu des Causses into an omelette for added flavor, or into a sauce or over vegetables for a spicy kick. Partner this cheese with a Cornas or a Rivesaltes.

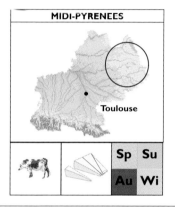

MIDI-PYRENEES

Toulouse

		Sp	Su
		Au	Wi

Carré d'Aurillac

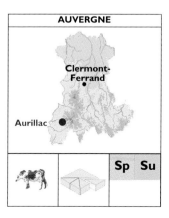

SOLD LOOSE, THIS RATHER NOVEL COW'S-MILK CHEESE IS A SPECIALTY "BLUE." CREATED OVER TEN YEARS AGO, IT'S PRODUCED IN SAINT-FLOUR IN THE AUVERGNE, IN A DAIRY THAT SPECIALIZES IN THE MANUFACTURE OF A.O.C. CHEESES SUCH AS BLEU D'AUVERGNE, SAINT-NECTAIRE, OR FOURME D'AMBERT.

Description
Shaped like a square slab, Carré d'Aurillac measures 16 inches long by 8½ inches wide by about 3¼ inches high, and weighs just under 5 pounds. It is ripened for sixteen days in air-conditioned cellars at a temperature of 48°–50°F, before being dispatched to its different points of sale. Sold cut, its ivory-colored interior, delicately marbled with blue, can be admired. Carré d'Aurillac has a thin, delicate rind and contains 50 percent fat.

Serving suggestions
After three weeks' ripening, Carré d'Aurillac has a mild, creamy flavor. It's a pleasant table cheese that goes well with walnut bread and slightly tart apple quarters. Accompany it with a Bordeaux or a Madiran.

AUVERGNE

Clermont-Ferrand

Aurillac

		Sp	Su

FOURME D'AMBERT A.O.C.

MADE FROM RAW COW'S MILK, THIS AUVERGNE CHEESE IS A MEMBER OF THE BLUE-VEINED FAMILY. IT CAN BE FOUND IN THE LOIRE REGION, IN THE *DÉPARTEMENT* OF PUY-DE-DÔME, AND IN FIVE CANTONS OF CANTAL AROUND SAINT-FLOUR.

In the beginning
Originating in the Forez mountains, Fourme d'Ambert appeared in the Auvergne in the eighth or ninth century. Having said this, it's probable that this cheese already existed in the *Pays arverne* (former Auvergne) at the time of Caesar. Farmers collected the milk from their cows grazing in the uplands, at an altitude of between 1,970 and 5,250 feet. The word *fourme* is derived from *forme*, the vat that contained the curds. In bygone days, the cheese was produced in *jasseries*, little dairies scattered about the Forez mountains. Fourme d'Ambert is ripened in a cellar for at least four weeks. Its shape is very different from that of the other *fourmes*, and easily recognizable, being a cylinder that is taller than it is wide (7½ inches high by 5 inches across). Fourme d'Ambert weighs around 4½ pounds.

Choosing wisely
The dry, yellowish rind of this cheese is enveloped in a gray down. Inside, the rich paste is dotted with a pronounced mold. Fourme d'Ambert is whiter than Fourme de Montbrison. Although it gives off an odor of a cellar, this cheese leaves a mild, fruity taste in the mouth. Serve it with a Loupiac or a Barsac.

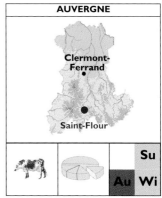

AUVERGNE

Clermont-Ferrand

Saint-Flour

Su
Au Wi

FOURME DE MONTBRISON

THIS COW'S-MILK *FOURME* BELONGS TO THE FAMILY OF BLUE-VEINED CHEESES. IT IS FOUND IN THE AUVERGNE NEAR MONTBRISON, THE TOWN THAT GIVES IT ITS NAME, AS WELL AS IN THE LOIRE REGION.

In the beginning
Fourme de Montbrison originated in the Forez mountains, in the Auvergne. The word *fourme* is derived from *forme*, the vat that contained the curds. Farmers collected the milk from their cows grazing in the uplands, at an altitude of between 1,970 and 5,250 feet. In former times, this cheese was produced in little dairies dotted around the hillsides. It is ripened in a cellar for a minimum of four weeks. Like Fourme d'Ambert, Fourme de Montbrison is shaped quite differently from the other *fourmes*. Cylinder-shaped, it measures 7½ inches high by 5 inches across, and weighs about 4½ pounds.

Serving suggestions
The dry, yellowish rind of this cheese is strewn with orange-red marks. Its rich paste, considerably yellower than Fourme d'Ambert's, contains a fairly unpronounced mold. Although it gives off an odor of a cellar, this cheese leaves a mild, fruity taste in the mouth. It should be eaten with slightly stale bread and accompanied by a Loupiac or a Barsac. In order to standardize the production of Fourme d'Ambert and Fourme de Montbrison, the two cheeses are grouped together under a single A.O.C. label.

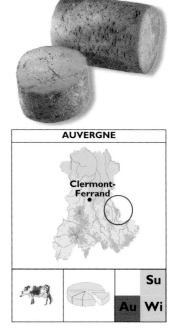

AUVERGNE

Clermont-Ferrand

Su
Au Wi

Fourme d'Ambert A.O.C.

A centuries-old cheese

According to some sources, Fourme d'Ambert existed even before the creation of the Roman Empire. What is certain, however, is that it had appeared on the scene by the eleventh century A.D. at the latest. On the facade of a chapel at Chaulme in Puy-de-Dôme, there are a series of carved stones illustrating the different commodities that the lord exacted in payment from his serfs: butter, ham, sausage, eggs, hay, grains, and *fourme*. Until the nineteenth century, Fourme d'Ambert was produced in *jasseries*, ancient buildings that served as a dwelling, cheese dairy, and stable all rolled into one. During the fine weather, women and children would go there to make the *fourme*, while the men would remain on the farm for the haymaking. From the beginning of the twentieth century, increasingly sophisticated cheese dairies were set up to replace the *jasseries*.

As a matter of interest, it was Henri de la Tour d'Auvergne Viscount of Turenne and Marshal of France (1611–1675), who declared, "God is with the big batallions, especially when his soldiers have a piece of *fourme* in their satchels!"

An artisanally produced cheese

In the past, this cheese, with its cellar odor, was made with a number of artisanal tools that have since fallen into disuse. Today Fourme d'Ambert is produced in factories in a more mechanized manner, while still respecting tradition, from the milk of cows grazing in the Forez mountains at an altitude of 1,970 to 5,250 feet. The milk is renneted under heat; the resulting curds are cut up and stirred, then hand-molded, after which they are drained, dried, turned, and pricked with needles to allow the blue veining to develop. The cheeses are then ripened in a cellar for a minimum of twenty-eight days. It takes 5¼ to 6½ gallons of milk to produce a traditional *fourme* weighing about 4½ pounds.

Fourme d'Ambert has been an A.O.C. cheese since May 9, 1972.

Short history of the town of Ambert

The capital of the Livradois, located in a poor region of granite cliffs, Ambert is famous for its cheese and its circular town hall. The present-day nucleus of the town dates from the tenth century; from the fifteenth century, Ambert has been famed for its paper windmills.

In Ambert, you can visit the Musée de la Fourme et des Fromages (Fourme and Cheese Museum), which traces the history of the production of this cheese with the aid of supporting documents. The museum also boasts a demonstration workshop, an exhibition on the cheeses of the region, and of course a tasting room, where you can become acquainted with other regional specialties.

If you are interested in how the *fourme* is produced, and wish to learn more about the region's traditions, you should visit the Musée des Vieux Métiers (Museum of Old Trades) in Olliergues, a small town between Thiers and Ambert. There, you'll become acquainted with the big names in the history of this ancestral cheese.

Which wine?

Partner the delicate flavor of Fourme d'Ambert with a gentle red or rosé—Côtes-d'Auvergne, Côtes-du-Forez, Côte-Roannaise, or even a white such as Côteaux-du-Layon. Fourme d'Ambert is delicious accompanied by a few slices of apple, as well as dried fruit or walnuts.

Goat Cheeses

The cheeses in this family share just one common denominator—goat's milk—which gives Sainte-Maure, Chabichou, or Bouton de Culotte a unique aroma and subtle taste all their own.

Morning and evening milkings

After the goats are milked, the acidity of the milk is checked. The milk from the evening milking is mixed with that of the morning milking in order to obtain a "mixed milk" of more uniform composition. Coagulation is achieved either naturally or with lactic ferments or rennet, at a temperature that varies according to the cheese in question.

Dry-salting

The cheeses are then removed from their molds and drained for twelve to twenty-four hours, then dried again in a ventilated drying room for about a week. During this drying stage, penicillin mold develops spontaneously on the surface of the cheeses and turns slightly blue from oxidation. The cheeses are salted generously, then transferred to a cellar for one to five weeks, depending on the consistency desired.

To dust or not to dust

At the beginning of this ripening stage, some cheeses are dusted with powdered charcoal. In the past, the ashes of vine shoots were used, as is still common practice with Valençay. At the same time, other cheeses may be sprinkled with seasonings or spices, or wrapped in a vine leaf, as is the case with Banon à la Feuille or Cabécou du Lot. As for Sainte-Maure, it is pierced with a rye straw to drain off moisture and facilitate removal from the mold.

Ripening: the crucial stage

After two weeks' ripening, these goat cheeses sport an increasing number of blue dots on their rind. The cheese develops a characteristic aroma. At this stage, Picodon de l'Ardèche is dry and makes for delicious eating. After three to four weeks, the cheese's interior hardens and becomes dry, in some cases brittle and crumbly. The taste is noticeably sharper without being piquant. The cheese—Crottin de Chavignol or Selles-sur-Cher—is semi-dry or very dry. If the ripening stage is prolonged even further, the goat cheese is said to be *repassé* ("sharpened"), with an even more pronounced taste.

The season for chèvre

A nanny goat yields twice as much milk in one milking as a productive cow. In ten days, a 110-pound nanny goat yields her weight in milk. The lactation period, however, lasts only for eight months, between March and October. Thus, the first farmhouse chèvres are spread out between mid-February and the end of March, and the last ones arrive on the market at the end of November. It makes sense, therefore, to enjoy these cheeses perfectly ripened during their best season.

Half-chèvre or pure chèvre?

The law authorizes the manufacture of *mi-chèvre* ("half-goat") cheeses, i.e., made with half cow's milk and half goat's milk. The proportion of goat's milk must never be lower than 50 percent.

A *pur chèvre* cheese is made entirely from goat's milk. All other cheeses made from a mixture of goat's and cow's milk are labeled *fromages au lait de chèvre* ("goat milk cheeses.")

No mistaking goat cheese!

The taste is highly pronounced, the texture firm, the edges well defined, the thin rind free from rough patches, and the compact curd very white. Chèvre doesn't soften and isn't runny like a soft cow's-milk cheese. A pure goat's cheese hardens evenly, while its aromas concentrate. The traditional shapes—cylinders or pyramids—are reserved exclusively for goat's cheeses, which must contain 45 percent fat.

ANNEAU DU VIC-BILH

A FARMHOUSE CHEESE, ANNEAU DU VIC-BILH IS A RECENT INVENTION. PRODUCED IN THE PYRENEES REGION, IT'S MADE FROM RAW GOAT'S MILK. THIS CHEESE SEDUCES CONNOISSEURS WITH ITS GENTLE TASTE OF HAZELNUT AND ITS PLEASANT, MILKY AROMA.

Description
Disk-shaped, measuring 4 inches across by ¾ inch thick and sporting a 1¼-inch hole in the center (*anneau* means "ring"), this cheese weighs between 7 and 9 ounces. It is ripened for a minimum of ten days. Anneau du Vic-Bilh has a natural rind coated with powdered charcoal and a soft, delicate, white interior. It contains 45 percent fat, making it a rich, creamy-to-soft cheese.

Serving suggestions
The taste of this cheese is perfectly balanced between acidity and saltiness. Enjoy it on a cheeseboard with a selection of close-crumbed breads—cumin, six-grain, or rye. Its shape makes for easy slicing into bite-sized pieces that melt in the mouth. Serve it at room temperature, taking it out of the refrigerator at least one hour before you plan to eat it. Pair it with a wine hailing from the same area, such as a Pacherenc du Vic-Bilh, or a dry white Jurançon.

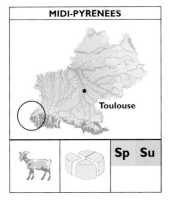

MIDI-PYRENEES

Toulouse

Sp Su

BANON À LA FEUILLE

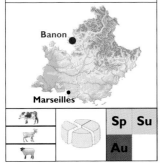

L IKE THE OTHER BANONS, THIS ONE IS PRODUCED ACCORDING TO TRADITIONAL TECHNIQUES. IT RIPENS UNDER WRAPS, ENVELOPED IN CHESTNUT LEAVES.

Method of production
Depending on the season, this cheese is made from cow's, goat's, or ewe's milk. A soft, unpressed, uncooked cheese, Banon à la Feuille is wrapped in four to five chestnut leaves ten days before being removed from its mold. Tied with raffia, these leaves may have been soaked for a while in eau de vie. Ripening lasts for ten to forty days in a humid cellar.

Serving suggestions
During this maturation period, the cheese takes on the aroma of the leaves that envelop it. Its thin rind, white to pale yellow in hue, takes on the brown of the leaves, as well as their veining. Banon has a lactic flavor, and gives off, bit by bit, an odor of humus. Enjoy Banon à la Feuille with *pain à l'ancienne* (a traditional cold-fermented bread), and a Provence wine such as a white Bandol, or a dry white Côtes-de-Provence.

PROVENCE-ALPES-CÔTE-D'AZUR

Banon

Marseilles

Sp Su

Au

Banon Herbes de Provence or Tomme à l'Ancienne

The jewel of Provençal cheeses is surely this Banon seasoned with local herbs, also known as Tomme à l'Ancienne (old-style tomme); both locals and tourists are devoted to it! This little mountain cheese is made according to a traditional farmhouse recipe. It's delicious at each stage of ripening, whether young and fresh or drier.

In the beginning
Banon is the invention of a couple living in the Provençal village of Puimichel, near Banon, a village in the Alpes-de-Haute-Provence region. It is also produced in the adjoining *départements*. Banon is produced from ewe's milk in winter, goat's milk in spring, and cow's milk throughout the year. It's made with several minced herbs that are mixed through its curd. This tomme-style cheese is ripened for two to three weeks, during which time its natural rind becomes speckled with white mold and its curd even-textured and creamy.

Serving suggestions
The curd of this cheese tastes of cream. Its mild flavor and hazelnut taste become stronger and spicier when ripening is extended. Serve this cheese with a baguette, accompanying it with a crunchy romaine salad dressed in walnut oil. Coteaux-d'Aix and Provençal wines are the ideal partners.

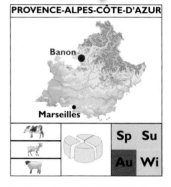

PROVENCE-ALPES-CÔTE-D'AZUR

Banon

Marseilles

		Sp	Su
		Au	Wi

Banon Poivre

Sprinkled with a few grains of black pepper, this Banon is without doubt one of the best cheeses of Provence.

Method of production
This little mountain cheese is made from cow's, goat's, or ewe's milk. A farmhouse cheese, it is delicious fresh or riper and drier. Disk-shaped, Banon Poivre measures 3 to 3½ inches across by ½ to 1¼ inches thick, and weighs about 3½ ounces. Its thin rind, enclosing a tender, highly perfumed curd, becomes yellower as ripening progresses.

In the beginning
The invention of a couple living in the Provençal village of Puimichel, this cheese was first made near Banon, a village in the Alpes-de-Haute-Provence region. It is also made in the neighboring *départements*. After three weeks' ripening, it is matured to perfection for eating.

Serving suggestions
The curd of the young Banon is sprinkled with a few grains of pepper. The flavor of this cheese is spicy and slightly piquant. Banon Poivre is delicious with country bread and a glass of white Provençal wine.

PROVENCE-ALPES-CÔTE-D'AZUR

Banon

Marseilles

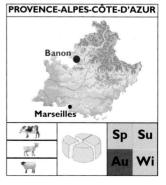

		Sp	Su
		Au	Wi

BANON

ONE CHEESE, SEVERAL VARIETIES

Named after a little village near the market town of Forcalquier in the *département* of Alpes-de-Haute-Provence, this cheese comes in different forms: Banon Herbes de Provence (herbs), Banon Poivre (pepper), Banon Sarriette (savory), and Banon à la Feuille (wrapped in chestnut leaves). Recently, the Association for the Defense and Promotion of Banon, established in 1993, filed a request for an A.O.C. with the INAO, the French body that awards protected designations of origin. This prestigious award would protect the consumer against cheeses masquerading as authentic Banon. Certain gourmets who think they are sampling Provence on a plate when they consume a morsel of so-called Banon could actually be eating a pale imitation of the cheese, made elsewhere.

WELL-DEFINED QUALITY CRITERIA

The requirements relating to the request for an A.O.C., ratified by the INAO, subject the production of Banon to strict rules and standards. The cheese must, for example, be made entirely from raw goat's milk, its rind must be white to creamy yellow in color, it must measure 3¼ to 3½ inches across by ⅜ to ¾ inch high, and weigh around 3.35 ounces (give or take 0.35 of an ounce). It must come wrapped in brown chestnut leaves, which may have been soaked in vinegar water, eau de vie, or grape marc brandy, and tied with genuine raffia rather than synthetic fibers.

Like all products awarded an A.O.C., Banon will have to be produced in a specific area: Alpes-de-Haute-Provence (except for Ubaye and Haut Verdon); the cantons of Laragne and Serre in Hautes-Alpes; the cantons of Montbrun and Séberon, in Drôme; and the cantons of Sault, Apt, Bonnieux, Cadenet, and Perthuis in the Vaucluse.

CHOOSING THE RIGHT METHOD

In point of fact, two methods are currently used to make a Banon—the "sweet-curd" method, common in the southern half of the country, and the "lactic-acid curd" method, predominant in the northern half of the country. The former technique requires the use of one quart of goat's milk with added rennet in order to obtain, within half an hour, an elastic paste molded in cheese strainers. Used since time immemorial, this method is the only one recognized by the experts. The latter technique requires the use of just 8½ ounces of goat's milk, to which rennet and a large amount of whey are added; coagulation, which takes place over twenty-four hours, yields curds of higher acidity, which will be used to make crumbly cheeses that don't soften through to the core, unlike the Banons that are made by the "sweet-curd" method.

AN ANCIENT CHEESE

Banon has been enjoyed since the Gallo-Roman era. According to the legend, the Roman emperor Antoninus Pius (A.D. 86–161) consumed so much of this cheese that he perished of indigestion. Much later, Jules Verne opined that the village of Banon produced "some highly esteemed cheeses." In their novel *Lavender Sky*, M. and P. Augier evoke Banon without actually naming it: "It was one of those cheeses made from goat's and ewe's milk, wrapped in walnut or chestnut leaves, for want of vine leaves, and placed in a stone or earthenware jar to ripen to perfection . . ." This poetically-tinged description leaves no doubt as to which cheese is alluded to!

BANON SARRIETTE

Banon

Marseilles

		Sp	Su

THIS JEWEL OF PROVENÇAL CHEESES IS COVERED IN SAVORY—A VARIANT THAT PRODUCES A SLIGHTLY ACID CURD.

In the beginning
The phrase "Banon cheese" appears for the first time in 1270, in the arbitral sentences of Banon and Saint-Christol, in Alpes-de-Haute-Provence. Legend even has it that the Roman emperor Antoninus Pius died of indigestion after overindulging in this cheese!

Description
This Banon, sprinkled with an herb from the Garrigue known as *pebre d'aï* ("donkey pepper") in the Provençal dialect, and "winter savory" in English, gives off the fragrant, sunny scent of its native soil. *Pebre d'aï* Banons come in farmhouse, artisanal, or factory-produced varieties. This one measures 3 to 3¾ inches across by ½ to 1¼ inches thick, and weighs about 3½ ounces.

Serving suggestions
This Banon melts like a dream on toast for enjoying as a first course with a salad. It's also eaten as a snack with Viennese bread. Match it with a wine from Provence, such as Coteaux-d'Aix or Bandol Rosé.

BARATTE CHÊVENET

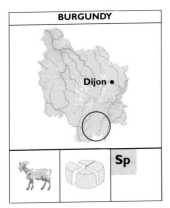

BURGUNDY

Dijon •

		Sp

PRODUCED IN THE MÂCONNAIS, THIS GOAT'S-MILK CHEESE IS EXCELLENT AT ALL STAGES OF RIPENING. ITS GOATY TASTE AND FINE FLAVOR ARE PARTICULARLY ENJOYED BY CHÈVRE FANS. BARATTE CHÊVENET IS A REGISTERED TRADEMARK.

Method of production
The coagulated milk is ladled into small molds and left to drain gently. In four to five days, the cheese is ready. Ripened only very slightly, this cheese is consumed quickly. Because it is an artisanal and homemade cheese, however, it is eaten year-round.

Description
In the past, this cheese was chiefly found at the Lyons market. One inch high, it can be recognized by its truncated-cone shape. A straw is stuck in its center like a churn stick, hence its name (*baratte* means "churn" in French.)

Serving suggestions
Fresh, dry, or ripened, this white cheese is eaten on walnut or cumin bread, which sets its flavor off nicely. Baratte Chêvenet is a real delight with a mesclun and shallot salad. Some also like it melted on toast. Serve it with a Côtes-du-Rhône or a Mâcon wine.

BARATTE DE CHÈVRE

A 100 PERCENT GOAT'S-MILK CHEESE, BARATTE DE CHÈVRE IS A DELIGHT IN THE SPRING, WHEN ITS PRODUCTION IS IN FULL SWING.

Choosing wisely

Like Baratte Chêvenet, this goat cheese is also produced in the Mâconnais. It can be recognized by its small (1 to 1¼ inches high) cylinder shape. A bit of vine shoot is planted in its center like a churn stick, which accounts for its name. The interior of the cheese is white, its rind barely flecked with mold, the sign of a short, ten-day ripening period. The cheese-seller/*affineur* receives the little cones completely fresh and waits for them to ripen before "planting" the piece of vine.

Serving suggestions

Whether fresh, dry, or ripened, this cheese has its devotees. It should be savored on country bread, accompanied by a mesclun salad with shallots. Some also like it served hot on toast. It can be served with an apéritif as an appetizer. Match it with a Côtes-du-Rhône or a Mâcon wine.

BURGUNDY

Dijon •

Sp

BONDE DE GÂTINE

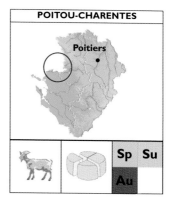

MANUFACTURED IN POITOU-CHARENTES, IN THE GÂTINE AREA OF POITOU, THIS CHÈVRE IS MADE FROM RAW GOAT'S MILK. MELLOW, WITH A SLIGHT GOATY TASTE, BONDE DE GÂTINE IS A FAR-TOO-UNCOMMON DELIGHT THAT MELTS DELICIOUSLY ON THE PALATE.

Description

This farmhouse chèvre is shaped like a small cylinder 2 to 2⅜ inches across by 2 to 2⅜ inches high. Bonde de Gâtine weighs 5 to 5½ ounces and contains 45 percent fat. Its tender white paste is enclosed in a slightly bluish natural rind.

Serving suggestions

After six weeks this cheese is mellow and flavorful, and ready to be savored. If the ripening period is extended to ten weeks, it develops a thoroughly agreeable acidity. Partnered with fancy breads, it leaves a rich, penetrating flavor in the mouth. This cheese is never aggressive, however, its slightly acid side being largely responsible for its charm. Enjoy it at the end of a meal with a wine from the Haut Poitou or a fruity Côtes-du-Rhône.

POITOU-CHARENTES

Poitiers •

Sp Su

Au

Bouchée de Chèvre

These bite-sized goat cheeses (*bouchée* is French for "mouthful") are flavored with pepper, cumin, chopped hazelnuts, paprika, and a variety of herbs. They add a stunning touch of color to a buffet.

Method of production
The milk is set to coagulate with lactic ferments and rennet. The curds are then placed in little strainers that are perforated at the sides and bottom to allow for rapid draining. While still entirely fresh, before their rind has had a chance to dry, the little goat cheeses are removed from the strainers and dispatched to the dairies that prepare them with five different seasonings, according to their customers' preferences.

Serving suggestions
According to tradition, goat cheese was served from Easter until All Saints' Day, the period when it was at its best. The Bouchées de Chèvre are rolled in chopped chives, herbs, pine nuts, paprika, pepper, or any other spice. They may be passed around with a dry white wine as an appetizer, or served with a green salad. Accompany them with a pleasant, lively wine such as a Menetou-Salon or a fresh Sancerre.

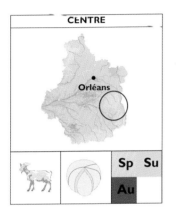

CENTRE

Orléans

Sp Su

Au

Bouchon de Sancerre

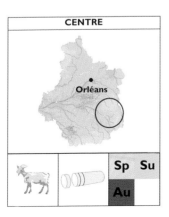

This farmhouse specialty from the Sancerrois area is well suited to its name (*bouchon* is French for "cork" or "stopper"). Made from whole goat's milk, this bite-sized cheese is reminiscent of Crottin de Chavignol in terms of its slightly goaty flavor. The winegrowers of the region are fond of it as a snack during the harvest between September and October.

Description
Cork-shaped Bouchon de Sancerre measures about 1½ inches across by ½ inch thick, and weighs between 1¾ and 2¾ ounces. At one time, this chèvre would develop a thin, natural rind flecked with white and bluish mold during its ripening period, which might last several months. This little cheese loses weight as it dries.

Serving suggestions
Ivory to light yellow in color, this cheese has a smooth, even-textured interior. When fresh (after one week's ripening), its curd is tender and mild-tasting. As ripening progresses, the curd becomes harder, with a more highly pronounced flavor. Bouchon de Sancerre can be enjoyed at any stage of ripeness with a batavia salad, as a snack, or as a pick-me-up between breakfast and lunch, as traditionally eaten in Lyons. Enjoy it with a fresh, lively glass of white Sancerre.

CENTRE

Orléans

Sp Su

Au

BOUGON

A MEMBER OF THE GOAT-CHEESE FAMILY, BOUGON IS MADE IN A COOPERATIVE FROM RAW MILK OR SOMETIMES FROM PASTEURIZED MILK (FOR SALE ABROAD). BY VIRTUE OF THE NATURAL FLORA OF ITS RIND, THE CHEESE'S INTERIOR GOES FROM SLIGHTLY ACID TO SUPPLE, DEVELOPING A MELT-IN-THE-MOUTH TEXTURE.

Description
This cheese resembles a small Camembert, but may also take the shape of a little Chaource. It has a naturally bloomy rind. When Camembert-shaped, Bougon is packaged in a box made from wood shavings. It may also come in the form of a large log, in which case it is sold loose at supermarket cheese counters.

Serving suggestions
This is the perfect cheese for making hot chèvre toast—slices of cheese are arranged on slices of country bread and put under the broiler for a few minutes. Its slightly acid, almost piquant flavor then harmonizes beautifully with a crisp green salad. Remember to take it out of the refrigerator at least one hour before you serve it. This firm, sharp-tasting cheese is delicious with a slightly sour Poilâne-style bread. Serve it with a red wine from the Haut Poitou or a lively Côtes-du-Rhône.

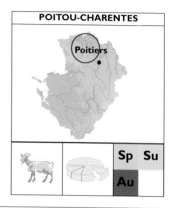

POITOU-CHARENTES

Poitiers

Sp Su
Au

BOUTON DE CULOTTE

T HIS LITTLE GOAT CHEESE HAS AN EVOCATIVE, COLORFUL NAME THAT SUITS IT TO PERFECTION— "PANTS BUTTON." OFTEN FOUND AT NIVERNAIS OR BURGUNDY MARKETS, IT IS SOMETIMES MADE FROM COW'S MILK OR EVEN FROM A MIXTURE OF GOAT'S AND COW'S MILKS. IN THE MÂCON COUNTRYSIDE, THIS CHEESE IS CALLED MÂCONNAIS OR CABRION DE MÂCON.

In the beginning
Bouton de Culotte was made and kept for the fall and eaten in its region of production during the grape harvest. Measuring 1¼ to 1½ inches across by ½ inch thick, this cheese weighs 1⅜ to 1¾ ounces. Depending on the length of the ripening period, which can last from two weeks to two months, patches of bluish mold appear on the rind, then become grayish, while the interior turns yellow. From young and soft, the cheese becomes mature and hard.

Serving suggestions
The greater the degree of ripening, the stronger the aroma of this cheese. The hard curd may turn brittle. Bouton de Culotte has a piquant, slightly acid flavor that goes well with wheat bread. It should be served with a red Burgundy or a dry white Mâcon.

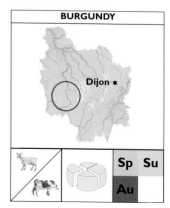

BURGUNDY

Dijon •

Sp Su
Au

BRIQUETTE DE LA DOMBES

A FARMHOUSE OR ARTISANAL CHEESE, BRIQUETTE IS MADE FROM WHOLE GOAT'S MILK IN AIN, NEAR THE FAMOUS PONDS OF THE DOMBES, A MECCA FOR WATERFOWL HUNTERS. IT IS TRADITIONALLY EATEN DURING THE GRAPE HARVEST. THIS CHEESE HAS A FAT CONTENT OF 45 TO 50 PERCENT. IT IS PRIMARILY SOLD IN ITS REGION OF PRODUCTION.

Description
Shaped like a little brick 3¼ inches long by about 2 inches wide, Briquette de la Dombes weighs 5¼ to 7 ounces.

Choosing wisely
This cheese is ripened for a minimum of ten or so days, which gives it its sought-after freshness and creamy-to-soft texture. Its uncooked curd is light in color. Fresh, it has a goat's-milk scent and a soft consistency. Its flavor is mild and velvety. Creamy, Briquette de la Dombes is delicious on brown or six-grain bread. Connoisseurs love it as an appetizer, with a green salad, or at the end of a meal, served with a white Mâcon.

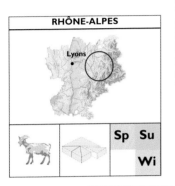

RHÔNE-ALPES

Lyons

Sp Su
Wi

BÛCHE DE CHÈVRE

S HAPED LIKE A LOG, THIS GOAT'S-MILK CHEESE IS SOLD LOOSE IN FRENCH GROCERY STORES. ITS SUBTLE, PENETRATING TASTE IS GENERALLY HIGHLY PRIZED BY CHÈVRE FANS.

Method of production
A factory-produced cheese, Bûche de Chèvre is sometimes cultured with *Penicillium candidum*. It has a white, even-textured curd surrounded by a fairly thin rind. The cheese boasts a delicate hazelnut flavor.

Serving suggestions
As ripening progresses, the cheese takes on an increasingly acidic flavor, which can sometimes become piquant. Its almost chalky curd melts deliciously on the palate. Sliced thinly over slices of bread, Bûche de Chèvre may be broiled for a few minutes before being served with an oak-leaf salad. Partner it with black grapes, slices of apple, and walnuts. Bûche de Chèvre is also good chopped finely in a salad or cubed in a cheese tart. Serve it with a dry, fruity white Touraine and some cumin bread.

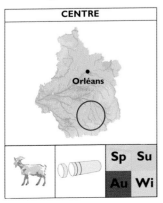

CENTRE

Orléans

Sp Su
Au Wi

BÛCHETTE AU ROMARIN

WITH ITS ELONGATED SHAPE, THIS RAW GOAT'S-MILK CHEESE RESEMBLES A SAINTE-MAURE DE TOURAINE. THIS IS A CHEESE THAT'S STILL YOUNG, ALMOST FRESH, OWING TO ITS SHORT RIPENING PERIOD, WITH A PLEASANT, MILKY SCENT. MADE IN BANON-EN-PROVENCE, BÛCHETTE AU ROMARIN IS FLAVORED BY THE SPRIG OF SAVORY OR ROSEMARY DECORATING ITS RIND.

Choosing wisely
The interior of this cheese is white, compact, and slightly moist. The aroma is clear-cut, the taste slightly acid. After a week's ripening, the curd becomes more compact and drier. The taste then becomes more pronounced, persistent in the mouth, and almost tacky on the palate.

Serving suggestions
Bûchette au Romarin is eaten fresh, perhaps at the beginning of a meal with a green salad dressed with raspberry vinegar—the acidity harmonizes well with the aroma of the rosemary sprig. Serve this cheese with "Passion" bread and a lively Bandol or a Beaujolais-Villages.

PROVENCE-ALPES-CÔTE-D'AZUR

Banon

Marseilles

Sp Su
Au

CABÉCOU DE ROCAMADOUR A.O.C.

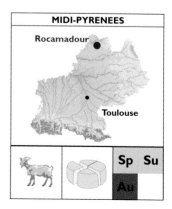

A RAW GOAT'S-MILK CHEESE, CABÉCOU DE ROCAMADOUR IS PRODUCED ON THE LIMESTONE PLATEAUS OF QUERCY—THE GREATER PART OF THE *DÉPARTEMENT* OF LOT AND SEVERAL *COMMUNES* OF AVEYRON, CORRÈZE, DORDOGNE, AND TARN-ET-GARONNE. IN LANGUE D'OC, THE DIALECT SPOKEN IN THE SOUTH OF FRANCE, *CABÉCOU* MEANS "KID."

In the beginning
This cheese is one of the oldest products of the limestone plateaus of Quercy. In a fifteenth-century treatise, Cabécou de Rocamadour is cited as a means of payment of taxes and rent. This small, disk-shaped farmhouse cheese measures 2 to 2⅜ inches across by ½ inch thick, and weighs about 1¼ to 1⅜ ounces. Its thin, striated rind encloses a tender, creamy, aromatic, ivory-colored interior. It is ripened for a minimum of ten days. Cabécou de Rocamadour has a goaty scent and a texture that is runny and soft on the palate.

Serving suggestions
This cheese is enjoyed creamy or dry, depending on its degree of ripeness. It should be savored at the end of a meal, with a salad. It is also a key ingredient in regional recipes such as Quercy Rocamadour tart, cabbage-wrapped Rocamadour with honey, and Rocamadour wrapped in pan-fried eggplant and tomatoes and baked. Serve it with a Cahors wine.

MIDI-PYRENEES

Rocamadour

Toulouse

Sp Su
Au

CABÉCOU DU PÉRIGORD

THIS LITTLE GOAT'S-MILK CHEESE IS MADE IN PÉRIGORD. A COUSIN OF CABÉCOU DE ROCAMADOUR, IT IS PROTECTED BY AN ASSOCIATION GROUPING TOGETHER FARMHOUSE AND SMALL FACTORY PRODUCERS. CABÉCOU DU PÉRIGORD ACQUIRES EVEN MORE PERSONALITY AND PRESENCE AS IT AGES.

In the beginning
The origins of this cheese are said to date back to the Moor invasion, which introduced goat cheeses to this region. Cabécou du Périgord has a pale yellow rind, a fine, even texture, and a regular shape. It gives off a hazelnut aroma and has a lactic flavor.

Serving suggestions
In the spring, this cheese is enjoyed fresh, giving off a fine scent of grass and pastures; in the summer, when it is more fully ripened, it will be drier. In the fall, Cabécou du Périgord becomes hard and brittle, but still has its fans! Some like it hot on a bed of salad; others enjoy it at the end of a meal with raisin bread. This cheese shines in the company of a red Loire wine.

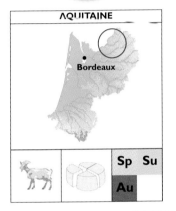

AQUITAINE

Bordeaux

Sp Su
Au

CABRETTE DU PÉRIGORD

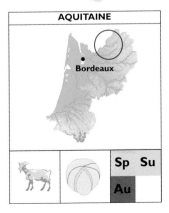

FASHIONED IN THE SHAPE OF A FIG, THIS FRESH GOAT'S-MILK CHEESE IS A TRUE DELIGHT, LIGHT AND AROMATIC.

Description
Measuring 2⅜ to 2¾ inches across, Cabrette du Périgord weighs between 5 and 7 ounces. This cheese is ripened for just a few days, which prevents the formation of a thick rind. The very white curd remains slightly moist, since its extremely short ripening period, which gives it quite a creamy taste, leaves it no time to dry. Well wrapped in its paper packaging, it can be kept in the refrigerator for ten days or so, after which it develops a chalky taste.

Serving suggestions
This cheese is primarily artisanally produced, so it is mainly known locally. Cabrette du Périgord should be eaten at the end of a meal with rye bread or German-style black bread. Accompany it with a red Bordeaux or a Madiran.

AQUITAINE

Bordeaux

Sp Su
Au

CABRI ARIÉGEOIS

THE CHEESEMAKER PHILIPPE GARROS MAKES GOAT'S-MILK CABRI ARIÉGEOIS ON A FARM NEAR FOIX, IN THE ARIÈGE. THIS CHEESE IS NEARLY IDENTICAL IN APPEARANCE TO THE VACHERIN PRODUCED IN SAVOIE.

Description
Like Vacherin, Cabri Ariégeois is sold in a wooden box. This cheese measures 4¾ to 5 inches across by 1½ to 2 inches high, and weighs 17½ ounces. Cabri Ariégeois will have been ripened for eight weeks by the time it arrives at its place of sale. It will spend another four weeks in a well-ventilated cellar before being marketed, since it must be extremely creamy to be considered good. This cheese is eaten with a spoon, like its cow's-milk cousin, Vacherin.

Serving suggestions
Use a knife to peel off the orange-hued, washed rind of the Cabri Ariégeois, exposing the ultra-creamy yellow interior, which can only be eaten with a spoon. This cheese comes into its own on a bit of toast or baguette. Serve it with a light local wine.

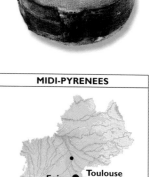

MIDI-PYRENEES

Foix · Toulouse

Sp Su
Au

CABRI DES GORS

SOMETIMES WRAPPED IN CHESTNUT LEAVES THAT GIVE IT A GENTLE WOODSY SCENT, THIS LITTLE GOAT CHEESE IS MADE IN THE DEUX-SÈVRES.

Description
Disk-shaped, Cabri des Gors measures 2¾ inches across by 1 inch thick, and weighs about 7 ounces. It is ripened for two weeks, at which point its natural rind is covered with white and reddish flora, and its silky white curd has turned creamy. Unlike Crottin de Chavignol, the interior of Cabri des Gors becomes runnier as ripening progresses—this is what makes the difference and gives the cheese an inimitable flavor.

Serving suggestions
Cabri des Gors is a delicious farmhouse cheese that can be enjoyed as a first course with a green salad seasoned with shallots. Served on a cheeseboard, Cabri des Gors should be accompanied by rustic breads. Enjoy it with a dry white Sancerre.

POITOU-CHARENTES

Poitiers ·

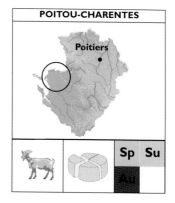

Sp Su
Au

CABRIOULET

PRODUCED IN LOUBIÈRES, NEAR FOIX IN THE ARIÈGE, THIS PYRENEAN GOAT'S-MILK *TOMME* HAS A SEDUCTIVE, PRONOUNCED TASTE AND A SCENT OF MILDEWY CELLAR THAT HAS ITS DEVOTEES.

Description
This farmhouse cheese is made from raw goat's milk. Measuring 8 to 8¼ inches across by 2 to 2⅜ inches thick, Cabrioulet weighs from 4½ to 5½ pounds. Before it is sold, it is ripened in a cellar for two months, during which time its rind is washed in brine. When the ripening period is extended for an extra two or three months, the cheese's rind turns as dry as a stone, its aroma becomes concentrated, and its flavor turns spicy. Cabrioulet's fat content is variable, fluctuating between 40 and 50 percent.

Serving suggestions
Cabrioulet's washed rind is moist and tacky; its yellow-brown, semihard, uncooked interior is sprinkled with holes. Its pronounced, slightly salty flavor is fairly balanced and rich. This cheese goes well with a tender, fresh country loaf with a loose crumb, or a Moisan loaf and a little butter. Serve it with a white Jurançon or a Limoux.

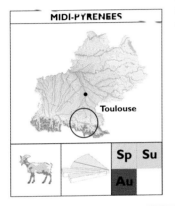

MIDI-PYRENEES

Toulouse

		Sp	Su
		Au	

CAMISARD

PRODUCED BY MICHEL DUBOIS IN THE CÉVENNES IN SAINT HIPPOLYTE-DU-FORT, CAMISARD IS A FRESH GOAT CHEESE WRAPPED IN THIN SLICES OF BACON. ITS NAME RECALLS THE PROTESTANT INSURGENTS OF CÉVENNES, WHO TOOK UP ARMS AFTER THE REVOCATION OF THE EDICT OF NANTES.

Description
Two slices of bacon are wrapped around a small disk of chèvre. Camisard slightly resembles Pélardon, from the same region: a little disk 2¾ to 2¾ inches across by ¾ to 1¼ inches thick, weighing 2 to 3½ ounces. It's made primarily during the goat-cheese production period, from spring to fall. Refined for only a few days, Camisard has practically no rind; its curd is compact, with a slight hazelnut taste.

Serving suggestions
This fresh goat cheese should be slipped into a hot oven for a few minutes. The bacon turns crisp and serves as a protective shell for the cheese, which melts gently. Camisard is therefore strictly eaten hot, on toast. Pair it with a Corbières or a Saint-Joseph served at room temperature.

RHÔNE-ALPES

Lyons

		Sp	Su
		Au	

CAPRINU

THIS LITTLE *TOMME*, MADE FROM WHOLE GOAT'S MILK AND SOLD IN WEDGES, IS MANUFACTURED ON THE ISLE OF BEAUTY BY THE ISULA CHEESE DAIRY. ANGE SANTONI, ITS PRODUCER, IS FOND OF POINTING OUT THAT CORSICAN GOATS ARE KNOWN FOR MUCH LOWER YIELDS PER MILKING THAN THEIR COUNTERPARTS ON THE MAINLAND, BUT BY CONTRAST PRODUCE A PARTICULARLY PROTEIN-RICH MILK. NEARLY 7½ QUARTS OF MILK ARE REQUIRED TO PRODUCE SLIGHTLY OVER 2 POUNDS OF CAPRINU.

Description

Caprinu comes in the form of a small, dense, and heavy *tomme* weighing 5¼ pounds and measuring over 8½ inches across by 4 to 4¾ inches high. Its rind is covered with orange and white flora. Its interior is white- to cream-colored. This little *tomme* is ripened for six months in a ventilated cellar. During this aging period, the rind becomes wrinkled and takes on brown hues. The curd becomes firm, developing sustained aromas.

Serving suggestions

For an apéritif, Caprinu is eaten cut into cubes with a glass of fresh wine, preferably Corsican to strike the right note. It can also be enjoyed at the end of a meal, with brown bread, in which case it should be accompanied by a red or white Patrimonio or a lively Côtes-du-Rhône.

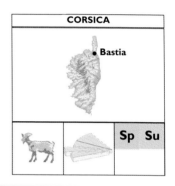

CORSICA
• Bastia

Sp Su

CARRÉ DE CHAVIGNOL

IN TERMS OF BOTH APPEARANCE AND FLAVOR, CARRÉ DE CHAVIGNOL IS LIKE A SQUARE CROTTIN DE CHAVIGNOL. IT WAS INVENTED ABOUT FIFTEEN YEARS AGO BY GILLES DUBOIS, THE CURRENT PROPRIETOR OF A CHEESE DAIRY ESTABLISHED IN 1896 BY HIS GREAT-GRANDFATHER. A CHEESEMAKER SPECIALIZING IN CROTTIN DE CHAVIGNOL, MONSIEUR DUBOIS INTENDED IN THIS MANNER TO DIVERSIFY WHILE CONTINUING TO PRODUCE GOAT CHEESES.

Description

There are two sizes of Carré de Chavignol. The small Carré is a 1¾-inch square weighing 4¼ ounces when fresh, and no more than 2 to 2¾ ounces after two weeks' ripening. As aging progresses, its white rind becomes covered in blue and white specks. In terms of weight and size, a small Carré de Chavignol represents one-and-a-half Crottins.

Serving suggestions

After two weeks' ripening, the curd of this cheese develops a pleasant goaty scent. Carré de Chavignol melts on the palate, leaving a slightly acid aftertaste. Its flavor is balanced and a bit salty. This chèvre, which should be enjoyed semidry or very dry, is delicious on a bed of salad as a first course. At the end of a meal, serve it on a cheeseboard with a crusty baguette, accompanied by a white Sancerre.

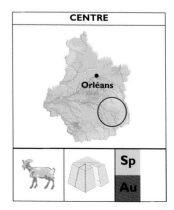

CENTRE
• Orléans

Sp
Au

CARRÉ DE CHAVIGNOL—GRAND FORMAT

CREATED SOME FIFTEEN YEARS AGO BY GILLES DUBOIS, THE DESCENDANT OF A FAMILY THAT'S BEEN IN THE CHEESEMAKING BUSINESS FOR OVER A CENTURY, THE LARGE CARRÉ DE CHAVIGNOL RESEMBLES A CROTTIN DE CHAVIGNOL IN BOTH APPEARANCE AND FLAVOR. THIS IS A GOAT CHEESE WITH A CHARACTERISTIC HAZELNUT TASTE.

Description
A large Carré de Chavignol is the size and weight of three Crottins de Chavignol, being a 3¼-inch, 8½-ounce square. After ten to twelve days' ripening on shelves, when the cheeses are dry enough not to run, they are placed in crates and transferred to a ripening cellar. After three weeks' ripening, their rinds, white when they emerged from their molds, turn bluish.

Serving suggestions
During the course of ripening, the cheese develops a pleasant goaty aroma. Soft in the mouth, it melts on the palate, leaving a slightly acid aftertaste. Its flavor is balanced and a bit salty. Carré de Chavignol is delicious plain on a bed of salad, as a first course. At the end of a meal, serve it on a cheeseboard with a crusty baguette, accompanied by a white wine such as a Pouilly.

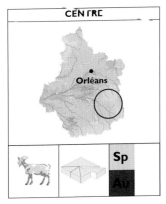

CENTRE

Orléans

Sp
Au

CARRÉ DU TARN

THIS SQUARE CHEESE MADE FROM RAW, WHOLE GOAT'S MILK WAS CREATED SOME TWENTY YEARS AGO BY A MONSIEUR THÉOSKI, A CHEESEMAKER BY TRADE. IT'S PRODUCED ON THE FARM FROM THE MILK OF HIS HERD OF 150 GOATS, NEAR ALBI IN THE TARN.

Description
Carré du Tarn is a 3¼-inch square weighing 6⅓ to 7 ounces. After three weeks' ripening, its downy surface develops a natural ivory rind. Its white interior is even-textured and creamy-to-soft. Carré du Tarn contains 45 percent fat.

Serving suggestions
Like all well-made goat cheeses, this one has a curd that is tender, moist, and tacky in the mouth. The goat's-milk aroma is noticeable. Unlike Crottin de Chavignol, which becomes harder and drier as ripening progresses, Carré du Tarn turns creamier as the aging period is extended. It can be enjoyed at various stages of ripeness, fresh or soft. It makes a fine apéritif, cut into pieces and served with a dry white wine. Carré du Tarn is also amenable to being broiled on toast and served with a salad. It harmonizes brilliantly with a white Gaillac from the same region, or a white Pouilly.

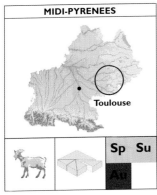

MIDI-PYRENEES

Toulouse

Sp Su
Au

CATHARE

THE OCCITAN CROSS IMPRINTED ON THE RIND OF THIS RAW, WHOLE GOAT'S-MILK CHEESE GIVES IT A FINE APPEARANCE. THE CROSS IS A PROUD REMINDER OF ITS PLACE OF ORIGIN, THE LAURAGAIS, AND THE HISTORY OF THE CATHARS.

Description
Shaped like a flat disk half an inch thick, Cathare measures 5½ to 6 inches across and weighs 7 ounces. It can be recognized by the cross on its rind, imprinted by "negative" dusting with wood-ash. Its crumbly curd requires a fairly long ripening period of at least three weeks in order to develop a smooth, fine texture. Its goaty taste is well asserted, a plus for gourmets partial to slightly acidic tastes, who should choose a semidry or dry Cathare, with a noticeable aroma.

Serving suggestions
This cheese may also be enjoyed fresh and tender, when it is full of a lively lactic flavor—in which case it should be eaten without delay. According to its degree of ripeness, serve Cathare with a traditional Rétrodor baguette or a delightfully crusty Baguépi. Accompany this limited-production farmhouse cheese with a dry white wine from the Tarn.

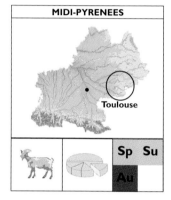

MIDI-PYRENEES

Toulouse

		Sp	Su
		Au	

CHABICHOU DU POITOU A.O.C.

THIS WHOLE-MILK CHEESE IS ONE OF THE BEST FRENCH CHÈVRES. ITS AREA OF PRODUCTION IS LIMITED TO THE LIMESTONE HAUT POITOU.

Description
This cheese is shaped like a small cylinder or *bonde* ("bung") 2⅜ inches high by 2 to 2⅜ inches across, and weighing 4¼ to 5¼ ounces. Chabichou du Poitou is said to date from the eighth century, when it was reputedly manufactured by the Saracens. The word *chabi*, a shortened form of "chabichou," is said to be a deformation of the Arabic *chebli*, or "goat." The fame of this cheese spread throughout the region, so that in 1782, Charles de Cherge remarked, "We may speak of excellent cheeses which, known by the people by the name of Chabichou, enjoy a justly deserved reputation." Made from whole goat's milk, this cheese from the Poitou is hand-ladled into molds, the bottoms of which are inlaid with the initials C.D.P. (Chabichou du Poitou.)

Serving suggestions
This cheese's rind is white, tinged with gray-blue mold. The firm interior may turn brittle after an extended ripening period. Its aroma is goaty and light. Chabichou is mild, without a hint of aggression, and smooth and creamy on the palate. This is a cheese for serving at the end of a meal, accompanied by walnut bread and a wine from the Haut Poitou.

POITOU-CHARENTES

Poitiers

		Sp	Su
		Au	

CHABIS SECONDIGNY

ALTHOUGH IT DOESN'T HOLD AN A.O.C. ITSELF, THIS WHOLE, RAW GOAT'S-MILK CHEESE RESEMBLES CHABICHOU. *CHABI*, AS MENTIONED EARLIER, IS DERIVED FROM THE ARABIC *CHEBLI*, MEANING "GOAT." THIS CHEESE IS PRODUCED IN POITOU-CHARENTES.

Description
Slightly bigger than Chabichou, Chabis measures 2½ inches across at its base and 2 inches across at its top, is 2¾ inches tall, and weighs about 4¼ ounces. Its traditional bung or stopper shape entitles it to the typically Poitou designation of *bonde*.

Choosing wisely
Chabis develops a whitish flora that, on ripening, turns blue-gray, sometimes speckled with red. Some of these cheeses are also dusted in charcoal powder. Chabis is ripened for between ten and twenty days.

Serving suggestions
Chabis is delicious at the end of a meal. Choose it according to its stage of ripeness—fresh or drier. This cheese is good in a number of dishes, such as a quiche or a soufflé. On a cheeseboard, it should be served with a red Sancerre.

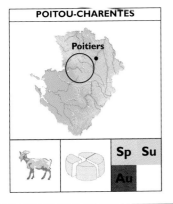

POITOU-CHARENTES

Poitiers

Sp Su
Au

CHAMPDENIER

THIS SPECIALTY GOAT CHEESE IS PRODUCED NEAR NIORT, IN THE DEUX-SÈVRES. CHAMPDENIER IS A FRESH FARMHOUSE CHEESE. ACCORDING TO THE TRADITION ASSOCIATED WITH ALL GOAT CHEESES, IT IS SERVED FROM EASTER TO ALL SAINTS' DAY, THE TIME OF YEAR WHEN CHÈVRE IS AT ITS BEST.

Description
This is a barely ripened goat cheese, marketed rindless and in a round cheese strainer. When drained very soon after purchase, Champdenier is still moist. A very white cheese, it has a light, goaty aroma.

Serving suggestions
This farmhouse cheese should be enjoyed plain or with fresh herbs. Its taste is slightly salty, smooth, creamy, and soft in the mouth. Served at breakfast with preserves, honey, or dried fruit, it makes a very pleasant alternative to other dairy products such as yogurt or *fromage blanc*. It can also be served at the end of a meal, accompanied by a light wine that won't overwhelm it.

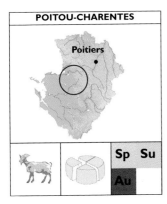

POITOU-CHARENTES

Poitiers

Sp Su
Au

CHAROLAIS

FARMHOUSE OR ARTISANALLY MADE FROM GOAT'S OR COW'S MILK, CHAROLAIS MELTS DELICIOUSLY IN THE MOUTH. THIS CHEESE IS PRODUCED ON THE GRANITE PLAINS OF CHAROLAIS IN BURGUNDY, THE RECIPE HANDED DOWN ON THE FARMS OF THE REGION FROM MOTHER TO DAUGHTER.

Description
Charolais is an unpressed, uncooked cheese. Cylinder-shaped, it measures about 3¼ inches tall by 2 inches across, and weighs 7 ounces. Its natural rind is covered with white-to-bluish flora, the result of at least six weeks' ripening. At this stage of ripeness, the cheese develops a marked lactic taste and a pronounced flavor.

Serving suggestions
This goat cheese should be enjoyed with a salad as a first course, cut into slices and melted on toast. It's by no means amiss on a cheeseboard, especially when served slightly dry, with a penetrating taste. Serve it with a Mercurey or a Rully, two wines from its native soil.

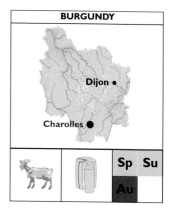

BURGUNDY

Dijon •

Charolles ●

		Sp	Su
		Au	

CHÈVRE AU MARC

UNUSUAL AND EXCEEDINGLY TASTY, THIS GOAT CHEESE RIPENED WITH BURGUNDY MARC IS A GENUINE CURIOSITY. IT IS MADE IN THE HEART OF BURGUNDY BY SEVERAL PRODUCERS.

Description
This little farmhouse cheese is made from raw goat's milk. Disk-shaped, it measures 2 to 2⅜ inches across by 1¼ to 1¾ inches thick, and weighs between 3½ and 4½ ounces. Creamy-white in color, its curd is even-textured and compact, although the longer the ripening period, the more crumbly it becomes. Like Époisses, this cheese is ripened with Burgundy marc, which gives it a characteristic flavor and hazelnut aroma.

Serving suggestions
This goat cheese, excellent from spring through fall, can be enjoyed plain with a sip or two of Burgundy wine to bring out its flavor. The locals accompany it with a mesclun salad dressed in walnut oil. Serve it with a dry white wine from its native soil or a glass of marc.

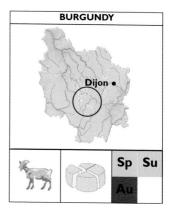

BURGUNDY

Dijon •

		Sp	Su
		Au	

CHÈVRE DU MORVAN

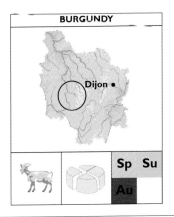

BURGUNDY

Dijon •

Sp Su
Au

THIS THOROUGHLY DELICIOUS LITTLE GOAT CHEESE CAN BE ENJOYED AS A QUICK SNACK ON THE FLIMSIEST OF PRETEXTS—OR JUST TO TREAT YOURSELF.

Description
Measuring 2¾ inches across by 1⅜ inches thick, this cheese weighs about 5¼ ounces. It is ripened for a minimum of ten days.

Serving suggestions
This cheese is eaten in various ways, depending on its stage of ripeness. Just out of the mold, it's enjoyed as a fresh, white cheese, sprinkled with pepper and chives. After a week, its initial fresh flavor gives way to a pleasant goat's-milk taste; it's then delicious in a green salad. After two weeks, when the rind develops a white flora speckled with blue, it's eaten on country bread. At this stage, it is inimitably soft with a more pronounced taste. Finally, beyond four weeks, Chèvre du Morvan hardens and its interior turns brittle and crumbly; it becomes stronger tasting, without being sharp. At this stage, it can be served on a cheeseboard, accompanied by walnut bread and a fruity white wine.

CHEVRION

AQUITAINE

Bordeaux •

Sp Su
Au

BOASTING A HIGHLY NOVEL TRIANGULAR SHAPE, THIS CHEESE IS MADE IN LOT-ET-GARONNE BY A SINGLE PRODUCER. IN OTHER WORDS, CHEVRION, A GENUINE WHOLE GOAT'S-MILK CHEESE, IS A RARE AND PRECIOUS PRODUCT!

Description
Shaped like a pyramid 2 to 2⅜ inches tall, Chevrion weighs between 7¾ and 8½ ounces. Ripened in wildflowers for at least three weeks, it has a fatty, creamy-to-soft texture and a sustained flavor. Chevrion gives off a rather delicate, goaty aroma. This cheese is mainly produced during the time of year when the goats are being grazed and nature is in full bloom—in spring, summer, and fall.

Serving suggestions
This cheese will delight true connoisseurs with its strong yet delicious flavor; serve it with a slice of multigrain bread. It may also be kept for two to five months; it then develops a full, "generous" strength all its own. Serve Chevrion with a robust, sunny Cahors.

CHEVROTIN DES ARAVIS

HAILING FROM SAVOIE, THIS RAW GOAT'S-MILK CHEESE IS PRODUCED ON ONLY A FEW FARMS, ACCORDING TO TRADITIONAL METHODS. IT RESEMBLES REBLOCHON, A CHEESE ON WHICH IT WAS MODELED.

Method of production
Made only on the farm using artisanal methods, Chevrotin des Aravis is a rare and precious cheese. Its method of production was inspired by that of Reblochon. Chevrotin des Aravis is made from the milk of goats grazing the flowery pastures of the Alps. During the three-to-six-month ripening period, the rind of this cheese is washed regularly. Disk-shaped, Chevrotin des Aravis measures between 3¼ to 4 inches across by 1¼ to 1½ inches thick, and weighs about 9 ounces.

Serving suggestions
The surface of this cheese is covered with white and brown flora. Its delicate, soft interior is pale yellow. Giving off a scent of goat's milk and flowers, it has an almost honeyed flavor. At the end of a meal, accompanied by dried fruit and assorted bread, Chevrotin des Aravis melts in the mouth, leaving a distinct hazelnut taste. Serve it with a Seyssel or a Savoie wine.

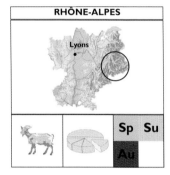

RHÔNE-ALPES

Lyons

Sp   Su   Au

CLACBITOU DU CHAROLAIS

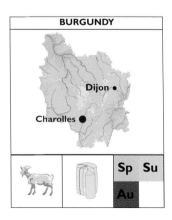

PREPARED FROM RAW MILK, THIS FARMHOUSE GOAT CHEESE RESEMBLES CHAROLAIS. INVENTED FAIRLY RECENTLY, IT'S PRODUCED IN BURGUNDY. IT'S SPRINKLED WITH SEASONAL HERBS AND GARLIC TO YIELD CLACBITOU, A DISH TRADITIONALLY SERVED DURING THE GRAPE HARVEST.

In the beginning
As soon as it was drained, Clacbitou, a cheese of variable shape and size, was covered with a mixture of chives, tarragon, and a chopped clove of garlic. This preparation was featured at the *goûtaillon*, the meal served to the grape pickers during the harvest, accompanied by a wine from the same region.

Serving suggestions
Although best when fresh and unripened, Clacbitou is also sold salted and peppered. At the end of its production, it's left to marinate for between one and two weeks in a cool room. It then takes on a different, spicier flavor. Accompany it with a Burgundy Aligoté or a Chablis. Clacbitou is enjoyed from the spring to the fall, when the goats graze freely on the grass and wildflowers.

BURGUNDY

Dijon •

Charolles ●

Sp   Su   Au

COEUR D'ALVIGNAC

H EART-SHAPED, AS INDICATED BY ITS NAME, THIS GOAT CHEESE IS PRODUCED BY THE ROCAMADOUR CHEESE DAIRY IN ALVIGNAC IN THE PÉRIGORD. IN APPEARANCE, IT BEARS A SLIGHT RESEMBLANCE TO COEUR DE NEUFCHÂTEL, ITS COUSIN FROM NORMANDY.

Description

Coeur d'Alvignac is molded, then ripened for seven days in the cellars of this artisanal cheese dairy—artisanal meaning that the dairy employs no more than ten employees. The different cheeses are then placed on straw matting in poplar-wood crates. In this packaging, they're dispatched throughout the whole of France, to retailers and dairy proprietors. This handcrafted cheese made from whole, raw goat's milk has a fat content of 45 percent and weighs 3½ ounces.

Serving suggestions

Coeur d'Alvignac has a pronounced taste without being too strong. The interior of the cheese is soft, with a lactic character. Enjoy it with whole-wheat or sesame-seed bread. Serve Coeur d'Alvignac with a generous red Cahors or a fresh white Bergerac.

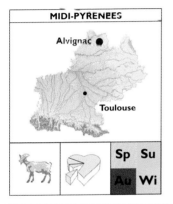

MIDI-PYRENEES

Alvignac ●

Toulouse

Sp | Su
Au | Wi

COEUR DE CHÈVRE CENDRÉ

A MEMBER OF THE SELLES-SUR-CHER FAMILY, THIS ARTISANAL CHEESE IS MADE FROM RAW GOAT'S MILK. THE RIND OF THIS CHEESE IS ALSO EDIBLE—ITS SCENTED FLORA IS VERY AROMATIC.

Method of production

Fashioned in the shape of a heart, this goat cheese is dusted with powdered charcoal. Its ripening period lasts two to three weeks, at which point its natural rind turns bluish to slightly grayish.

Serving suggestions

Coeur de Chèvre Cendré has a very white paste, as is typical of genuine goat cheeses. Hard at the outset, then tender and tacky, it melts agreeably in the mouth, sometimes leaving a slightly acid, salty aftertaste. During ripening, the cheese develops a mixed goat's milk/cellar flavor. Coeur de Chèvre Cendré should be served with walnuts and raisin bread. An oak leaf salad dressed with walnut oil will set it off to best advantage. Accompany it with a glass of well-chilled Quincy or Sancerre.

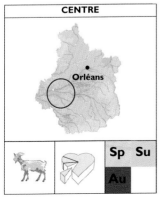

CENTRE

Orléans

Sp | Su
Au

CROTTIN DE CHAVIGNOL DEMI-AFFINÉ

A FAVORITE SNACK OF FARMERS AND WINEGROWERS IN THE SANCERROIS, THIS LITTLE CHEESE MADE FROM WHOLE GOAT'S MILK IS FARMHOUSE- OR DAIRY-PRODUCED. WHILE IT'S BEEN MADE SINCE THE SIXTEENTH CENTURY, THE NAME CROTTIN DE CHAVIGNOL WAS ONLY ADOPTED IN 1829. TODAY, ITS PRODUCTION EXTENDS FROM THE SANCERROIS TO THE CHAMPAGNE BERRICHONNE REGION.

Description
Shaped like a flat cylinder with a slightly concave top, this cheese measures 1½ to 2 inches across by 1¼ to 1½ inches thick. Fresh, it weighs about 5 ounces. After two weeks' ripening, it loses an ounce in weight and begins to develop a bluish mold. At this point, its curd is tender and velvety. Soft-textured, the semiripened Crottin Demi-Affiné is white inside.

Serving suggestions
Young and semiripened, Crottin de Chavignol should be enjoyed on crusty bread. It's prized for its velvety curd and its characteristic goat-cheese taste, which is particularly light in the spring. Sample it with a Sancerre or a Pouilly.

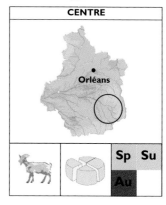

CENTRE

Orléans

Sp | Su
Au

CROTTIN DE CHAVIGNOL SEC

A SMALL CHEESE MADE FROM WHOLE GOAT'S MILK, CROTTIN DE CHAVIGNOL IS BOTH ARTISANALLY- AND FACTORY-PRODUCED. ITS PRODUCTION EXTENDS FROM THE SANCERROIS TO THE CHAMPAGNE BERRICHONNE REGION. NEVERTHELESS, IT IS ALWAYS RIPENED IN ITS A.O.C. AREA.

Description
Cylindrical in shape with a slightly concave top, Crottin de Chavignol measures 1½ to 2 inches across by 1¼ to 1½ inches thick, and weighs a minimum of 2 ounces. Its white or ivory-colored paste is covered with a fine bluish down. To obtain a dry Crottin (Crottin Sec), the ripening period must be extended. Fresh, the Crottin weighs 5 ounces. After two weeks, it weighs no more than about 4 ounces, and its rind is beginning to develop a blue flora. After five weeks, it has shrunk and dried out even more. Now blue and brittle, it gives off a more powerful aroma and is just right for devotees of strong-tasting cheeses.

Choosing wisely
A Crottin Sec can be recognized by its blue rind, its firm, even texture, and its brittle interior. It has a dry flavor and a hazelnut taste, light in the spring, more pronounced in the fall. Savor it with a white Sancerre or a Pouilly.

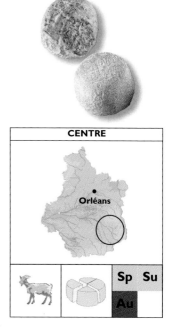

CENTRE

Orléans

Sp | Su
Au

Crottin de Chavignol Repassé A.O.C.

WHETHER DAIRY- OR FARMHOUSE-PRODUCED, CROTTIN DE CHAVIGNOL IS ONE OF THE BEST CHÈVRES AROUND. CHEESE-LOVERS ADORE ITS FRUITY FLAVOR. MADE FROM WHOLE GOAT'S MILK, THIS LITTLE CHEESE IS PRODUCED FROM THE SANCERROIS RIGHT INTO THE CHAMPAGNE BERRICHONNE REGION.

In the beginning
Farmers in the Sancerrois have been making goat cheeses since the sixteenth century; however it wasn't until 1829 that their product was dubbed "Crottin de Chavignol." At the time, the word *crottin* referred to a small terra-cotta oil lamp whose shape evoked that of the cheese. Cylindrical in shape and slightly concave at the top, Crottin de Chavignol measures 1½ to 2 inches across by 1¼ to 1½ inches thick, and weighs a minimum of 2 ounces. Its white or ivory-colored paste is covered with a fine bluish down.

Choosing wisely
Fresh, the Crottin weighs 5 ounces. After two weeks it weighs no more than 4 ounces and its rind starts to develop a bluish flora. It's now ready to eat. Some prefer to extend the ripening to obtain a (dry) Crottin de Chavignol Sec. As time passes, the cheese continues to shrink and dry out. Now firmer, its interior develops a stronger smell. After five weeks the cheese's rind is obviously bluish in color and its curd, firm and even-textured, has turned brittle. The flavor of this cheese is light in the spring and more pronounced in the fall. Enjoy it with a Sancerre or a Pouilly.

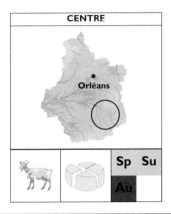

CENTRE

Orléans

Sp Su

Au

Fort de la Platte

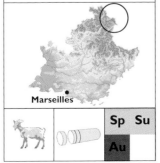

NAMED AFTER AN OLD MILITARY FORT, THIS GOAT CHEESE IS PRODUCED NEAR THE FRENCH-ITALIAN BORDER, IN THE VICINITY OF BRIANÇON.

Description
A small goat's-milk *tomme*, Fort de la Platte belongs to the family of pressed cheeses. During its ripening period, which lasts between two months and a year, it develops a natural rind with an abundant flora. The interior of the cheese is white, fairly smooth and even-textured. Fort de la Platte measures 6¾ inches long by 2⅜ to 2¾ inches thick, and weighs 1¾ pounds. These vital statistics may vary, however, depending on where the cheese was produced.

Serving suggestions
Although eaten between June and December, Fort de la Platte is best in the fall. A cheeseboard cheese par excellence, it should be enjoyed with walnuts and grapes, which bring out its goaty taste. It can also be served in slices on a piece of bread at a picnic. Accompany it with a Gamay de Touraine.

PROVENCE-ALPES-CÔTE-D'AZUR

Marseilles

Sp Su

Au

GROÛ DU BÂNE

MADE FROM GOAT'S MILK, THIS FARMHOUSE CHEESE IS PRODUCED IN PROVENCE AND BEARS THE NAME OF THE PROVENÇAL MASSIF ON WHICH THE GOATS GRAZE. CHEESE CONNOISSEURS ENJOY ITS UNUSUAL FLAVOR. GROÛ DU BÂNE IS UNFORTUNATELY HARD TO COME BY, AS ITS PRODUCTION IS LIMITED.

Description
Groû du Bâne resembles a Selles-sur-Cher in terms of shape. Round and thick, it measures about 3¼ inches across by 1½ to 2 inches in height. After ten days' ripening, its rind is naturally covered in cream-colored flora. Its tender, unpressed, and uncooked paste becomes even-textured and smooth. After three weeks' ripening, the cheese has dried, but its various hazelnut aromas become concentrated, giving off a strong scent.

Serving suggestions
The longer the ripening period is extended, the more robust the delicate scent of Groû du Bâne becomes. Its curd develops a very pleasant, slightly acid flavor. The cheese melts on the palate, leaving a hazelnut aftertaste in the mouth. Serve this unusual cheese with a Viennese baguette and enjoy it with a fresh white Côtes de Provence.

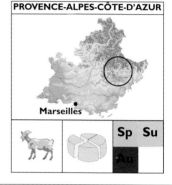

PROVENCE-ALPES-CÔTE-D'AZUR

Marseilles

Sp Su
Au

LINGOT ARDÉCHOIS

CREATED IN THE ARDÈCHE, THIS FARMHOUSE CHEESE IS FASHIONED IN THE SHAPE OF A SMALL BRICK, HENCE ITS NAME LINGOT, WHICH MEANS "INGOT" IN FRENCH. MADE FROM GOAT'S MILK BY JUST A HANDFUL OF PRODUCERS, THIS CHEESE DESERVES TO BE BETTER KNOWN AND MORE WIDELY AVAILABLE.

Method of production
Lingot Ardéchois is ripened for three to four weeks in a well-ventilated cellar. Its naturally furrowed rind becomes covered with a uniform ivory-white flora. Fully ripe, this cheese is soft and its curd develops a strong goat-cheese scent. When the ripening period is extended, it becomes drier and gives off fairly persistent, concentrated aromas. Lingot Ardéchois is rectangular in shape, measuring about 3¼ inches long by 1¼ to 1½ inches wide, and weighing 6⅓ ounces.

Serving suggestions
Lingot Ardéchois has a creamy-to-soft interior. Its strong goat-cheese taste harmonizes well with a slightly sour bread, such as a Poilâne loaf. With its abundance of personality, this is one to introduce to cheese lovers. Accompany it with an Ardèche wine.

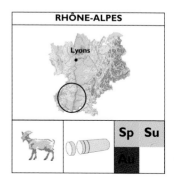

RHÔNE-ALPES

Lyons

Sp Su
Au

LINGOT DU BERRY

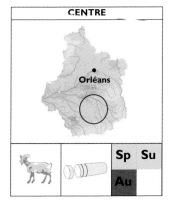

CENTRE

• Orléans

CREATED IN THE BERRY REGION, THIS FARMHOUSE CHEESE IS FASHIONED IN THE SHAPE OF A LITTLE BRICK, HENCE ITS NAME LINGOT, WHICH MEANS "INGOT" IN FRENCH. LINGOT DU BERRY IS MADE FROM GOAT'S MILK.

Description
This cheese is ripened for three to four weeks. Its naturally furrowed rind becomes colonized with a uniform ivory-white mold. Fully ripe, this cheese is soft and its curd develops a strong goat-cheese scent. When the ripening period is extended, it becomes drier and gives off rather persistent, concentrated aromas. Lingot du Berry is rectangular in shape, measuring about 3¼ inches long by 1¼ to 1½ inches wide, and weighing 6⅓ ounces.

Serving suggestions
Lingot du Berry has a creamy-to-soft interior. It's generally eaten with country bread or a crusty baguette. Some like to eat it with a salad dressed in walnut oil. Accompany this cheese with a fruity white wine from Sancerre or Touraine.

Sp Su
Au

MÂCONNAIS

BURGUNDY

Dijon •

● Mâcon

PRODUCED IN THE VICINITY OF MÂCON, IN THE *DÉPARTEMENT* OF SAÔNE-ET-LOIRE, MÂCONNAIS IS MADE FROM RAW GOAT'S OR COW'S MILK, OR A MIXTURE OF THE TWO. THIS CHEESE IS ALSO KNOWN BY THE NAME OF CHEVRETON DE MÂCON OR CABRION DE MÂCON.

Description
After two weeks' ripening, a tender goat cheese is obtained. The longer ripening is extended, the harder and saltier Mâconnais becomes. This little cheese measures 1½ to 2 inches high by 1¼ to 1½ inches thick, and weighs between 1¾ and 2 ounces. It is farmhouse- or artisanally-produced.

Serving suggestions
Fairly rough to the touch, Mâconnais's natural rind is white or grayish. The interior of the cheese, tender or hard depending on the length of ripening, gives off a fresh, grassy aroma in the spring. This cheese has a fat content of 45 percent. Mâconnais is a fairly rare local cheese. It's eaten at the end of a meal, accompanied by rye bread. Ideally, Mâconnais should be tasted either fresh or fairly dry, in order to appreciate the difference. Serve it with a red Burgundy.

Sp Su

Pastille de Chèvre

Goat cheese in all its simplicity—this unpretentious little cheese has the whiteness of a breath mint and the delicacy of a genuine fresh chèvre.

Description
Shaped like a flat disk (*pastille* means "lozenge" or "tablet" in French) and as light as a feather, this cheese is produced in the Périgord by a Monsieur Soreda. It is made immediately after the milking and is hardly ripened at all—hence its soft texture and delicate taste. Rindless, this cheese has a beautifully white, delicate, creamy-to-soft curd.

Serving suggestions
Like most goat cheeses, Pastille de Chèvre can be served as a first course with a salad dressed in walnut or hazelnut oil. Like mozzarella, it also harmonizes beautifully with tomatoes drizzled with olive oil. Even better, you can accompany this cheese with fresh figs that have been baked for a few minutes. Lastly and most simply, serve it at the end of a meal with a Saint-Nicolas-de-Bourgueil.

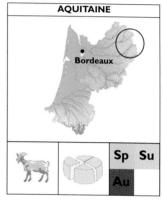

AQUITAINE

Bordeaux

		Sp	Su
		Au	

Pavé des Dombes

Hailing from the Dombes, a vast lake-studded plateau between Rhône and Saône, this cheese, whose reputation is too often eclipsed by that of its neighbor, Bleu de Bresse, deserves to be better known.

Description
This ingot-shaped cheese is made from goat's or ewe's milk, depending on the season. After ten to fifteen days' ripening Pavé des Dombes develops a beautiful, soft, ivory-colored natural rind that encloses a light-colored, creamy-to-soft, smooth interior. This cheese is at its best in the spring, when made from the milk of animals that have grazed on the marvelously rich and tender new grass.

Serving suggestions
Creamy and delicious, Pavé des Dombes is best enjoyed at the end of a meal. It can be served with walnut or raisin bread and accompanied by a light wine, for example a slightly fresh Côtes-du-Rhône, which won't overwhelm its very delicate taste.

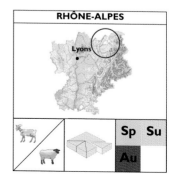

RHÔNE-ALPES

Lyons

		Sp	Su
		Au	

PÉCHEGROS

NO MORE THAN ONE OR TWO CHEESE DAIRIES PRODUCE THIS FARMHOUSE GOAT CHEESE CREATED BY A MONSIEUR REMOND. ITS NAME, PÉCHEGROS, INDICATES THE LOCALITY. THIS CHEESE, MANUFACTURED IN A MEDIEVAL WALLED TOWN IN THE TARN, COMES FROM PENNE, A SMALL VILLAGE LOCATED BETWEEN ALBI AND MONTAUBAN. THREE HERDS OF GOATS SUPPLY THE MILK REQUIRED TO MAKE THIS CHEESE. THE PRODUCER HANDCRAFTS 350 TO 400 OF THESE CHEESES A WEEK.

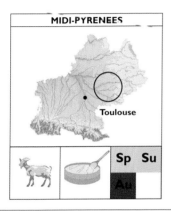

MIDI-PYRENEES

Toulouse

Sp Su
Au

Description

This soft, pressed-curd cheese is encircled with a strip of spruce bark. It is then ripened for at least three weeks in a humid cellar. Its rind is washed in brine during the first two weeks of ripening. This cheese measures about 4 inches across by ¾ to 1¼ inches thick, weighs 12 ounces, and has a fat content of 50 percent.

Serving suggestions

Thanks to the strip of spruce bark, the cheese acquires a thoroughly delectable, subtle smoky taste. The rind develops a resinous aroma. The longer the ripening period, the creamier and runnier the cheese's paste becomes. After two months, Péchegros can be eaten with a spoon, like a Vacherin. Serve it with a Cahors or a local white wine.

PÉLARDON DES CÉVENNES A.O.C.

INVENTED ONLY RECENTLY, THIS CHEESE WAS AWARDED AN A.O.C. LABEL IN 2000. PÉLARDON DES CÉVENNES IS A DELICATE GOAT CHEESE PRODUCED NEAR ALÈS, IN THE GARD.

In the beginning

In the Cévennes region, the term *pélardon* refers to all the little goat cheeses made in the Gard and the southern part of the Ardèche. Goats have long been the livestock of choice here, able to graze the arid land more successfully than cows or sheep.

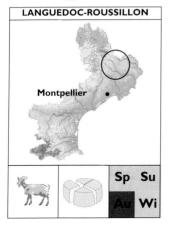

LANGUEDOC-ROUSSILLON

Montpellier

Sp Su
Au Wi

Description

A small, hockey-puck-shaped cheese, Pélardon des Cévennes measures 2⅜ to 2¾ inches across by about 1¼ inches thick, and weighs between 2 and 3½ ounces. It bears a slight resemblance to Cabécou de Rocamadour. Made from whole, raw milk, this cheese boasts a tender interior and a very thin rind. Pale yellow in color, its surface develops a light mold and its white paste a delicious hazelnut taste.

Serving suggestions

Like most goat cheeses, Pélardon des Cévennes can be enjoyed both fresh and dry. You could include it on a cheeseboard with a generous selection of chèvres, accompanied by a simple Côtes-de-Provence, or better yet, a spicy, rounded Costières-de-Nîmes.

PICODON DE L'ARDÈCHE A.O.C.

ALL THE PIQUANCY OF THIS CHEESE IS ALLUDED TO IN ITS NAME (*PICODON* MEANS "SPICY" IN THE OCCITAN DIALECT). SAMPLE IT TO DISCOVER A DELICIOUS, ROUND, AND PERFUMED CHEESE.

In the beginning
This cheese hails from the mountains of the Ardèche and the Drôme—goat country. As these beasts yield little milk in winter, the inhabitants of these arid regions invented a cheese that would keep all winter long. Before being eaten, the cheeses were rehydrated by successive washings.

Description
This is a cheese made from whole milk, to which a small amount of rennet is added. Shaped like a hockey puck measuring 2 to 2¾ inches across, Picodon weighs between 1¾ and 2¾ ounces. It is ripened for at least twelve days. With the passage of time, its rind becomes covered with blue, white, or yellow flora. It has a firm, even-textured interior. This cheese boasts a slight acidity and is pleasantly piquant on the tongue when fully ripened.

Serving suggestions
The cheese is eaten either young or very dry, with a mesclun salad. Preserved in white wine or olive oil, it makes a very pleasant and novel variation on a theme. Picodon de l'Ardèche is best served with a Côtes-du-Rhône.

RHÔNE-ALPES

Lyons

Sp Su
Au

POULIGNY-SAINT-PIERRE A.O.C.

SHAPED LIKE AN ELONGATED PYRAMID, THIS GOAT CHEESE HAS BEEN NICKNAMED "EIFFEL TOWER," NOT LEAST BECAUSE OF ITS SILVERY GLINTS.

Description
Produced in the valley of Brenne, in the Berrichon area, this is a 4¾-inch-high, pyramid-shaped cheese weighing about 9 ounces. A goat cheese with a tender paste, Pouligny-Saint-Pierre develops a thin, slightly bluish natural rind. Its very white interior is firm to the touch, but should remain supple; sometimes it is slightly crumbly. The cheese has a pleasant, slightly acidic flavor, with a hazelnut aftertaste.

In the beginning
Hailing from a tranquil region watered by the Gartempe, the Creuse, and the Indre rivers, Pouligny-Saint-Pierre first saw the light of day in the village of Levroux. In the nineteenth century, a farmer's wife reputedly had the idea of reshaping old cake pans into pyramid shapes. The recipe inspired numerous imitators, and the tradition stuck.

Serving suggestions
Pouligny-Saint-Pierre can be eaten at all stages of ripeness. White and fresh, it harmonizes beautifully with a green salad, or can be served hot on toast. Speckled with blue mold, it is eaten with a baguette. Very blue, and hence very ripe, it is eaten in the fall with slices of pear, fresh walnuts, and a dry white wine such as a Reuilly, Sancerre, or Touraine.

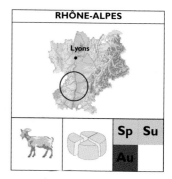

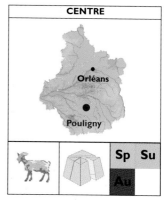

CENTRE

Orléans

Pouligny

Sp Su
Au

ROCAMADOUR A.O.C.

NOT CONTENT WITH HAVING TAKEN THE NAME OF ONE OF THE MOST STRIKING PLACES IN QUERCY, ROCAMADOUR IS ALSO THE OLDEST CHEESE MADE IN THIS AREA, AND ONE OF THE SYMBOLS OF LOCAL GASTRONOMY.

In the beginning

Written references to this cheese have existed since the fifteenth century, at which time it would appear to have represented a unit of value in the calculation of taxes and payments in kind.

Method of production

Made from raw, whole goat's milk renneted under heat, Rocamadour is hand-molded and ripened for at least six days. Shaped like a small hockey puck, it measures 2⅜ inches across and weighs about 1¼ ounces. During ripening, its rind is gradually covered with a delicate, velvety down, which takes on a creamy, then yellow-brown hue. Its white or ivory-colored interior is supple and creamy.

Serving suggestions

The longer Rocamadour ripens, the more assertive its goat-cheese flavor becomes. Fresh or creamy, it may be eaten with a salad, hot over toast, or absolutely plain at the end of a meal. Drier, it is best served on a cheeseboard. A red Cahors is the perfect partner for this cheese. Rocamadour also features as an ingredient in numerous regional dishes, such as *tarte quercinoise* (Quercy tart) and *fritot* (baked eggplant, tomato, and Rocamadour).

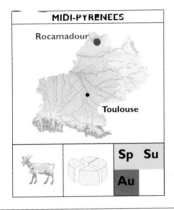

MIDI-PYRENEES

Rocamadour

Toulouse

Sp Su

Au

RONCIER

THIS CHEESE, WITH ITS RATHER NOVEL APPEARANCE, IS PRODUCED FROM RAW, WHOLE GOAT'S MILK AT THE LAUZÉRAL FARM IN THE VAUCLUSE. RONCIER IS SOLD WRAPPED IN THREE FINE BLACKBERRY LEAVES, FROM WHICH THE CHEESE TAKES ITS NAME (RONCIER MEANS "BRAMBLE THICKET").

Description

A single producer supplies this little marvel of a cheese to the Maison Quatrehomme cheese sellers in Paris. A very creamy rind encloses a perfumed, creamy-to-soft interior. Roncier measures about 2⅜ inches across by 1 inch thick, and weighs 7¾ ounces. This farmhouse cheese is made exclusively during the goat-cheese production season, from spring to fall (Easter to All Saints' Day.) Roncier is barely ripened, which preserves its pleasant goaty taste.

Serving suggestions

Roncier is delicious eaten young and fresh, when its rich milkiness is at its best. After carefully removing the very decorative blackberry leaves, you can enjoy this melting cheese on a bit of country bread. Accompany it with a slightly fresh Côtes-du-Rhône.

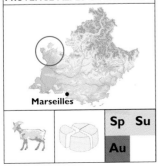

PROVENCE-ALPES-CÔTE-D'AZUR

Marseilles

Sp Su

Au

ROUELLE BLANCHE

A DISTANT COUSIN OF ANNEAU DE VIC-BILH, THIS CHEESE IS ALSO SHAPED LIKE A HOCKEY PUCK HOLLOWED OUT IN THE CENTER. THOUGH OBVIOUSLY LACKING A "HEART," IT HAS THE SOUL OF A TRADITIONAL CHÈVRE.

Description
Produced in the Tarn region, Rouelle Blanche ("White Wheel") is a small, flat cylinder with a hole in the middle. Measuring 4 inches across by ¾ inch in height, it weighs between 7 and 9 ounces.

Method of production
This is a handcrafted, raw goat's-milk cheese made with a respect for tradition. Ripening lasts for two to three weeks, producing a natural rind covered with mold. Inside, the cheese's curd is white, even-textured, and very tender, with an agreeable hazelnut flavor, and to cap it all off, a fine, pleasant-tasting acidity.

Serving suggestions
Like the majority of goat cheeses, Rouelle Blanche harmonizes beautifully with a salad dressed in walnut oil. At the end of a meal, serve it with multigrain or raisin bread, accompanied by a fairly fresh white Bordeaux.

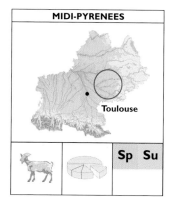

MIDI-PYRENEES

Toulouse

Sp Su

ROUELLE CENDRÉE

A LSO SHAPED LIKE A HOCKEY PUCK HOLLOWED OUT IN ITS CENTER, ROUELLE CENDRÉE IS A DELICATE GOAT CHEESE WITH A FINE HAZELNUT AROMA AND AN AIR OF RENEWED TRADITION.

Description
This small, flat cylinder with a hole in the middle is made in the Tarn region. Measuring 4 inches across by ¾ inch in height, Rouelle Cendrée weighs between 7 and 9 ounces.

Choosing wisely
This raw-milk chèvre should be supple to the touch. Its natural rind, dusted in powdered charcoal, is covered with patches of gray mold. Inside, the cheese's curd is white, even-textured, and very tender, with an agreeable hazelnut flavor and a fine, pleasant-tasting acidity.

Serving suggestions
Serve Rouelle Cendrée at the end of a meal with a range of chèvres for sampling with a crusty baguette. Accompany it with a Quincy or a Reuilly, two white wines that set off goat cheeses to perfection.

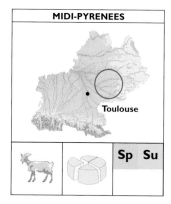

MIDI-PYRENEES

Toulouse

Sp Su

ROCAMADOUR A.O.C.

ROCAMADOUR AND CABÉCOU

Rocamadour is a member of the Cabécou family of cheeses—the only one to have been deemed worthy of receiving the prestigious Appellation d'Origine Contrôlée guaranteeing the customer a quality product.

Cabécou, from the Occitan dialect word for "kid," is a small cheese (1½ by ⅜ in.), and a typical product of the south west of France. Fresh and young, it is referred to as Cailladou; riper and drier, it is called Cabécou.

HISTORY

Rocamadour is a small cheese made from goat's milk. Long ago, it was called *Cabécou de Rocamadour* in certain areas, and it is still referred to by this name. A treatise dating from the fifteenth century indicates that it was once taken as the unit of value for payment by sharecroppers, and was also used for tax payment purposes. The story has it that it was made by the Saracens who, when they were abandoned in the Poitiers area after the victory of Charles Martel in 732, were forced to make their own cheese to feed themselves. Later, the writings of André Theuriet, a nineteenth-century author from the region, contained this homage to Chabichou (yet another synonym for Cabécou and Rocamadour): "A *pâté de Ruffec*, largely consumed, gave off an exquisite scent of partridges and truffles, opposite the local cheese, the Chabichou with its goaty aroma."

METHOD OF PRODUCTION

Rocamadour is made from raw, whole goat's milk rennetted under heat. The resulting curds are left to coagulate for a minimum of twenty hours, then subjected to a draining process lasting at least twelve hours. The curds are then kneaded and salted, after which the cheeses are ripened in an *hâloir* or a cellar at a temperature of around 34°F for a minimum of six days.

According to each individual producer's own techniques, Rocamadour may be ripened with marc brandy, then wrapped in leaves, which imparts an extremely appealing rustic flavor and appearance to the cheese.

About 550 tons of Rocamadour are made each year in France. This production is carried out by five private and cooperative manufacturers, forty-one farms, a private company that oversees the ripening, and sixty-nine dairies.

THE A.O.C.

LABEL

The A.O.C. label awarded to Rocamadour is relatively recent, dating from March 16, 1996.

The area where Rocamadour is produced extends over the communes of the limestone plateaus of Quercy; it covers a large portion of the *département* of Lot, as well as several *communes* in Corrèze, Aveyron, Garonne, and Tarn.

The *commune* of Rocamadour in the Lot has a picturesque setting. A focal point of the Cult of the Virgin Mary, it is a very important place of pilgrimage, like Santiago de Compostela in Spain.

EATING AND STORING

You can't go wrong by accompanying Rocamadour with a Cahors wine. You can also enhance the aroma of this cheese by serving it with a Gaillac, a Bergerac, or a dry, white Vouvray. In the south of France and in the mountains, the chèvres that have been overdried are placed in preserving jars, which are then filled with olive oil, white wine, or eau de vie. As a general rule, unpreserved cheeses keep well for a week under refrigeration. Keep them wrapped in their original packaging to keep them from drying out.

Sainte-Maure de Touraine A.O.C.

With its elongated cylinder shape and central straw running its entire length, this cheese is hard to mistake. Its origins may date as far back as the Moor invasions.

In the beginning
This cheese's name (*Maure* means "Moor") recalls the North African invaders who occupied this region in the eighth to ninth centuries and were the first in the area to raise goats and make goat cheeses.

Description
Weighing 9 ounces and measuring 5½ to 6¼ inches long, this cheese is molded in a cylindrical container, after removal from which a long straw is inserted lengthwise through its center for stability and aeration. During the ten-day to one-month ripening period, the rind becomes covered in flora and turns bluish or ash-colored.

Choosing wisely
The curd gives off a slight goaty aroma. As time passes, the flavor becomes more acid and takes on a hazelnut taste. After four weeks' ripening, Sainte-Maure begins to dry and shrink. Its curd becomes harder and its taste saltier, but still fairly round in the mouth.

Serving suggestions
This cheese is eaten fresh with crudités or nuts and grapes, broiled on toast with an oak leaf salad, or fully ripened. Serve it with a young red Chinon or a Gamay—or if a white wine is preferred, a dry Vouvray or a Montlouis.

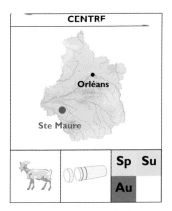

CENTRE

Orléans

Ste Maure

Sp Su
Au

Selles-sur-Cher A.O.C.

Another great classic from the "Garden of France," this cheese is a bit of a change from the log-shaped Sainte-Maure or Valençay's truncated pyramid.

Method of production
Hailing from south of the Loire, Selles-sur-Cher is produced in a strictly delimited area astride the *départements* of Loir-et-Cher and Indre-et-Loire. The center of this region is the village from which the cheese takes its name. Selles-sur-Cher is a cheese with a tender curd made with goat's milk. It is molded, salted, and dusted with charcoal powder, then ripened for between ten days and three weeks.

Description
Shaped like a hockey puck 3¼ inches across by 1¼ inches thick, Selles-sur-Cher weighs 5¼ ounces. Its natural rind is highly irregular and covered with gray-blue mold. The interior of the cheese is tender and melting, tart and slightly salty, with a hazelnut aftertaste.

Serving suggestions
The locals eat this cheese with its rind, which gives it an inimitable flavor. Selles-sur-Cher is best served at the end of a meal, with a crusty loaf and a salad containing shallots. Accompany it with a Gamay or a white Touraine.

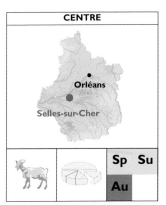

CENTRE

Orléans

Selles-sur-Cher

Sp Su
Au

TOMME AU MUSCADET

MADE IN THE NANTES AREA, THIS UNUSUAL *TOMME* IS FLAVORED WITH THE LOCAL WINE, A DRY, FRUITY WHITE WITH ITS FAIR SHARE OF AROMA.

Description
Shaped like a big wheel, this goat's-milk cheese measures about 12 inches across by 3¼ to 4 inches high, and weighs nearly 5½ pounds.

Method of production
This *tomme* is ripened in a ventilated cellar, where it remains for between two months and one year. During this time, its rind is washed and brushed several times a week with a mixture of Muscadet and water. This procedure develops a supple rind with a lovely orange color, which in turn perfumes the light yellow curd of the cheese.

Serving suggestions
The interior of this cheese has a light, perfumed aroma. This *tomme* makes an unusual and tasty first course, served with a green salad. Sliced thinly over toast and baked for several minutes, it's quite simply delicious. It can also be served as an apéritif, cut into cubes or sticks, with a glass of (what else?) Muscadet-sur-Lie.

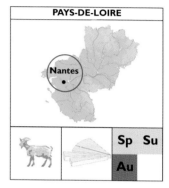

PAYS-DE-LOIRE

Nantes

Sp Su Au

TOMME DE CHÈVRE

ALTHOUGH ITS RATHER GENERIC NAME GIVES LITTLE AWAY, THIS IS A DELIGHTFUL CHEESE FROM PROVENCE. MADE FROM GOAT'S MILK, ITS AROMAS OF THE GARRIGUE WILL MAKE YOUR TASTE BUDS SING.

Description
Shaped like a hockey puck, this traditional little raw-milk cheese measures about 4 inches across by 1 inch thick, and weighs between 7¾ and 9 ounces. Its reddish-hued rind is washed in brine twice a week during the ripening period, which lasts at least three weeks. Tomme de Chèvre's mild interior has a slightly goaty taste that develops hazelnut aromas as it ages. In the mouth, this cheese offers a range of thoroughly interesting, unique flavors.

Serving suggestions
This goat cheese should be savored at the end of a meal, with a slightly sour rye or wheat loaf. Its delicate aromas will blossom to perfection in the company of a white Bandol or a white Côteau-d'Aix.

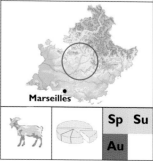

PROVENCE-ALPES-CÔTE-D'AZUR

Marseilles

Sp Su Au

Tomme Sainte-Cécile

Produced on a farm in Burgundy, this straightforward, generous cheese is a must-try with a local red wine, and will appeal to all gourmets in search of new flavors.

Description
Round and fairly tall, this goat *tomme* is ripened in a ventilated cellar for a minimum of two months, sometimes up to a year. Its natural rind is rough and quite bloomy. Its smooth, even-textured interior develops a pronounced goaty taste, the acidity of which varies according to the degree of ripeness. You are unlikely to find Tomme Sainte-Cécile in a cheese shop, since it is primarily sold in its area of production.

Serving suggestions
Cut into cubes, this firm cheese is ideal as an appetizer. Shaved or cut very thinly, its taste is more delicate, and it melts deliciously in the mouth. It can also be served at the end of a meal, with a really fresh country loaf. Accompany it with a white Burgundy such as a rich and generous Pouilly-Fuissé or a red Mâcon.

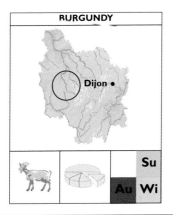

BURGUNDY

Dijon •

Su
Au Wi

Truffe de Valensole

Hailing from Haute Provence, where the goats graze freely in the pastures, this new-style "truffle" has an incomparable taste. This cheese's name—"Valensole truffle"—is not just an invitation to indulge, it's also the promise of a flavor to be savored!

Description
Measuring 2⅜ inches in diameter and weighing just under 4½ ounces, this delicate goat cheese is shaped like a truffle—hence its name. During the ripening period, which lasts at least two weeks, the cheeses are dusted in powdered charcoal, which gives them their grayish cast. This covering of ash causes the growth of patches of blue mold.

Serving suggestions
The very white interior of this cheese becomes harder and more brittle as ripening progresses. It has a very pronounced, slightly acid taste that persists in the mouth. Truffe de Valensole can be eaten hot as a first course on a slice of toast with an oak leaf salad, or at the end of a meal with country bread. Accompany this cheese with a white Côtes-de-Provence or a really fresh Sancerre.

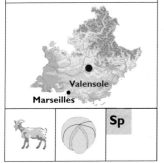

PROVENCE-ALPES-CÔTE-D'AZUR

Valensole •
Marseilles •

Sp

VALENÇAY

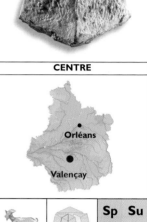

T HIS FARMHOUSE OR FACTORY-PRODUCED CHEESE, MADE FROM RAW OR PASTEURIZED GOAT'S MILK IN TOURAINE AND BERRY, RESEMBLES A TRUNCATED PYRAMID DUSTED WITH CHARCOAL.

In the beginning
The story has it that at one time this cheese was shaped like a true pyramid, with a point at the top. Returning from Egypt after his ill-fated campaign, Napoleon Bonaparte stopped off at the castle of Valençay, and espying the cheese, which reminded him of the Pyramids and his recent defeat, drew his sword and lopped off its tip.

Choosing wisely
This cheese measures about 2⅜ to 2¾ inches across at its base by 2⅜ inches high, and weighs 7 to 9 ounces. Valençay has a fat content of 45 percent. It is ripened for three weeks in a ventilated cellar at a relative humidity of 80 percent. It is then dusted with charcoal powder. This cheese develops a natural surface flora. Its white interior sticks slightly to the palate and has a slightly acid taste. Valençay should be served with country bread, accompanied by a Quincy or a Reuilly.

CENTRE

Orléans

Valençay

Sp Su
Au

VIEILLEVIE

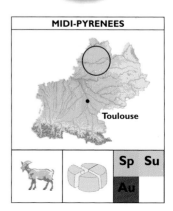

T HIS LITTLE ROUND GOAT CHEESE HAILING FROM THE LOT IS THE EPITOME OF SMOOTH CREAMINESS. HOWEVER, THIS FARMHOUSE SPECIALTY IS QUITE DIFFICULT TO TRACK DOWN.

Description
Shaped like a small hockey puck, Vieillevie is the size of a Cabécou, 2 inches across by ¾ inch thick. Ripened for about two weeks, it develops a very slightly bluish flora. Vieillevie has a thin rind and a tender, creamy interior with a delicate aroma of mold. This goat cheese is only found in a few very well-stocked cheese shops.

Serving suggestions
Vieillevie can be eaten fresh, just starting to develop its bluish mold, and with a very present goaty flavor, or else riper and drier, with an almost chalky taste. Avoid heating this cheese, which will spoil its delicate flavor. Serve it instead with a crusty baguette, accompanied by a green salad with shallots, and partner it with a Sancerre or a really fresh white Reuilly.

MIDI-PYRENEES

Toulouse

Sp Su
Au

Processed Cheeses

These cheeses quite naturally came into being in countries producing large-format pressed, cooked cheeses such as Emmental. Today, numerous varieties such as Cantal, Roquefort, and other blues are used to make processed cheeses.

A cheese for all ages

Back in the nineteenth century, the Swiss had already begun recycling large-format cheeses that had been poorly ripened, and hence were probably unsaleable. This recycling gave rise to the first processed cheeses. Today these cheeses are made by mixing several varieties. To do this, the cheeses are derinded, cut up, shredded, and milled, then melted with other dairy products such as butter, milk, or cream. Sometimes seasonings or spices are added. The mixture is then cooked at a high temperature to yield a product with excellent keeping qualities.

Mild-flavored varieties

Industrial producers have had great success with these products that, while lacking a highly pronounced taste, present obvious advantages in terms of ease of transportation, keeping qualities, and consumption. There are many varieties of processed cheeses—plain, and those containing ham, walnuts, cumin, and herbs, to name a few. To obtain a variety of tastes, young cheeses with a fresh, acid flavor are often combined with ripened cheeses contributing their own specific qualities. Every year, new cheeses arrive on the market, many of which are appealing and inexpensive.

These cheeses are exported abroad, where they are highly regarded—particularly in the Middle East. They may be packed in individual-size portions, in boxes, or even in tubes. They are sometimes referred to as "crème de . . ." ("cream of . . ."), in which case they consist only of the cheese mentioned.

Members of the processed-cheese family include Laughing Cow, Kiri, Apéri-Cube, and Crème de Roquefort.

A fairly new invention

Processed cheeses are rather new arrivals to our tables. The first one, made from Emmental, was launched on the market by a Swiss company in 1911. During World War I in 1916, a German engineer hit on the idea of melting certain very mild-tasting, low-fat cheeses. He noticed that these cheeses had a very long shelf life. In the same year, an American researcher obtained the first government patent for the melting process that he had perfected. Back in France, the first processed-cheese factory was established in Dôle in the Jura in 1917.

An easygoing cheese

Thanks to their hermetic packaging, sometimes in individual portions, it's easy to slip a Kiri or a small round Babybel in your pocket. Good year-round, these products can easily be stored refrigerated for two to three weeks.

Processed cheeses, containing 40 to 50 percent fat on average, are therefore supple and soft. They spread like a dream on walnut or raisin breads, and make delicious ham-and-grilled-cheese sandwiches or cheeseburgers. Processed cheese slices enhance vegetable gratins or endives with ham. A few slices of kiwi or apple on some bread spread with processed cheese makes an energy-filled snack.

Matching wines

Processed cheeses harmonize well with light, dry white wines such as Sancerre or Chablis, which you should serve chilled to between 53°–57°F. Moreover, a Rambol spread on crackers is perfect served with a red Burgundy or a Touraine wine. Don't forget beers and their varied flavors. Some, like the French Angélus, are delicious with garlic- or pepper-flavored pastes.

CANCOILLOTTE

A MEMBER OF THE PROCESSED CHEESE FAMILY, CANCOILLOTTE HAS A FAIRLY LONG TRADITION OF PRODUCTION. THE PRIDE OF THE FRANCS-COMTOIS, THIS SKIM COW'S-MILK CHEESE IS MADE FROM METTON—A HIGHLY AROMATIC, GREENISH PASTE OBTAINED FROM THE WHEY COLLECTED DURING THE PRESSING OF COMTÉ CHEESES.

Method of production
To make Cancoillotte, the metton is left to ferment for several days in a warm cellar. Once it has turned a lovely golden color, it's heated together with some butter and salt water while being stirred constantly. Once it has cooled, the Cancoillotte is poured into stoneware or cardboard containers. This cheese is a granular yellow paste with a very pungent flavor, to which white wine and seasonings are added.

Serving suggestions
Cancoillotte can be eaten hot or cold, as a topping for bread, or with vegetables and meat. It's a very popular dish in Franche-Comté, where it originated. Serve it with a Jura wine.

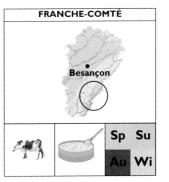

FRANCHE-COMTÉ

Besançon

Sp Su
Au Wi

RAMBOL AUX NOIX

T HIS FACTORY-PRODUCED, COW'S-MILK CHEESE FIRST CAME INTO BEING IN THE YVELINES, NEAR RAMBOUILLET—HENCE ITS NAME. IT'S MORE OF AN URBAN CURIOSITY THAN A GASTRONOMIC JEWEL.

Description
Factory-produced from pasteurized cow's milk, this processed cheese decorated with shelled walnuts is sold in a clear plastic cover, which shows off its creamy consistency—the reason for its popularity. You're more likely to find Rambol aux Noix at the supermarket than in a specialty cheese shop.

Serving suggestions
Easy to spread, Rambol aux Noix is ideal as an afternoon snack for gastronomes who haven't yet learned to appreciate the intense flavors of a Muenster or the subtleties of a chèvre. It can be served on a cheeseboard for guests who are averse to strong tastes. Rambol goes well with a light, unpretentious wine such as a Beaujolais.

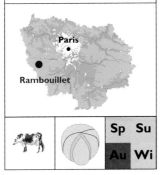

ÎLE-DE-FRANCE

Paris

Rambouillet

Sp Su
Au Wi

VACHE QUI RIT

THIS LEGENDARY CRÈME DE GRUYÈRE WAS CREATED IN 1921, THE BRAINCHILD OF LÉON BEL, SON OF THE FOUNDER OF THE FAMOUS BEL CHEESE COMPANY.

In the beginning
In 1865, Jules Bel founded a company that ripened and sold Gruyères. At the end of World War I, his son Léon turned his attention to a revolutionary new development—processed cheese—perfecting Vache Qui Rit (Laughing Cow) in Jura in 1821. The fame of this new product soon spread throughout the world. It was the cartoon artist Benjamin Rabier who created the now-legendary image of the red cow that appears on the packaging.

Method of production
Made from a variety of cheeses such as Emmental, Gouda, or Comté, the Laughing Cow comes in the form of a uniformly smooth, spreadable paste. This processed cheese contains 50 percent fat.

Description
Five different-sized boxes of this cheese are on the market, to suit singles and big families alike. Over the last few years, Bel has developed new formats and flavors for Vache Qui Rit, selling it in little dishes in netting; in cubes flavored with goat cheese, olives, ham, or tomato; and as a dipping cheese with breadsticks.

Serving suggestions
Serve any way you like—except on a cheeseboard. This processed cheese is adored by children, who devour it at school, on picnics, or after sports.

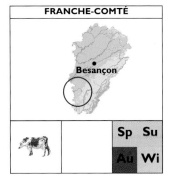

FRANCHE-COMTÉ

Besançon

| | | Sp | Su |
| | | Au | Wi |

a short
cheese
glossary

GLOSSARY

ABOMASUM, RENNET STOMACH
Stomach pouch of young ruminants, from which rennet is made.

ANNATTO
Natural orange coloring obtained from the annatto tree that grows in Central America, used to color certain cheeses such as Langres or cheddar.

ARTISANAL
Handcrafted; said of a cheese made by hand according to traditional methods.

ATMOSPHERIC HUMIDITY
Amount of moisture in the air. A certain level of humidity is essential for the fermentation or ripening of the cheeses and the growth of their surface mold.

BACTERIA
Living organisms that play a role in the transformation of organic matter.

BLOOMY RIND
Said of cheeses whose rinds are covered with a fine white mold, the "bloom."

BRINE
Water- and salt-saturated solution used to rub the rinds of soft cheeses such as Muenster.

BURON
In the Auvergne, a small mountain hut in which farmers made cheeses during the summer grazing.

BUTTERMILK
Sour-tasting liquid residue left over from the butter-making process.

CASEIN
Protein contained in milk that allows it to curdle when rennet is added. It is also used to manufacture the little labeling plates imbedded in the rinds of certain cheeses such as Comté or Reblochon.

CAVE
French for both "cave" and "cellar": a natural or man-made place, often with a high level of humidity, in which ripening of the cheese takes place.

CENDRÉ
Refers to a cheese that has been dusted with powdered charcoal.

CHEESE STRAINER
Mold pierced with holes into which the curds are poured to drain. Incorporated in the packaging of some cheeses.

CHURN
Container in which the cream skimmed off the milk is beaten in order to produce butter.

COAGULATION
The transformation of a liquid organic substance into a semisolid mass. With milk, this is the curdling caused by the addition of rennet.

COOPERATIVE
A company whose associates have an equal share in the work, management, and profits. By extension, a dairy cooperative is formed when milk producers pool their processing, ripening, and/or marketing resources in order to make optimum use of their milk production.

CULTURING
The addition of ferments to the milk, which are necessary for the production of cheese.

CURDLING

The coagulation of the milk after rennet is added. The still-warm, reheated, or cool milk is placed in large copper vats, where it curdles or coagulates due to the addition of a given quantity of rennet coupled with manual or mechanical stirring.

DEHYDRATION

Process by which all the water is removed from a product, leaving only the dry matter.

DESICCATION

Drying out, dehydrating. The dry matter (proteins, fats, mineral salts) is the part of the milk remaining after desiccation.

DRY MATTER

The solid residue obtained after desiccation of a dairy product.

ENZYME

Organic substance that triggers a biochemical reaction.

FARMHOUSE

Describes a cheese made on the farm with milk from the farm's own herds.

FAT CONTENT

The fat content printed on the packaging of cheeses is calculated with respect to 100 g of dry matter. French legislation is very precise: the cheese is low-fat (*maigre*) if it contains under 20% FDB, "light" (*allégé*) between 20–30%, and high-fat or rich (*gras*) between 50–60%. Cheeses containing between 60–75% FDB are referred to as "double cream" (*double-crème*), and those above 75% as "triple cream" (*triple-crème*).

FDB (FAT ON DRY BASIS)

The fat content of a cheese, expressed as a percentage of the milk solids. The latter is calculated by subtracting the water weight from the total weight of the cheese, then dividing the fat into the solids. Example: 100 g of cheese, of which 60 g is water and 22 g is fat: total weight (100 g) less water weight (60 g) leaves 40 g; divide weight of fat (22 g) into solids (40 g) to give the result of 55% FDB.

FERMENTATION

The process of development or maturation of a dairy product, such as cheese or yogurt, with the addition of ferments that may be lactic (for fresh cheeses), caseic (for soft cheeses), or propionic (for hard cheeses). By extension, and more particularly for cheeses, we speak of "ripening."

FONDUE

A typical mountain dish based on cheese, fondue is of Swiss origin. It consists of shavings of Gruyère and Emmental melted in an earthenware or cast-iron fondue pot with white wine and possibly seasonings. Small pieces of bread are then speared on a fork and dipped in the mixture. Fondue is often served accompanied by local charcuterie specialties and wines.

FRESH CREAM

This term is used for both raw and pasteurized cream (either heavy or light).

FRUITIÈRE

Small cooperative in regions such as Jura, Savoie, or the Swiss Alps, where the milk is collected and made into large wheels of cheese.

FULLY RIPE

In French, *(fait) à coeur*, literally "(ripe) to the core": Describes a cheese that is just right for eating—soft and creamy, neither overly strong nor underripe.

HÂLOIR

Ventilated "resting" room for ripening certain cheeses, particularly soft cheeses. This is the stage at which the rind starts developing a bloom.

JASSERIE
Stone building in which cheese is made in the Forez region in the Auvergne.

LOW-FAT MILK
In France, the fat content of liquid low-fat milk must lie between a minimum of 1.5% and a maximum of 1.8%. It is obligatory for the container to bear the wording *demi-écrémé* ("low-fat"). In France, low-fat milk comes in predominantly blue packaging.

METTON
Curdled milk used to make the processed cheese Cancoillotte.

MILLSTONE (FRENCH, *MEULE*)
Describes the large-wheel format of cooked, pressed cheeses such as Comté, Emmental, or Beaufort. The term evokes the huge wind- or water-mill stones used to grind grain.

NEEDLES
Producers of blue-veined cheeses use needles to pierce the curd of a cheese in order to aerate it and encourage the development of penicillium strains seeded beforehand.

NON-FAT OR SKIM MILK
The fat content of liquid skim milk must not be greater than 0.3%. In France, this milk comes in predominantly green packaging.

PASTEURIZATION
Heat treatment consisting of heating the milk to a minimum temperature of 161.6°F and a maximum of 185°F for 15–20 seconds, then cooling it quickly to 39.2°F.

PDO (FRENCH, AOP)
Protected Designation of Origin (French, *Appellation d'Origine Protégée*). This term was implemented by the European Community in 1996.

pH VALUE
An index of the relative acidity or alkalinity of a solid or liquid substance.

PRESS
Piece of equipment that speeds up the draining process by applying pressure to the curds over several hours or days.

RAW MILK
Milk that is not pasteurized or otherwise heat-treated, but merely cooled.

RENNET
Substance that causes curdling of the milk, obtained from the rennet stomach or abomasum of young ruminants such as calves or lambs.

RENNETING
Operation consisting in the addition of rennet of animal or plant origin to the milk in order to facilitate curdling.

RIPENING (FRENCH, *AFFINAGE*)
The period in which the cheese, placed in a cellar at a constant or progressive temperature and humidity, receives a great deal of care and attention, being turned, brushed, and washed in brine. Subject to the action of ferments and yeasts, the cheese reaches a point of perfect ripeness and is ready to be eaten.

RUNNY (FRENCH, *COULANT*)
Describes a cheese of unsatisfactory consistency. The term also describes the runny paste of a cheese that has not been kept cool or refrigerated.

SEDGE

The rush leaves traditionally wrapped around a Livarot, which earned the cheese its nickname of "colonel." Today, paper bands are used.

STERILIZATION

Heat treatment that destroys all microorganisms. There are two different procedures: Simple sterilization, when the product is packaged, then heated to 239°F for 15–20 minutes; and UHT sterilization, in which the product is heated to 302°F for 2–3 seconds, then chilled quickly. Simple sterilized milk can be kept for 150 days, as compared with 90 days for UHT milk.

TRANSHUMANCE

The moving of grazing animals to high pastures in the summer.

TRIPLE-CRÈME

Fresh cream cheese containing a minimum fat content of 75%.

WHEY

The liquid that is expelled when the cheeses are drained; also sometimes referred to as "lactoserum."

WHOLE MILK

Liquid whole milk has a minimum fat content of 3.5%. Whole evaporated milk must contain at least 7.5% fat; whole condensed milk, at least 9%; and powdered whole milk, a minimum of 26% fat. In France, whole milk usually comes in predominantly red packaging.

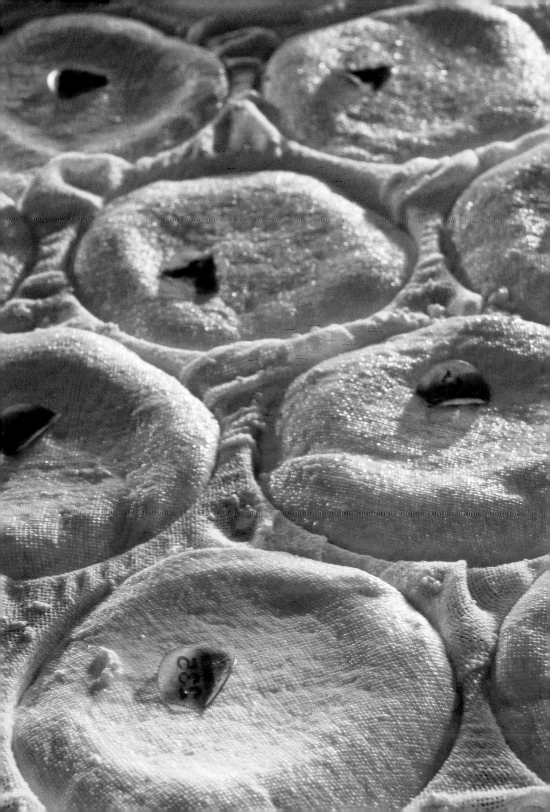

indexes

INDEX OF CHEESES

INDEX OF ACCOMPANIMENTS

This guide was drawn up by Alix Baboin-Jaubert

with the collaboration of : Alexandra Bentz, Élizabeth Boyer, Pascale Le Hec, Marielle Pfender, and Fella Saïdi-Tournoux.

Maps on pages 33 to 41:
Agence Idé Infographie: Thomas Grollier

Pictograms:
Agence Idé Infographie: Ludovic Raczkowsky

Layout:
JAD-Hersienne

Photographs:
(c) Alain Muriot, Studio Soleil Noir

Côté vues, p. 57, 87, 97, 123, 160 165
Fromagerie Bel D.R., p. 199
Fromagers de France D.R., p. 1, 2, 23
Inside, p. 6, 8, 202
Option Photo, p. 73, 103
Aline Périer, p. 141, 157, 193
Photonica, p. 16 (bottom), 17, 20, 27, 42, 44

Acknowledgments:
The author particularly wishes to thank the CIDIL (Centre Interprofessionnel de Documentation et d'Information Laitière), and especially Pomme Goldenberg for her patience and information, as well as Pascale Le Hec, Ninon Brunet, and Catherine Vallery-Radot for their friendship.

Likewise, many thanks to:
Marie Quatrehomme, La Maison du Fromage, 62 rue de Sèvres, 75007, Paris
Tel: 0033 1 47 34 33 45

Philippe Olivier
43 rue Thiers, 62200 Boulogne-sur-Mer
Tel: 0033 3 21 31 94 74

Laurel Glen Publishing
An imprint of the Advantage Publishers Group
5880 Oberlin Drive, San Diego, CA 92121-4794
www.laurelglenbooks.com

All notations of errors or omissions should be addressed to Laurel Glen Publishing, editorial department, at the
above address. All other correspondence (author inquiries, permissions and rights) concerning the content of this
book should be addressed to Hachette Livre, 43 Quai de Grenelle, 75905 Paris.

ISBN 1-57145-890-5
Library of Congress Cataloging-in-Publication Data available upon request.

English translation by Translate-A-Book, Oxford, U.K.
Typeset by Organ Graphic, Abingdon, U.K.

Printed in Singapore.

1 2 3 4 5 06 05 04 03 02

About the Author

Alix Baboin-Jaubert is a journalist who works on a
variety of cooking magazines in France.

Marie Quatrehomme runs the Maison du Fromage at 62, Rue de Sèvres in Paris,
and collaborated with the author to complete the book.